The Security of Korea

Westview Special Studies in International Relations

The Security of Korea: U.S. and Japanese Perspectives on the 1980s
edited by Franklin B. Weinstein and Fuji Kamiya

Any discussion of the security of Korea has implications for U.S.–Japan relations, but the Carter administration's announcement in 1977 of its intention to withdraw U.S. ground-combat forces from Korea by 1982, which brought to the surface deep-rooted Japanese and American frustrations with one another, made it clear that neither side fully understood the other's view of Korea.

This book, a collaborative effort by specialists of diverse expertise and viewpoints, clarifies U.S. and Japanese perceptions of the Korean problem and explores alternative approaches to the maintenance of peace and security on the Korean peninsula. Demonstrating that much of the conventional wisdom about Korean security rests on oversimplifications, exaggerated fears, and mistaken assumptions, the authors assert that the prospects for avoiding conflict grow brighter despite existing pitfalls, and offer recommendations for the U.S. and Japanese governments.

Franklin B. Weinstein is director of the Project on United States–Japan Relations at Stanford University, where he also teaches in the Department of Political Science. Fuji Kamiya is professor of international relations at Keio University and serves as research director of the Japan Institute of International Affairs.

Prepared under the auspices of the
Project on United States–Japan Relations
Stanford University

The Security of Korea: U.S. and Japanese Perspectives on the 1980s

edited by Franklin B. Weinstein and Fuji Kamiya

Coauthors:

Selig S. Harrison
Ryukichi Imai
Fuji Kamiya
Masataka Kosaka
Makoto Momoi
Daniel I. Okimoto
Henry S. Rowen
Kiichi Saeki
Franklin B. Weinstein
Allen S. Whiting

Westview Press / Boulder, Colorado

Westview Special Studies in International Relations

Published in 1980 in the United States of America by
    Westview Press, Inc.
    5500 Central Avenue
    Boulder, Colorado 80301
    Frederick A. Praeger, Publisher

Library of Congress Cataloging in Publication Data
Main entry under title:
The Security of Korea.
    (Westview special studies in international relations)
    1. United States—Relations (military) with Korea. 2. Korea—Relations (military) with the United States. 3. United States—Foreign relations—Japan. 4. Japan—Foreign relations—United States. I. Harrison, Selig S. II. Weinstein, Franklin B. III. Kamiya, Fuji. IV. Series: Westview special studies in international relations and U.S. foreign policy.
E183.8.K7S43   355'.033'0519   80-13544
ISBN 0-89158-668-7
ISBN 0-89158-758-6 (pbk.)

Printed and bound in the United States of America

Contents

Coauthors

Selig S. Harrison is senior associate at the Carnegie Endowment for International Peace. He covered North and South Korea during many years in Asia as a correspondent for the *Washington Post.* He is chairman of the University Seminar on Korea at Columbia University.

Ryukichi Imai is general manager, engineering, of the Japan Atomic Power Company. He is also a special assistant to the minister of foreign affairs, dealing mainly with nuclear and arms-control matters.

Fuji Kamiya is professor of international relations at Keio University and serves as a trustee of the Japanese Institute of International Affairs, the Japan Association of International Relations, the Japan Association of International Law, and the Research Institute for Peace and Security. He has been appointed to the Foreign Advisory Committee of the Korean Institute of International Studies.

Masataka Kosaka is professor of international politics at Kyoto University.

Makoto Momoi is director of international security studies and professor of international relations at the National Defense College of Japan.

Daniel I. Okimoto is assistant professor of political science at Stanford University.

Henry S. Rowen is professor of public management in the Graduate School of Business at Stanford University. He has served as president of the Rand Corporation, as assistant director of the Bureau of the Budget, and as deputy assistant secretary of defense.

Kiichi Saeki is chairman of the Nomura Research Institute. He formerly served as president of the National Defense College of Japan.

Franklin B. Weinstein is director of the Project on United States–Japan Relations at Stanford University, where he also teaches in the Department of Political Science.

Allen S. Whiting is professor of political science at the University of Michigan.

Introduction

Both Americans and Japanese find it hard to think about the security of Korea without coming to dwell on the implications for U.S.–Japan relations. Korea has, of course, an intrinsic importance for the United States and Japan, but their respective relations with Korea also have a major impact on the way Washington and Tokyo view each other. For many Americans, a critical part of the rationale behind the U.S. commitment to Seoul is the latter's importance to Japan. If the Japanese did not consider a U.S. commitment to South Korea vital to their security, the character of that commitment might change dramatically. From a Japanese perspective, the prospects for Korean security depend largely on what the United States is prepared to do; Japanese discussions of Korea's future tend to become debates about U.S. policy. And the Japanese inevitably view U.S. policy toward Korea as an indicator of the strength of the U.S. commitment to Japan itself.

The Carter administration's 1977 announcement of its intention to withdraw U.S. ground-combat forces from Korea by 1982 brought to the surface Japanese and U.S. frustrations with one another. Many Japanese were concerned not only about the substance of the decision, but, more importantly, about the manner in which the policy was decided and communicated. Many U.S. observers, for their part, found the Japanese demanding of the United States but unwilling to make sacrifices themselves. U.S. officials were especially puzzled about Tokyo's apparent inability even to express its views forthrightly concerning the U.S. role in Korea. In July 1979, President Carter announced that the troop withdrawals would remain suspended until at least 1981, but the deeper frustrations and concerns evoked by the previous withdrawal decision remained in evidence.

Stanford University's Project on United States–Japan Relations has, since 1975, brought together Japanese and U.S. specialists on security affairs for discussions and collaborative research. Korea has been an important item on the agenda since the outset. Discussions of Korea have always been lively and provocative, but they have also evidenced the frustrations to which allusion has been made. Some of the Japanese have asserted that the United States simply does not understand how the Japanese view Korea and, in some respects, does not understand Korea itself. Therefore, a study was undertaken in 1977 to elicit Japanese perceptions of the Korean problem, as well as to clarify U.S. views on the subject.

The working group that undertook the study followed a somewhat novel procedure. Through consultations among the ten-member group, which included an equal number of U.S. and Japanese specialists, a lengthy list of questions for study was compiled under three categories: (1) force reductions and withdrawals, (2) nuclear nonproliferation, and (3) nonmilitary measures to deter conflict. At the initial meeting, held in June 1977, the group surveyed those questions in order to identify the key issues, and ascertained which questions should be covered by several people to ensure the representation of divergent perspectives. In some cases, as many as five or six members were subsequently asked to study the same question. Each member agreed to write a working paper, the paper to consist of a series of researched answers to the questions he was assigned to study, for discussion at the group's second meeting in December 1977. The initial draft of this manuscript grew out of the working papers, the comments made at the two meetings, and additional contributions prepared in the spring of 1978. The draft was discussed further at a general conference of the Project on United States–Japan Relations in July 1978. Further revisions were undertaken in late 1978 and mid-1979, and additional sections were prepared to take into account developments in late 1979, including the assassination of South Korean President Park Chung-hee. Revisions were completed in early 1980, a time of considerable uncertainty concerning the future development of South Korea's political system.

The book follows the basic question-and-answer format that provided the structure for the working group's research. Each chapter but the last contains contributions from most of the group's members; the authors are identified at the start of the sections they contributed. The concluding chapter was prepared by the editors on behalf of the entire group.

This book would not have been possible without the support of numerous institutions and individuals. The principal funding for the study came from the Henry Luce Foundation's Fund for Asian Studies and from Japanese funds made available through a cooperative arrangement with the Japan Center for International Exchange (JCIE), directed by Tadashi Yamamoto. We were also fortunate in being able to draw on continuing support from the Sumitomo Fund for Policy Research Studies, administered by the Japan Society, and from Stanford's Arms Control and Disarmament Program, directed by John W. Lewis. We would like to express our appreciation to the JCIE staff members who worked on this project, particularly Yoji Yamamoto and Makita Noda. We are also grateful to Barbara Johnson and Jacquelyn Miller for secretarial assistance and to Barbara Sullivan for her help in typing the manuscript. Of course, none of the institutions or individuals acknowledged here bears any responsibility for the book's content.

Franklin B. Weinstein
Fuji Kamiya

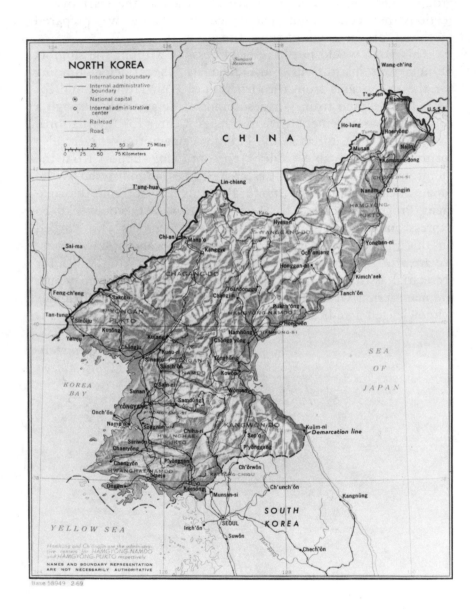

NORTH KOREA

—— International boundary
----- Internal administrative
      boundary
● National capital
○ Internal administrative
   center
+ Railroad
— Road

0   25   50   75 Miles
0   25   50   75 Kilometers

CHINA

Sampori
Reservoir

Wang-ch'ing

T'u-men

Namyang

U.S.S.R

Ho-lung

Hoeryŏng

Musan

Najin

Lin-chiang

Komusan-dong

CH'ŎNGJIN-SI

Nanam

Ch'ŏngjin

T'ung-hua

HAMGYŎNG-
PUKTO

Hyesan

CHANGGANG-DO

Sai-ma

Chi-an

Manp'o

Yongban-ni

Kanggye

Och'onjang

Hongyan-Ri

Feng-ch'eng

CHAGANG-DO

Kimch'aek

T'oandongni

Changjin

Tanch'ŏn

Tan-tung

Sakchu

P'YŎNGAN
PUKTO

Pukch'ŏng

HAMGYŎNG-NAMDO

Sinŭiju

Kusŏng

Hongwŏn

HAMHUNG-SI

Yŏmju

Hamhŭng

Kujang

Hamhŭng

Ch'ŏngju

Ch'ŏngp'yŏng

Kusu-ri

KOREA
BAY

Sinanju

Yŏnghŭng

Sŏnch'ŏn

Kowŏn

P'YŎNGAN
NAMDO

Sain-ni

Sunan

Samdŭng

Wŏnsan

SEA

OF

JAPAN

P'YŎNGYANG

Onch'ŏn

P'YŎNGYANG-SI

KANGWŎN-DO

Kuŭm-ni

Demarcation line

Namp'o

Songnim

Chiha-ri

HWANGHAE-
PUKTO

Sep'o

Sariwŏn

P'yŏnggang

Chaeryŏng

Ch'ŏrwŏn

Chaengyŏn

P'yŏngsan

HWANGHAE-NAMDO

Ch'unch'ŏn

Haeju

SŎNG-CHIGU

Ongjin

Kaesŏng

Kangnŭng

Munsan-si

SOUTH
KOREA

YELLOW SEA

Inch'ŏn

SEOUL

Suwŏn

Chech'ŏn

Hamhŭng and Ch'ŏngjin are the administrative names for HAMGYŎNG-NAMDO
and HAMGYŎNG-PUKTO respectively

NAMES AND BOUNDARY REPRESENTATION
ARE NOT NECESSARILY AUTHORITATIVE

Base 58949 2-69

South Korea

Internal administrative boundary
National capital
Internal administrative capital
Railroad
Road

0   25   50   75 Miles
0 25 50 75 Kilometers

Chŏngju
Hamhŭng
Wŏnsan
North
Korea
Pyŏngyang
Sariwŏn
Changyŏn
Haeju
Ongjin
Kaesŏng
Munsan
Kyŏnggi-do
Seoul
Seoul Exp'obi
Suwŏn
Ch'ŏnan
Ch'ungch'ŏng-namdo
Taejŏn
Kunsan
Chŏnju
Chŏlla-pukto
Kwangju
Chŏlla-namdo
Mokp'o
Yŏngdang
HŬKSAN-CHEDO
Chindo
Cheju
Cheju-do

Pyŏnggang
Ch'ŏrwŏn
P'yŏng-gang
Kansŏng
Demarcation Line
Ch'unch'ŏn
Kangnŭng
Kangwŏn-do
Parhan-ni
Samch'ŏk
Wŏnju
Yŏju
Ansŏng
Ch'ungch'ŏng-pukto
Ch'ŏngju
Chŏngju
Yŏngju
Ham'chang
Andong
Yŏngdŏk
Kyŏngsang-pukto
Kamch'ŏn
P'ohang
Changgi-ap
Taegu
Kyŏngju
Kyŏngsang-namdo
(Administrative seat at Pusan)
Chinju
Masan
Chinhae
Ulsan
Pusan-si
Pusan
Samch'ŏnp'o
Sunch'ŏn
Yŏsu
Kŏje-do

Sea of Japan

Ullŭng-do

Yellow
Sea

Korea
Strait

Tsushima

Korea Strait

Japan
Kyushu

NAMES AND BOUNDARY REPRESENTATION
ARE NOT NECESSARILY AUTHORITATIVE

Base 501382 12-72

Images and Interests: U.S. and Japanese Assumptions About Korea

WEINSTEIN: Differences between U.S. and Japanese views of Korea's security reflect, at least in part, the dramatically contrasting historical relationships that the two countries have had with Korea. In this chapter, we examine basic Japanese and U.S. images of Korea, their perceptions of the economic and military balance between the two Koreas, and the extent to which U.S. and Japanese interests in Korea overlap.

What Are the Basic Images That Japanese and Americans Have of the Two Koreas? What Assumptions Do They Make About the Nature of the Korean Political and Economic Systems?

KOSAKA: Japanese images of Korea are pervaded by a sense of awkwardness about the relationship between Japanese and Koreans. This awkwardness stems not merely from the painful historical relationship between the two countries but also from the failure of many Japanese to understand Korean society. Although there are many similarities between the Japanese and Korean societies, the differences are important. For example, the Koreans tend to be more dogmatic than the Japanese. In this respect, Koreans are truer to Confucianism. Thus, while the Japanese may believe that realism demands the acceptance of a divided Korea, the Koreans find it hard to renounce the symbol of a unified country, even if in their hearts they know it is unattainable.

The Japanese have been inclined to see in the Korean peninsula two features that they consider basic to an understanding of the peninsula's future: (1) the rapid modernization of the South and (2) the prevalence for many years of dictatorships in both

Koreas. The Japanese view South Korea as a modernizing country—one that has "taken off." Whatever one may conclude about the military balance between the two Koreas, it is apparent that in most areas the self-confidence of the South Koreans is rapidly increasing. South Korea's economic development is healthy and very promising.

Given the history of Korean government, it is in keeping with tradition that authoritarian regimes should prevail in both the North and the South. The Koreans have never had a democratic or constitutional system. Since the fourteenth century, Korean governments have been highly centralized, with control extending down to the village level. Viewed in this context, the dictatorship of Park Chung-hee in the South was very natural. Some U.S. observers may be impressed with the degree of pluralism in South Korea. Unlike their counterparts in North Korea, people in the South are at least willing to express dissent. But one should not mistake these factions for the kind of pluralism associated with a democratic system.

The Japanese image of South Korea is thus one of a modernizing economy with a dictatorial, though not totalitarian, political system. This basic view is unlikely to change. Although the removal of Park has already led to some easing of controls and more significant moves toward liberalization cannot be ruled out, Korea's tradition of authoritarianism poses a formidable obstacle to the establishment of a democratic system.

KAMIYA: While the Japanese may feel awkward about Korea and have therefore been reluctant to become too directly involved in Korean security affairs, it is worth noting that the United States, which is deeply involved in Korea, has sometimes failed to grasp the basic facts concerning that country. South Korea's economy has not only "taken off," but the country is in fact already quite industrialized. In perhaps ten years, South Korea will be one of Japan's strongest economic rivals. Indeed, this competition could lead to serious problems, because Korea and Japan—unlike the United States and Japan—have no reservoir of good feeling to fall back on when their economic relationship is strained. Although most U.S. specialists would acknowledge that South Korea's economic development is impressive, they have not shown enough respect for Korean achievements. The Korean economy has grown faster than the United States predicted. If the United States genuinely appreciated the magnitude of South Korean economic progress, it would not be so critical.

The Carter administration's policies concerning human rights in Korea also seem to be based on an insufficient appreciation of the realities of the Korean situation. It is true that Park Chung-hee, like Kim Il-sung, saw himself as a god. Both Koreas have felt the need for a dictatorial system. But it is inappropriate for Carter to expect the Koreans to practice democracy or to respect human rights as defined by the United States. Korean and U.S. standards simply are not the same. The United States ought to recognize that if Koreans were to visit New York, they would probably be shocked to see the unbelievably dirty streets in some parts of the city. From one perspective, it might be said that there are real limitations on human rights in New York. Perhaps Carter should devote his energy to cleaning up the streets of New York before he makes such an issue of human rights in other countries.

There have been two possible evaluations of the position Park held among the Korean people. Some have contended that he was supported by a majority of the South Korean people, others that he lacked popular support and thus remained in power only by using the army, the police, and the Korean Central Intelligence Agency (KCIA) to suppress the populace. Adherents of the latter view predicted that if the South Korean people had an opportunity to express their opinions without inhibition, they would opt for someone like Kim Dae-jung. I believe that the former evaluation was correct.

In the Syngman Rhee period (1945-1960) in South Korea, both anti-Communist and anti-Japanese feelings were strong. This was a consequence of (1) the sudden liberation of Korea from Japanese colonialism through the intervention of outside forces; (2) the division of the peninsula into two Koreas at the time of liberation; and (3) North Korea's antagonistic policies, leading to the Korean War. Under these circumstances, South Korea was temporarily obliged to pursue anti-Japanese and anti-Communist policies in order to establish a national identity. Rhee's policies, however, were fundamentally weak regarding economic development. By the end of the 1950s, South Korea seemed unable to free itself from economic and military dependence on the United States. In contrast, North Korea had achieved a measure of success in raising production and had grown more independent in military affairs. In 1958 the last of the Chinese volunteers withdrew from North Korea. At that time, North Korea (the Democratic People's Republic of Korea—D.P.R.K.) appeared to be the only bastion of Korean nationalism.

In the early 1960s, the South Koreans sought a change in policy, especially with respect to economic development and independence. Park, who came to power in 1961, a year after Rhee's fall, substituted for the anti-Japanese policy one that involved cooperation with Japan. He sought to use this cooperation to further South Korea's economic development.

Even before Park's assassination, it was very easy to list the shortcomings of his regime. In particular, after the new constitution of 1972 there were many difficulties from the standpoint of democracy. Criticism of Park does not, however, signify support for the position taken by people like Kim Dae-jung. In my view, Kim has lost a basis for public support for the following two reasons.

First, since Kim's expulsion from the leading political circles, South Korea's economy has developed dramatically. At the time when Park and Kim competed for the presidency, Kim based his political appeal on the gap between the cities and the countryside. Today, however, the countryside is advancing more rapidly than the urban areas. We no longer witness extreme poverty in the rural areas each spring. South Korea's economy has surpassed that of the North, and the South Koreans have grown more self-confident. Korean nationalism is no longer a monopoly of the North. Park's success in bringing a higher level of economic well-being and national pride to the South Koreans undoubtedly won him the support of a majority of the people, even if they did not regard him as flawless.

Second, I believe that Kim has lost a good deal of his previous support among the South Korean people because of his method of waging an antigovernment struggle. He and his colleagues appealed first to Japan and the United States, rather than to the South Korean people. The Kim group did this in hopes that Tokyo and Washington might intervene to influence the situation in South Korea. Before he was "kidnapped" by the KCIA while visiting Japan, Kim was mainly active in the anti-Park movement in Japan and the United States. At the time of the Myong Dong protest in April 1976, the protestors' antigovernment statement was initially distributed in Japan and the United States. This initial appeal to foreigners was characteristic of Kim's behavior, and, in an increasingly self-confident South Korea, such behavior is not respected.

MOMOI: Insistence on the adoption of a U.S.–style democracy in South Korea is likely to lead to the undermining of the Korean family structure and social system. A strong family structure is one of the chief characteristics of the Korean social system. It is questionable whether the Koreans should be pressured to abandon this system. In any case, it will take generations to produce any meaningful social change. Though some feel that such change is possible in ten years, I would estimate that it will take at least twenty.

The central characteristic of the Korean people is their competitiveness and their high degree of discipline. They overcame the "Carter shock" in a shorter time than it took Japan to overcome the "Nixon shocks." Their growing national pride and self-confidence may well make the South Koreans more amenable to compromise. There is already some evidence of greater rapport between Japan and South Korea, since both countries have experienced "shocks" stemming from the inconsistency of U.S. policy. As the South Koreans move closer to the Japanese in military, economic, and even political terms, this rapport may continue to develop, though one cannot ignore the parallel growth of a competitive relationship. Communication between Japanese and Koreans is likely to improve, especially since most Japanese find the younger generation of Koreans, many of whom have been educated abroad, more flexible and generally easier to communicate with than the older generation (even though the latter are more likely to speak Japanese).

Looking to North Korea, Japanese are well aware of the dangers of that country's isolation. The next fifteen years will be a crucial period for the Korean peninsula in general. The growth of South Korea's military power makes many Japanese uneasy, in particular the possibility that the South Koreans may receive sophisticated weaponry beyond such clearly defensive weapons as TOW antitank missiles. It is thus extremely important to find a way to maintain peace in Korea for at least the next fifteen years, either through arms-control measures or by other means.

WEINSTEIN: U.S. images of Korea differ significantly from those described by the Japanese. The United States is inclined to view North Korea in fairly undifferentiated terms as a rigid Stalinist dictatorship. Congresswoman Helen Meyner has noted the extra-ordinary residue of bitterness toward North Korea left among the U.S. populace as a result of the war. The Pueblo seizure and the August 1976 tree-cutting incident in which two U.S. army officers were slain by North Korean troops in the demilitarized zone (DMZ) have reinforced the image of the North Koreans as aggressive, almost barbarous, renegades. The United States tends to be much less concerned than Japan about the isolation of North Korea. On the contrary, many U.S. specialists feel that North Korea ought to remain in isolation until Pyongyang formally recognizes South Korea's right to exist.

The United States is increasingly aware of the economic accomplishments of South Korea. Indeed, the image of a strong, more self-confident South Korea figured prominently in the Carter administration's original conclusion that U.S. ground-combat forces could be safely withdrawn from Korea by 1982. There is a growing belief that South Korea will so outstrip the North economically that, in time, the North will see the futility of hoping for a collapse of the South. U.S. images of South Korea, however, generally remain focused on political questions—human rights, lobbying practices, and the strategic importance of the peninsula—which tends to make those images negative.

WHITING: U.S. criticism of South Korea tends to be along two basic lines, which may coincide at certain times. First, the Seoul government is criticized insofar as its policies arouse opposition that makes the regime unstable. Repressive policies run a risk of student demonstrations and urban discontent, which invites instability. Second, there is a more general criticism rooted in U.S. conceptions of what the cold war was about. Most U.S. citizens feel that we fought for democracy against communism and that we should continue to aid and defend only those countries that are democratic or have some direct security value to the United States. (For example, although Panama is a dictatorship, the U.S. populace is inclined to support this government because of its strategic importance to the United States.)

The religious aspect is also important to the United States. When the South Korean government attacks church leaders, people here tend to become aroused.

HARRISON: There is a more fundamental basis for questioning the stability of the South Korean regime—namely, the political consequences of the country's dependent pattern of growth. In the eyes of many U.S. and Japanese observers, the image of a booming economy in South Korea is clouded by the political and economic costs resulting from a pattern of deliberate economic dependence on Japan and the United States.

Many South Koreans are deeply disturbed by an extensive and ever-growing dependence on Tokyo so soon after their bitter encounter with Japanese colonialism. These South Koreans do not like to see the South cast in the role of subcontractor for Japanese and U.S. industry. They maintain that because many of the South's industries are heavily dependent on imported components and raw materials, the South's economy does not get much "value added" in this important sector of its development. In theory, as Raymond Vernon and others have explained, the principal advantage of foreign enterprise is that a country receives a steady trickle of new technology through the "product cycle" as ancillary domestic industries develop to supply the foreign enterprise with more and more of its components. But the new technology does not trickle down when previously developed technologies are brought in for predetermined export markets or when manufactured components are shipped in for assembly merely to take advantage of low wage rates. This has been demonstrated with reference to the electronics industry by Suh Sang Chul and other leading South Korean economists in a volume published by the Korean Development Institute.[1] Moreover, in the absence of the "product cycle," there is a built-in necessity to keep up a high rate of imports in order to maintain export growth. Thus, exports contribute little to the balance of payments and Seoul finds itself on a treadmill, with steadily increasing trade deficits, especially vis-à-vis Japan. There is also a parallel rise in national indebtedness to sustain industrial and other imports. Although there is nothing inherently mistaken in a development strategy that emphasizes exports and involves some foreign indebtedness, the extent and character of Seoul's dependence makes the South Korean economy dangerously vulnerable to fluctuations in the Japanese and U.S. economies.

Thus far, Seoul has maintained a satisfactory debt service ratio, and there are substantial benefits in economic expansion, particularly in the form of jobs for those employed in the export sector. But these advantages are offset to a considerable extent by

serious social inequalities that are a direct consequence of the lop-
sided development pattern now being pursued. In order to keep
wages low, thus making the South attractive for foreign investment, it has been necessary to depress the price of food grains as
a means of holding down the overall consumer price level. This
has forced many farmers off the land, producing, in turn, a series
of extremely undesirable consequences. One is that food imports
must be continued indefinitely by adding to balance of payments
deficits or by perpetuating U.S. food aid under Public Law 480.
Another consequence is that powerful industrial and real estate
combines that were close to the Park regime have been acquiring
vast farm acreage. And most important, perhaps, is the fact that
farmers forced off the land have gravitated to the cities, thus de-
pressing already low wages and aggravating urban unemployment.

According to official sources, unemployment dropped from
6.2 percent in 1967 to 3.5 percent in 1978 and no longer con-
stituted a serious problem in the South. Any South Korean who
has worked at least one hour a week is classified as "employed,"
however, and the number of workers who work fewer than 18
hours a week is greater than the number of unemployed.[2] The unemployment rate would be 8 or 9 percent if one included this
segment of the work force among the unemployed. Similarly,
official statistics on wages and per capita income are misleading
and tend to obscure the impact of economic distortions and in-
equities on the living standards of those at the bottom of the
economic heap.

Engel's law holds that as a family's income rises, a progressively
smaller share is spent for necessities and a larger share for educa-
tion, recreation, and consumer goods. In the case of South Korea,
however, consumer spending has lagged far behind increases in
national income. Although wages have been rising, a survey by
the General Confederation of Labor Unions showed the "Engel's
coefficient" to be 52.8 percent among the workers surveyed, in
contrast to a government estimate that only 40 percent of workers'
income is spent for necessities.[3] By international standards, a
52.8 percent figure, if authenticated, would indicate a precariously
low standard of living for those workers concerned. In any case, a
visitor need only go to the East Gate textile sweatshops or the
Chonggechon slum area of Seoul to find workers who earn as little
as $8.50 for what is generally a 50-hour work week.[4]

OKIMOTO: On the other hand, it should be noted that South Korea has succeeded in distributing income more equitably than most other developing countries. The Engel's coefficient may in fact be misleading as a measure of equity, since it is heavily influenced by the level of aggregate development and thus conveys no information about changes in income distribution over time. While no single measure can be regarded as definitive, the Gini coefficient (the most widely used measure of equity), shows that even in a period of dramatically rising GNP South Korea's income distribution has remained more equitable than that of any other non-Communist developing country in Asia, except Taiwan.[5]

WEINSTEIN: Moreover, South Korea has, by practically all accounts, achieved a remarkable degree of success in reducing the gap between urban and rural incomes. It was estimated that rural incomes, which had been only 60 percent of urban household incomes in 1967, had attained parity with urban incomes by the end of 1977; the average rural household income had reached $2,960, as compared to $2,903 for urban households. Because rural households were generally larger than urban ones, per capita income in the rural areas remained slightly lower. More recently, however, there has been increasing recognition that the country's continued rapid growth is producing a deterioration in income distribution. Studies published in 1979 made it clear that the wealthier elements, both urban and rural, have benefited disproportionately from the country's economic success, while unskilled workers have fallen further behind and the number of rural households falling below the poverty line has increased markedly. The World Bank noted in mid-1979 that South Korea's earlier record of maintaining an extraordinary degree of equity in income distribution during a time of rapid growth had suffered setbacks.[6]

Notwithstanding South Korea's impressive achievements, there is evidence of discontent with the impact of the country's economic growth on certain groups. In early 1979 church-based dissidents began to draw particular attention to the uneven character of the country's development, especially the impact of inflation on low-income workers. Although GNP increased by 12.5 percent in 1978, inflation rose at the rate of 16 percent, according to official statistics; labor unions and dissident groups claimed that the actual inflation rate was closer to 30 or 40 percent. The government's critics assert that there remain large pockets of un-

skilled workers in certain industries, such as textiles and electronics, laboring at well below subsistence wages. The government's minimum wage guidelines, set to rise from $60 to $72 a
month in 1979, have been criticized as completely unrealistic by
a dissident leader who cited an estimate by the Korean Federation
of Trade Unions that a worker's minimum living cost in 1979 was
more than $160 a month per person. By the start of 1980, unem-
ployment—having risen from 3.5 percent in 1978 to 4 percent in
1979, and projected to reach 5.3 percent in 1980—was again seen
as a significant problem.[7]

Another indication of discontent was the surprisingly strong
showing of the opposition in the December 1978 National Assembly elections, reportedly the most unfettered in the history of
the Korean republic. Although control of the National Assembly
was never in doubt, given the president's right to appoint one-third
of the body's members, the ruling Democratic Republican party
polled fewer votes than the opposition. The opposition was
especially successful in Seoul. To be sure, some interpreted the
election results more as a positive judgment on the viability of the
South Korean system than as a negative judgment on Park. These
observers pointed to the government's self-confidence in permitting such an open election and to the heavy turnout, which they
felt indicated that the populace had chosen to express its discontent through the electoral process, rather than heeding calls to
boycott the elections.[8]

In the same month as the election, Park gave amnesty to some
four thousand prisoners, including Kim Dae-jung and the dissident poet Kim Chi-ha. On his release, Kim Dae-jung resumed his
criticism of Park, asserting that failure to restore full democracy
to South Korea would lead the country down the road traveled
by South Vietnam and, more recently, Iran. In May 1979 Kim
Young-sam was chosen as president of the opposition New Democratic party, and Kim immediately launched an intensified campaign against Park's leadership. He implicitly criticized Park's
handling of relations with the North by offering to meet personally
with Kim Il-sung. He urged constitutional reform, sided with
workers protesting a controversial decision to close their factory,
and sharply criticized President Carter's June visit to Seoul as a
"big present" to Park's "minority dictatorial regime." He called
on the United States, which he said had already "interfered" in

Korea's domestic affairs by keeping its troops in the country, to exert "public and direct pressure" on Park in order to "bring him under control." By October Kim Young-sam's outspoken statements had led the government to have him expelled from the National Assembly. In protest against the expulsion of Kim, 69 National Assembly members—the entire opposition—resigned. Violent antigovernment demonstrations broke out in Pusan and Masan, where demonstrators not only protested Kim Young-sam's ouster but called for changes in the Yushin ("revitalizing") constitution and even for Park's resignation as president.[9]

HARRISON: While these developments may be subject to varying interpretations, it is my view that many of the Park regime's policies had long been extremely unpopular with the low-income majority of South Koreans. That is why Park had to rely on coercion to remain in power. There is a widespread feeling that these policies were basically designed to serve the political interests of Park and his in-group, regardless of their impact on the broader public interest. By the same token, it is my view that Park's policies were widely suspect in the foreign policy field. Many South Koreans believed that the Park government sought to exaggerate tensions with the North for political purposes. An atmosphere of tension provided a justification for authoritarian controls in the name of defense against Pyongyang. There have been strong undercurrents of support in the South for a more flexible policy toward Pyongyang, which would be more accommodating on such issues as the North's proposal for negotiations on mutual force reductions. Kim Dae-jung won broad support when he espoused a more flexible policy in his 1971 election campaign. He was cautiously moving toward advocacy of a limited North-South confederation when he was silenced by Park. Park was addressing domestic as well as international public opinion when he made his conciliatory January 1979 overture to the North for a resumption of talks.

KOSAKA: Japanese and Koreans are inclined to have little respect for the kinds of political undercurrents just mentioned. In Korea, there is a tradition of what the Japanese call *jidaishugi* ("submission to authority," or "kowtowing"). As Kamiya has noted, Koreans who have failed at home and go abroad to snipe at their government are not appreciated. While political rebels may be respectable figures to many Americans, they are not to Koreans.

WHITING: Nevertheless, the undercurrents of support for a more positive approach to North Korea represent a counterappeal, which Pyongyang might exploit. This may be what Park feared. If the economic prospects for South Korea should somehow dim, those political undercurrents could become considerably more important.

KOSAKA: Although that observation may be valid, two points should be made. First, the apparent absence of any comparable undercurrents in North Korea is a result of the fact that no opposition is permitted there. Second, the situation is simply not ripe for a genuinely productive North-South dialogue even though some contacts are possible, as became evident in early 1979. Perhaps a real dialogue will be possible in ten years, but not now. Even in the case of the two Germanies, which are more mature states, very little progress has been made. It is hard to avoid being skeptical about any Korean dialogue because it is so difficult to imagine anything significant on which the two Koreas might agree. The subject of relations between the two states is a sensitive one, filled with pitfalls. As for economic ties, the South Koreans have little to gain from a relationship with the North. Any agreement on a nonaggression pact or mutual force reductions would require prior recognition by both sides that it is impossible to change the status quo. And we are still a long way from any such recognition.

KAMIYA: Moreover, it is only partly correct to say that Park's fear of the North's political appeal prevented a North-South dialogue. It is also true that the North Koreans lost interest in the negotiations after their delegates saw, to their astonishment, the prosperity of the South. Although the South Koreans have indeed been hesitant to permit contacts with the North, the North Koreans have been even more reluctant to deal seriously with the South. Although the North-South talks that took place in early 1979 appeared to represent a certain softening in Pyongyang's attitude, there is, as yet, little evidence that North Korea is prepared to reach any overall modus vivendi with the South.

WHITING: In any case, even if the time is not ripe for agreements between the two Koreas, both of which must share responsibility for the failure of previous attempts at a dialogue, it would be a mistake to condition any discussion of how to stimulate and develop such a dialogue on this "ripeness."

What Are the Political Prospects for Post-Park South Korea? —
How Stable Is the Pyongyang Government?

KAMIYA: The fatal shooting of President Park on October 26, 1979, by the head of the KCIA, Kim Jae-kyu, was unexpected, and the initial reporting confused. First accounts called the incident a coup d' etat. A revised version quickly followed labeling the shooting an accident. The South Korean government statement also initially indicated that the KCIA chief had acted alone, but later announcements revised the story again, stating that the shooting was a premeditated act planned by Kim and abetted by his subordinates. Following this it was announced that the late president's top secretary, Kim Kae-won, and his associates were also being investigated.

Explanations of the incident as either an individual act or an accident were never credible. An editorial cartoon in one of the Seoul newspapers soon after the assassination was captioned "A Puzzle without a Key," but the horizontal and vertical lines of the crostic puzzle depicted were joined in various ways to spell "KCIA," "CIA," and "USA." Many Koreans were inclined to suspect U.S. involvement. Even if one did not share that suspicion, it was almost inconceivable, given the nature of the South Korean situation, that the KCIA chief—a man known for his loyalty to the president—could kill Park without being involved in a reasonably broad-based plot.

WEINSTEIN: In December, following a sixteen-day trial before a martial law court, Kim Jae-kyu and six others (five of them former KCIA men) were sentenced to death for their parts in the assassination. In his trial, Kim insisted that he had planned the killing alone in order to restore parliamentary democracy to South Korea. Testimony at the trials indicated an intense political rivalry for Park's ear—with Cha Chi-chol, commander of the Presidential Security Force, as the principal target of the animosity of Kim Jae-kyu and Kim Kae-won. According to Kim Kae-won's testimony, Cha was an arrogant hardliner who influenced Park to make "tough crackdowns" on dissidents, whereas Kim Kae-won and Kim Jae-kyu allegedly counseled moderation.[10]

KAMIYA: Although the assassination of Park could not have been predicted, there was ample prior evidence that the Yushin ("revitalizing") system, based on the constitution of that name promulgated in 1972 to assure Park's unchallenged rule, was under growing pressure. For example, Kim Young-sam, just prior to his expulsion from the National Assembly, made a scathing—and well reported—speech demanding that the Yushin system be completely scrapped and that the Yushin constitution be revised. In short, the speech seemed to reject the existing government system in its entirety. Such a speech, and the front page coverage it received in the press, would have been absolutely unthinkable at the peak of the Yushin system.

The so-called YH incident, which took place in June 1979 at a wig manufacturing company, provides another example of the changes that were occurring in Korean politics. A female worker appealed for redress of her grievances, the police interfered, and in the subsequent violence several people were killed. Another female worker wrote an open letter to her mother recounting in heart-rending detail the hardships she encountered, and this letter was published, in its entirety, by the Korean press. In the past, such a letter would have never appeared in a Korean newspaper. A newspaper that dealt with such a topic even superficially would have been forced to suspend publication. But in the case of the YH incident press coverage was permitted, and no action was taken against the newspaper. Some journalists suggested that certain elements within the government had come to doubt the wisdom of relying exclusively on coercion.

These signs of change cannot be viewed as irrelevant to the assassination of Park by Kim Jae-kyu. It is also interesting to note that after the assassination, the atmosphere was calm in Seoul. Even air travel was interrupted for only an hour or two. In fact, the air route from Seoul to Tokyo was reopened so soon that many people returned on the night of the incident.

According to Japanese in Seoul at the time of the shooting, Park's assassination provoked mixed feelings. Although Koreans typically described the assassination as unfortunate, there seemed to be a certain feeling of relief. The Koreans seemed to suspect that some kind of change was coming sooner or later, and they appeared relieved that it had finally occurred. Among Koreans in Japan there almost seemed to be a feeling of preparatory acceptance.

The role of the South Korean Army is significant. In my view, the army cannot be seen as entirely separate from the KCIA, and it is likely that undercurrents found in one institution existed in the other. It is noteworthy that the first meeting of the cabinet in the post-Park period took place at the Department of Defense, rather than at the central government offices. Following this important meeting with scarcely a moment's delay, the South Korean minister of defense and the army chief of staff were promising their allegiance to the acting president and his system. The smoothness of this process rouses the imagination.

We can also speculate about the role of the United States. Towards the end of the Park administration, Washington was clearly concerned about Park's reliance on authoritarian methods to maintain his regime. Kim Young-sam's expulsion from the National Assembly had evoked a negative U.S. reaction. The cancellation of a planned visit by Assistant Secretary of State Richard Holbrooke may be viewed as an expression of the serious U.S. concern about the political situation in South Korea.

It is unlikely that the Yushin system can be maintained in the post-Park period, but there is little basis for optimism that a new system founded on a broad national consensus will emerge in the near future. Politicians like Kim Dae-jung and Kim Young-sam have stood as the strongest opposition leaders, but their strength and ability to work together have partly sprung from the repressiveness of the Park system, to which they represented an antithesis. If the next election to select a new leader were absolutely free, the opposition parties would probably support one of the two Kims. Unfortunately, however, they might both stand for election, splitting their support. Whether the army leadership will, in fact, allow Kim Dae-jung to be a candidate is, of course, open to doubt. In any case, the strength of the political opposition is far from clear.

The situation is likely to remain unsettled for some time, but in the long run Park's removal may be seen as having provided an opportunity to move gradually from the narrowly based Yushin system to one which takes account of the opposition's position. Naturally, this will require considerable compromise on both sides. If the opposition should come to play a role as part of a coalition government, a major step will have been taken toward a more stable South Korean political system. If, on the other hand, South Korea should experience a protracted period of instability, the situation could become dangerous and might even lead the

United States to question the wisdom of any extended commitment. The possibility of such a reassessment, however, is slight, at least for the near future.

On balance, although the assassination of Park was an extremely unfortunate event, it may well lead to an improvement in the Korean situation. It is also likely that the new regime, regardless of who holds power, will work even harder to develop Seoul's relations with Communist countries. South Korea may well find that it can derive real benefit from the calamity of Park's assassination.

WEINSTEIN: The rush of optimism about South Korea's future that followed the initial shock of Park's assassination was tempered somewhat by developments toward the end of 1979. On December 12, General Chung Seung-hwa, the martial law commander, and some fifteen other senior officers were arrested by Major General Chon Too-hwan, the head of the Army Security Command. The arrests were accompanied by gun battles in what was described as the "most shocking breach of army discipline" in the 31-year history of the South Korean republic. It was alleged that General Chung and the other detainees had aided Kim Jae-kyu, but a report issued by the Defense Ministry on December 23 did not directly link any of those arrested to the assassination. There were, however, indications that General Chung had received certain payments from Kim Jae-kyu prior to the assassination.[11]

The move against General Chung and his supporters appeared to reflect a major division within the army leadership, running along generational and possibly political lines. General Chon and his colleagues were members of the South Korean Military Academy's class of 1955, a group with an unusually strong sense of cohesiveness because it was the first to complete four years in the academy. Some Korean sources have interpreted Chon's action as nothing more than a move by junior officers to wrest power from their seniors. In late January 1980, it was announced that some 35 officers senior to Chon and his associates would be retired by the end of the month. But there was also some evidence of concern on the part of General Chon about the new leadership's implicit repudiation of certain aspects of Park's rule. In the aftermath of the Park assassination, formal leadership had been assumed by Premier Choi Kyu-hah, who on December 6 was designated by the electoral college to serve out the remaining five years of Park's term as president. Choi, a bureaucrat said to have limited political ambitions, announced that he would back revision of the much criticized Yushin constitution. As early as November 10, Choi had made it clear that he would not serve a full term as president but would hold office only to prepare the way for democratic elections under a less authoritarian constitution. As a gesture of "national reconciliation," Choi revoked Emergency Decree 9, used by Park to ban all criticism of the government. A number of political prisoners were released, including Kim Dae-jung.

Even before General Chon made his move, there were signs that the path to liberalization would not be easy. Kim Jong-pil, who succeeded Park as head of the governing Democratic Republican party, had predicted that it would take two years before any elections could be held, while opposition members insisted that elections take place by August 1980. Dissidents were also concerned about the continuation of martial law, new arrests and torture by the martial law authorities, and persistent limitations on human rights and freedom of the press. But the prospects for at least some liberalization seemed good. General Chung, who, following the assassination, had been widely regarded as the nation's most powerful man, was said to favor at least a modest shift toward democratic rule.[12]

In contrast, General Chon was known as a hard-line backer of authoritarian rule who owed his position to a close personal relationship with Park. He was said to have been picked as a promising officer by Cha Chi-chol, whom he served as a senior staff officer. If he proved able to retain power, many observers expected Chon to slow any moves toward political liberalization.[13] Some U.S. officials, however, contended that the ideological differences between Chon and Chung had been exaggerated. In any case, the United States, known to be unhappy about General Chon's violation of established guidelines when he used troops under joint U.S.–Korean command in his December 12 move against General Chung, made clear to Chon that Washington would strongly oppose any moves to set back the trend toward "responsible political leadership." In late December, President Choi promised constitutional revision in "about a year's time." Elections, he said, would take place "as early as possible" after constitutional revision, "unless any unexpected contingencies arise."

President Choi's pledge of elections was clearly hedged, and the gap between the government and the opposition remained very wide. The unprecedented breakdown of army unity in December was a serious danger sign. As of January 1980, uncertainties concerning the future attitudes of generals and opposition leaders made it extremely difficult to predict South Korea's political future. But it seemed unlikely that the Yushin system could be maintained in Park's absence, for no other leader could command the necessary authority. Many observers felt that a failure to carry out promised reforms and to hold open elections would lead to significant unrest. Whether the army, especially the younger officers, would support a lengthy period of repression was open to question. And although President Choi was generally viewed as a weak leader, there was growing speculation that Prime Minister Shin Hyon-hwak, a man with substantial experience in economic affairs and a former member of the Democratic Republican party, might emerge as a presidential candidate, perhaps with the backing of a new political party.[14] In any case, there was at least some basis for hoping that the South Korean leaders, mindful of the economic and military risks of protracted instability, would show the restraint and compromising spirit needed to permit the country to move gradually toward a more stable, less authoritarian system.

KAMIYA: Turning to North Korea, Kim Il-sung's political position appears very strong. But the potential for instability in North Korea is high, given the extreme personality cult that Kim has fostered and the confusion surrounding the possibility that his son may succeed him.

WHITING: So long as Kim remains alive, however, there is no question about the stability of the North Korean regime. Aside from a protuberance on his neck (which has been present for years and shows no sign of change or constraint on his movement), Kim appears to be in excellent health. He is in his late sixties and is likely to be in power at least through the mid-1980s. Should he suddenly leave office, however, whatever intrigues occur at the top involving his son or others are unlikely to affect the basic stability of the system. For all intents and purposes, the regime is here to stay.

*What Assumptions Can Be Made About the Economic Balance
Between the Two Koreas in the 1980s?*

WEINSTEIN: Because of the paucity of data on North Korea's
economy and wide discrepancies in those figures that are available,
it is hard to make precise comparisons. Nevertheless, there can be
no doubt that the South's economic performance has been far
more impressive than the North's in recent years. From the mid-
1960s to the mid-1970s, the South's real GNP more than tripled,
enabling it to surpass North Korea in per capita GNP for the first
time since partition. A comprehensive analysis of the economic
balance between the two Koreas was published by the U.S. Central
Intelligence Agency (CIA) in early 1978.[15] The CIA reported that
South Korea's GNP in 1976 was slightly more than double that of
the North. The International Institute for Strategic Studies (IISS)
has presented a picture even more favorable to the South, placing
South Korea's 1977 GNP at $31.5 billion, more than three times
the North's estimated $9.8 billion. Figures released by Seoul
concur with the IISS estimates for the South but place North
Korea's 1977 GNP at only $6.7 billion, which would make South
Korea's 1977 GNP nearly five times that of the North. The *Far
Eastern Economic Review* reports that in 1978 South Korea's
GNP reached $46 billion (in 1978 dollars), more than five times
North Korea's estimated $8-9 billion. The South's per capita GNP
in 1978 was $1,242, and it reached $1,624 in 1979; per capita
GNP in the North could not have been much over $600 even if
the highest estimates are accepted.[16]

South Korea's most spectacular success has been in the expansion of its exports, which increased by 45 percent annually from
1970 to 1977. Exports nearly doubled between 1974 and 1976.
Seoul's exports, consisting mainly of manufactured products,
reached $7.7 billion in 1976, fourteen times larger than North
Korea's $555 million. The South's exports rose to $10 billion in
1977, compared to North Korean exports of $620 million. In
1978, South Korea's export earnings reached $12.7 billion, and
exports of $15.5 billion were projected for 1979. In addition,
South Korean receipts from services—overseas construction,
tourism, and shipping—totaled $5.8 billion in 1978.[17] The rapid
growth of foreign exchange earnings has facilitated the increased

capital import necessary for industrial development. In 1976, machinery imports in the South were already more than ten times those of the North. Although South Korea continues to maintain a large foreign debt, booming exports have made it possible to reduce the debt service ratio from the 20 percent level of the early 1970s to a manageable 11 percent in 1976, one of the lowest among the major non-OPEC less developed countries. The debt service ratio was estimated to have fallen further to 10.4 percent in 1977.

In contrast, North Korea's exports increased only 10 percent a year after 1970, which in late 1974 led to default on debt repayments. Large-scale defaults, which have continued to the present, have made it impossible for Pyongyang to finance an adequate level of capital goods imports. This places a severe constraint on future growth potential. By the end of 1976, Pyongyang's hard-currency debt to non-Communist creditors had reached $1.4 billion, about six times the annual hard-currency exports. This includes more than $350 million owed to Japanese companies for imports of industrial plants and goods contracted between 1971 and 1975. North Korea owed at least another $1 billion to Communist creditors. The debt service ratio has approached 100 percent, making further rescheduling essential. In December 1976 Japan agreed to a two-and-a-half-year moratorium on the debts, and early in 1979 Pyongyang requested another extension. In late August Japanese creditors and North Korean bank officials agreed on basic terms to settle the debt. As of mid-1979, North Korea's foreign debt was still believed to exceed $2 billion. Prospects for alleviating the problem in 1980 seemed poor. North Korea's total trade volume in 1979 was reported to be about $1.9 billion, a mere 13 percent of the South's exports for the year.[18]

The South has also achieved an impressive edge in industrial development. Since 1965, industrial production in South Korea has increased almost 25 percent annually—about twice as fast as that of the North and perhaps the fastest in the world. Government statistics released in April 1979 showed industrial production in the South up 29.2 percent from February 1978 to February 1979.[19] The most dynamic industries have been export oriented—clothing, footwear, and electronics. Recently, considerable progress has been made in such heavy industries as shipbuilding, steel, petrochemicals, and fertilizer. There are plans for a huge 100-plant machine-building industrial complex that by 1981 will produce $2 billion in industrial, electrical, and precision machinery; specialty steels; and industrial components. An ambitious nuclear energy program is also under way. In 1978, private sector investment in new plants and equipment was estimated at 47 percent.[20]

While North Korean statistics indicate 14 percent annual growth in industrial production, this has been erratic, with zero or negative rates in three of the years since 1965. Heavy industry and mining continue to dominate the economy. North Korea produces more coal, iron ore, nonferrous metals, machine tools, and military hardware than does the South. Although Pyongyang has taken pride in the North's self-sufficiency in such fields as agriculture and the production of machine tools and weapons, this self-sufficiency has meant a relatively low return on capital. North Korea has maintained high savings and investment rates by keeping private consumption down. Domestic savings rates have probably been between 25 and 35 percent of GNP. But a considerable portion of North Korean investment has gone to the defense sector, which does not lead to self-sustaining growth. Recognizing the North's low rate of return on capital, Pyongyang began to increase imports of modern machinery and equipment from the West in the early 1970s. But North Korea's foreign debt problem and suspicion of foreign technology have greatly reduced the productivity of imported equipment.

South Korea's domestic savings rate has also been high—up from less than 5 percent in the early 1960s to 21 percent in 1976. Although the South's foreign savings rate fell to 2 percent of GNP in 1976, it should be noted that foreign savings have financed about 40 percent of total investment since the early 1960s.

Both Koreas have made substantial progress in agriculture in recent years. Grain production has grown more rapidly in North Korea, though emphasis has been placed on corn, rather than rice, which is preferred and strictly rationed. North Korean agriculture is heavily mechanized, with high fertilizer application and extensive irrigation. Overall rural living conditions, however, appear to be better in the South. In 1971, Seoul launched the *Saemaul* ("New Community") movement to stimulate rural development through cooperative village self-help projects, funded partly by the government. This movement has resulted in improved farm roads and housing as well as expanded rural electrification. Rural incomes have risen as a result of government grain price supports and fertilizer subsidies. Rural industrial plants designed to employ surplus labor have also contributed to the rise in income.

The same factors that have favored South Korea over the past decade are likely to persist through the next several years. At the same time, the impact of North Korea's debt problem is expected to be greatest during this period. The CIA's 1978 report, based mainly on data through 1976, anticipated that by 1981 South Korea would have an economy nearly three times that of North Korea. As noted above, according to both Seoul's figures and those of the *Far Eastern Economic Review,* South Korea's GNP in 1978 had already attained a level five times that of the North. The South Koreans have consistently exceeded the targets that they set for themselves in the current five-year plan (1977–1981); as of early 1979, South Korea was said to be running at least six months ahead of the schedule set in the plan.[21]

To be sure, South Korea experienced a significant slowing of economic growth in 1979, due in large measure to international economic conditions, such as sharply rising oil prices. In 1979 South Korea's economy grew only 7.1 percent, after adjustment for inflation. This was the smallest increase since 1975, and a sharp decline from 1978's inflation-adjusted growth rate of 11.6 percent. Economic growth in 1980 was expected to decline further to an inflation-adjusted 3 to 5 percent, but government planners were optimistic that real economic growth would reach 7 or 8 percent in 1981. The latter prediction was dependent on a degree of stabilization in world oil prices and improvement in South Korea's overseas markets, particularly the United States, where restrictions on such imports as color television sets were seen as very damaging to Seoul's export economy. The inflation rate in 1979 approached 25 percent, South Korea's oil bill having jumped from $2.4 billion in 1978 to more than $3 billion in 1979. If crude oil prices in 1980 average $30 a barrel, South Korea's oil bill for the year is expected to approach $6 billion. In the last quarter of 1979, there were reports that industrial production had begun to fall; exports were starting to decline (if measured at constant prices); and the Park assassination and its aftermath were said to have damaged foreign bankers' confidence in South Korea. But the devaluation of the won in January 1980 was expected to boost South Korea's exports, and Seoul's December 1979 announce-ment of plans to significantly loosen the restrictions on foreign investment seemed likely to encourage foreign businessmen. Al-though exports were expected to rise only 13 percent to $17 billion in 1980, government economists anticipated a 23.5 percent rise to $21 billion in 1981, assuming that inflation could be controlled.[22]

South Korean development will continue to require heavy imports of modern plants and equipment, which will necessitate heavy foreign borrowing. But, according to the CIA report, there is every indication that Seoul will be successful in generating the necessary capital inflows. In contrast, North Korea's capital im-ports, which reached $2 billion between 1970 and 1976, are expected to fall to around $1 billion by 1981. North Korea was seized by a serious energy shortage in 1979, and, for the first time in many years, factories were asked to close for one day a week.[23]

North Korea has, of course, devoted a considerably higher percentage of its budget to defense, maintaining a military force roughly equal in manpower to South Korea's with only half the population and a much smaller GNP. It is uncertain, however, just how much higher this percentage is. The IISS reports that in 1977 North Korea allocated 34 percent of its government expen-ditures to defense, compared to 15 percent in the South. But the IISS cautions that international comparisons may be invalidated by differences in the scope of the governmental sector. According to the CIA report, annual North Korean defense spending from 1965 to 1976 was probably between 15 and 20 percent of GNP, while South Korea spent only 4 percent of GNP annually during the 1960s and early 1970s. The IISS indicates that by 1977 South Korea was spending 6.5 percent of GNP on defense, while North Korean defense expenditures were 10.5 percent of GNP, down from 11.2 percent in 1976. (A footnote in the report suggests, however, that the figures used for North Korea may be too low.) South Korean statistics, using a lower GNP estimate for the North, assert that Pyongyang spent 23 percent of its GNP on defense in 1977, compared to 6.2 percent in the South.

A particularly striking trend in recent years is the dramatic increase in South Korea's military expenditures. According to the IISS, South Korea spent $943 million on defense in 1975, $1.5

billion in 1976, $2 billion in 1977, and $2.6 billion in 1978. North Korean defense expenditures, in contrast, were said to have remained constant at about $1 billion in both 1977 and 1978. (The IISS states that no figures are available for the earlier years.) The numbers given for North Korea are, of course, open to doubt. U.S. diplomats reportedly asserted in mid-1979 that North Korean defense spending actually ranges between $1.8 billion and $2.4 billion. In any case, South Korea is now spending considerably more on defense than the North, and further sharp increases in Seoul's military expenditures may be anticipated. The CIA predicted in its early 1978 report that South Korea would double its 1976 defense outlay of $1.5 billion by 1981, but defense spending has actually risen at a much faster rate. By 1979 the defense budget had already reached $3 billion, and in response to a request from President Carter during his July 1979 visit to Seoul, South Korean officials indicated plans to increase defense spending in 1980 by an extra 1 percent of GNP (approximately $500 million). Seoul's 1980 budget, announced in November 1979, asked $4.4 billion for defense in 1980.[24] It is unmistakably clear that, given the growing gap between the two economies and the increasing readiness of the South Koreans to devote a high percentage of expenditures to defense, Pyongyang will find it very hard to keep pace.[25]

How Do the Military Capabilities of the Two Koreas Compare? What Are the Impacts of the 1977 and 1979 Upward Revisions of North Korean Strength?

WEINSTEIN: In May 1978, the Congressional Budget Office (CBO) published a comprehensive assessment of the military balance between the two Koreas.[26] The CBO analysis, which relied on a variety of techniques from Department of Defense (DOD) computer simulations of battles to independent traditional analyses by experienced military officers, took into account classified DOD studies. According to the CBO analysis, North Korea's advantages lay in the following areas:

1. large numbers of tanks (though not the latest Soviet models)
2. large numbers of artillery pieces, mortars, and rocket launchers

3. an extensive air defense system with large numbers of weapons, but virtually no modern radar-controlled mobile guns or late-model surface-to-air missiles
4. greater numbers of, but less capable, tactical aircraft
5. extensive unconventional warfare (commando) forces

South Korea was given the advantage in the following:

1. superior ground-force manpower, particularly with respect to division staying power and reserves
2. superior technical capability in tactical aircraft, in antitank guided missiles, and probably in tanks
3. prepared defense positions on advantageous terrain

(See Table 1.1 for a comparison of North and South Korean military indicators.)

The CBO's opinion was that "despite important asymmetries, the military balance between North and South Korea now seems even enough to present substantial risk to North Korea that an attack could fail." The report noted that the South Korean Force Improvement Plan would provide more and better tanks, tactical aircraft, antitank weapons, and artillery, with additional new programs to be launched in light of the then-planned withdrawal of U.S. ground-combat forces. The CBO predicted that "in the case of an unaided North Korean attack across the DMZ, South Korean ground forces appear capable of maintaining their own defenses." According to the CBO report, the assessment that South Korea "will be able to defend itself against North Korea without U.S. ground forces" was behind the decision to withdraw the Second Division. In explaining this assessment, the report drew attention to the importance of geography. Asymmetries in firepower favoring North Korea might be significant if the geography of Korea was like that of Europe. North Korean armored forces, though superior in number, cannot be used to maximum effect in the hills and ridges that dominate the DMZ approaches to South Korea. According to the CBO report, the South Korean Army had recently restructured its defenses to take better advantage of these geographic assets. Extensive and well-constructed tank barriers and prepared defensive positions further enhanced South Korean capabilities.

TABLE 1.1

Key Military Indicators, North and South Korean
Armed Forces, 1979

	North Korea	South Korea
Population	17,170,000	35,940,000
Total active forces	512,000 (622,000-672,000)[a]	642,000
Army	440,000 (550,000-600,000)[a]	560,000
Navy	27,000	32,000
Airforce	45,000	30,000
Marines	------	20,000
Reserve forces		
(includes paramilitary)	1,800,000	2,800,000
Ground forces		
Divisions[b]	28 (37-41)[a]	20
Marine divisions[b]	0	1
Brigades	15	11
Marine brigades	0	2
Regiments	35	0
Batallions	8	38
Tanks	2,100 (2,500-2,600)[a]	1,100
Armored personnel carriers	800 (1,000)[a]	520
Artillery	3,000 (3,500)[a]	2,000
Rocket launchers	1,300 (1,600)[a]	0
Mortars	9,000	5,300
Surface-to-air missiles	250	125
Antiaircraft guns	5,000	1,000
Navy		
Combat vessels	396	107
Air forces		
Combat aircraft	655	276
Older models[c]	515	113
Newer models[d]	140	163

Source: International Institute for Strategic Studies, The Military
Balance, 1978-1979 (London: 1978), pp. 63-64; Report to the Senate
Committee on Foreign Relations by Senators Hubert Humphrey and John
Glenn, U.S. Troop Withdrawal from the Republic of Korea, 95:2 (January
1978), p. 27.

[a]Revised U.S. intelligence estimates as reported in Los Angeles Times,
July 16, 1979; Far Eastern Economic Review, May 18, 1979, p. 49; and
Representative Les Aspin, "The Korean Troop Withdrawal Plan: A Reassessment," mimeographed, June 1979, p. 3. These sources are not
entirely consistent with one another.

[b]North Korean divisions are modeled after USSR/PRC divisions, and number about 10,000 men each--roughly 65 percent of the strength of South
Korean divisions, which follow U.S. division organization. Most of the
manpower differences, however, lie in combat support and logistics
troops. Actual deployed combat strength in a North Korean division,
including weapons, is roughly the same as that of a South Korean division.

[c]Older models include MIG 15/17/19, IL-28, F-86, F-5A, RF-5A, and S-2F.

[d]Newer models include MIG 21, SU-7, F-4D/E, and F-5E.

If, through miscalculation or some other unexpected development, war were to break out in Korea after the departure of the Second Division and a rapid U.S. response were deemed necessary, the following U.S. forces were identified as immediately available: 9 squadrons of land-based fighter/attack aircraft (3 squadrons in Korea itself); the 2 brigades of the Third Marine Amphibious Force (including its tactical air wing) in Okinawa; and the 20 to 25 combat ships of the Seventh Fleet, including 2 aircraft carriers. According to the CBO report, while Washington was planning to maintain a capability to reintroduce the Second Division if necessary, this would "probably add only marginally to the military effort against the attackers." Additional U.S. tactical air, as well as logistical, support would represent more valuable contributions.

Of course, not everyone in Washington accepted the assessments reported by the CBO. Major General John K. Singlaub, chief of staff of U.S. forces in Korea, created a furor in May 1977 when he was quoted in the press to the effect that the recent upward revision of estimates of North Korean firepower had invalidated the assumptions behind the president's withdrawal decision. It was generally accepted that there had been a substantial increase in the inventory of North Korean tanks. This was the result not of any sudden buildup by the North Koreans, but of an improvement in U.S. intelligence capabilities. Following the end of the Vietnam War, the United States intensified its intelligence efforts in Korea, which led in 1977 to a dramatic upward revision of the number of North Korean tanks.

There was, however, no consensus among government officials as to the implications of the new figures. As Singlaub acknowledged, the conventional wisdom in both military and civilian circles had held for some time that the ground forces of South Korea were equal, or superior, to those of North Korea. Some, like General Richard G. Stilwell, a former commander of U.S. forces in Korea, agreed with Singlaub that this conclusion was no longer valid. The CIA was said to be somewhat pessimistic in its estimates of South Korean capabilities. Senate Foreign Relations Committee staff members who visited Korea in June 1977 reportedly returned with some doubts about the ability of the South Koreans to hold their own.

I interviewed a cross section of U.S. officials in both the executive and legislative branches during September 1977. A few of the officials interviewed then felt that the North had an edge on the ground. But most, including some who emphasized the significance of the improved North Korean capabilities, refused to draw the conclusion that North Korea's ground forces were superior overall. They stressed that there can be few "hard facts" in a situation such as this. Although the North Koreans had marked advantages in certain areas, it was "hard to say what it all adds up to," according to one official with considerable Korean experience. We must consider not only the numerical balance and the terrain, but also such factors as training, the quality of equipment, leadership, combat experience, and scenarios as to how the conflict is likely to begin. Several policymakers pointed out that much of the discussion about numbers is of limited relevance. The central consideration is not the comparison of the number of tanks on each side, but the balance between the tank forces of North Korea and the antitank capabilities of the South. Despite the claims of generals like Singlaub and Stilwell, there was, in the words of one official with long experience, "nothing to suggest that North Korea can overcome the obstacles inherent in defensive terrain, fortifications, and the antitank defenses of South Korea, especially if one counts tactical air support." Many estimates are misleading, he noted, because they fail to include air support as an antitank weapon. Besides, calculations of the military balance must take into account nonmilitary factors, such as the economic base and population, that favor the South.

Another well-informed source reported that the question of the military balance had been discussed at length in interagency meetings. According to this source, the majority of the military felt that the new figures did not alter the overall balance. The predominant view was that even then, in 1977, South Korean forces could, if properly deployed, prevent the fall of Seoul against a North Korean attack without support from the Second Division. This estimate assumed that South Korean forces would be deployed in an anti-invasion mode, rather than an anti-infiltration mode, as they are at present. This was based on the judgment that the infiltration threat had become considerably less than it was some years before.

Like the CBO report, those who dismissed the claims of Singlaub and Stilwell stressed the central importance of terrain. Some made the point even more sharply than did the CBO report.

A military expert noted that there are only two major invasion routes to Seoul, and both are narrow corridors, greatly enhancing the effectiveness of antitank missiles. If North Korean tanks travel along those corridors, he asserted, they will be "torn to shreds" by the antitank weapons the South Koreans are acquiring. "Some people," he added, "think this is still 1950, when South Korean forces were not properly deployed, did not have the proper equipment, had weapons half of which did not fire, and faced a multitude of other problems."

Except for one congressman, even the most pessimistic of the officials interviewed agreed that the South Korean Army would be able to stand on its own without U.S. ground forces by 1982, assuming that the planned transfers of equipment were carried out. They expressed certainty that the proposed aid package would eliminate all of the South Korean deficiencies on the ground.

New North Korean tunnels under the DMZ were discovered in late 1978, and these gave rise to some concern in Seoul. The tunnels were a matter of concern less for the capabilities they represented than as a possible indicator of North Korea's intentions. Few have suggested that they dramatically alter the military balance, but many have assumed that they reflect Pyongyang's aggressive designs. Although it would be foolish to rule out aggressive plans on Pyongyang's part, there are other plausible, and less alarming, interpretations as to why the tunnels have been dug. Some have speculated that tunnel digging, which began in the early 1970s at about the same time as the opening of the first North-South dialogue, may have been a kind of "sop" to more militant elements at a time when Kim had decided to experiment with a more conciliatory line. The tunnels may have been viewed as a means of sustaining a sense of militance and revolutionary momentum through "preparations" for a reunification effort, even though like Taiwan's "preparations" for a return to the mainland, the North Korean efforts were beginning to seem a bit like "whistling in the dark." It is possible that some in Pyongyang, genuinely fearing the South's growing strength, may have concluded that the "best defense is a good offense." And, of course, there may well be a feeling that the tunnels would put the North in a position to take advantage of opportunities that might arise, should the situation in the South deteriorate dramatically. No one can say with confidence why the North Koreans have dug those tunnels, but it would be a mistake to assume unquestioningly that they can only signify a planned invasion.

In early 1979, the press reported on a new U.S. Army intelligence analysis, which had concluded that the North Korean Army was far stronger than previously estimated. Citing satellite photography and intercepted communications on the movements of North Korean units, the army study indicated that the North Korean Army had the equivalent of 41 divisions, rather than 28, as previously believed. Press reports, however, presented contradictory accounts concerning both the means by which the U.S. Army had reached such conclusions and the new totals for North Korean troops and tanks. First reports on the new assessment indicated that, despite the additional 13 divisions, there had not been any major increase in the size of the North Korean Army, still believed to number about 440,000. Rather, the increased strength of the North Korean ground forces was attributed to changes in organization, which apparently emphasized the maintenance of large numbers of ready units. Those press reports also stated that satellite photography had revealed 300 more tanks than previously estimated, bringing the total to 2,000.[27] Consistent with the press explanation, one government source indicated to me that North Korean forces formerly listed as reserves were now being counted as active forces, presumably because of their high state of readiness.

But a later report asserted that the new assessment had been based largely on an increase in the number of tanks from 1,900 to 2,600. The army apparently concluded that tank formations spotted in the satellite photographs revealed the presence of North Korean armored divisions. This conclusion was said to have been disputed by the CIA, which had tentatively concluded that the tanks belonged to tank brigades. The CIA was, however, prepared to accept the conclusion that the North Korean ground forces were stronger than previously estimated, though not as strong as the army believed. This later report also said that the army estimated the number of North Korean troops at 500,000, an increase of 60,000.[28] Subsequent estimates of North Korean ground forces ranged as high as 700,000, but by mid-May, there seemed to be an emerging consensus that the North Koreans had about 550,000–600,000 ground troops and 2,500–2,600 tanks.[29] Significant increases were also noted in artillery pieces (now estimated at 3,500), armored personnel carriers (now put at 1,000), and rocket launchers (now about 1,600).[30] As in the case of the 1977 revision, government officials claimed that the new figures were mainly the result of improved intelligence, not of any sudden upsurge in North Korean military strength. The recently discovered buildup of North Korean forces was believed to have taken place gradually since 1971, with the most dramatic increases coming between 1974 and 1976; since 1977, it has continued at a much lower rate.[31]

The new estimates raised a number of questions beyond the obvious ones stemming from the contradictory nature of the reports published in the press. Why did two of the reports described above refer to previous tank estimates (1,700 and 1,900) well below the 2,100 listed in the IISS 1978–1979 survey? The inexplicably low baseline did have the effect of making the reported increases appear more dramatic. To what extent did the new estimates represent merely a new method of tallying North Korean forces, rather than an actual increase in their size? Some suggested that analysts were now counting as active forces troops that were previously viewed as reserves. If so, then the North Koreans, rather than having more forces, were in a higher state of readiness—significant, of course, but a more subjective judgment. Several key officials in Washington indicated privately that a new method of counting was the major reason for the revised figures; other officials strongly denied this. Still others insisted that the "new methodology" consisted simply of a more rigorous step-by-step analysis of photographic intelligence data, a time-consuming approach not previously used in Korea.

A report issued by Congressman Les Aspin in June 1979 asserted that the reason for the previous underestimation had to do with the way North Korean units were deployed. Specifically, Aspin pointed out, many small North Korean military units were scattered around the countryside. Units once thought unaffiliated to any other unit were now identified as belonging together, and this discovery was said to have been responsible for the dramatic increase in the number of divisions. Aspin also noted that all of the newly identified forces were in the rear areas, while U.S. intelligence efforts were concentrated in the forward areas. According to Aspin, North Korea's presumed "forward defense" strategy had apparently been replaced by a "defense-in-depth" deployment strategy.[32]

The timing of the army report raised some questions. In 1977 the estimates of North Korean strength had been revised upward with the explanation that the end of the Vietnam War had made it possible to devote more intelligence resources to Korea. But two years later the same explanation seemed less persuasive to some people. There were suspicions that the army intelligence report— by assuming that tank formations indicated divisions where others had assumed only brigades—might simply have been drawing the most pessimistic conclusions in order to dramatize the North Korean threat. Indeed, certain administration officials reportedly expressed skepticism about the entire reassessment. These officials, who noted that the report was first disclosed to the *Army Times,* a newspaper with close ties to the Pentagon, suspected that the new assessment might have been designed to fit the opinions of some senior army officials opposed to the Carter administration's withdrawal plan. A senior official privately emphasized that the reasons for the new army estimates of North Korean strength could not be understood without reference to the army's very strong institutional interest in maintaining a substantial U.S. troop presence in Korea. Military officials, of course, denied that the new estimates had been influenced by their opposition to the withdrawal plan.[33] In any case, the new assessment did play an important role in strengthening the arguments of those who wished to stop the troop withdrawal. Thus, the administration announced in February 1979 that the troop withdrawals would be "held in abeyance" until Washington could assess "new developments, including the new intelligence data on North Korean strength, U.S.–China normalization, and the evolution of a north-south dialogue."[34] In July the suspension was extended to 1981.

Although they were certainly not displeased at the suspension of the troop withdrawal, the Japanese expressed a good deal of puzzlement about the meaning of the new assessment. According to a variety of sources contacted in Tokyo in early 1979, the Japan Defense Agency had concluded that while the new estimates might be useful as a political justification for opposing the troop withdrawal, they were questionable as an intelligence analysis. The assumption was that the reassessment was essentially a "numbers game," motivated primarily by a desire to provide support for those opposed to the troop-withdrawal plan. In the words of one Japanese, it gave Carter a face-saving way to back off from his withdrawal policy. The impression that the administration was searching for ways to justify the abandonment of a troop-withdrawal policy that had become a political liability was reinforced by the lumping together, in the administration's explanation of the suspension, of such disparate considerations as the new estimates, U.S.–China normalization, and the start of a North-South dialogue in Korea.

In any case, there was little evidence of Japanese concern about any North Korean military buildup. And the Japanese were relatively hopeful that the start of a North-South dialogue might help stabilize the situation, although resolution of the central issues between the two Koreas seemed remote. Of course, the Japanese did not rule out the possibility that the new estimates might reflect a substantial increase in North Korean strength.

Significantly, in July 1979 some Japanese specialists noted that if the dramatic revision of the estimates concerning North Korea was justified, then one had to be seriously concerned about the reliability of U.S. intelligence. After the spectacular failure of U.S. intelligence in Iran, it was unsettling to hear, for the second time in two years, that U.S. estimates of North Korean strength had been wrong. For the Japanese and others who rely on U.S. commitments, repeated admissions of intelligence failures, whether due to a shortage of intelligence resources or a decision that new methods of counting were needed, threatened to add a new dimension to the problem of maintaining the credibility of U.S. commitments.

MOMOI: The "new assessment" could have four possible explanations. First, it could be the result of a genuine reevaluation, with the conclusion that previous analyses simply underestimated North Korea's manpower strength. Second, it could, as South Korean sources claim, be the result of an extensive manpower buildup by the North Koreans. Third, the new assessment could be the product of an intelligence manipulation by U.S. officials desiring to justify the modification of the troop-withdrawal program. Or, finally, it could be the result of a simple mathematical recalculation.

It is premature to rule out any of these possibilities. But it is interesting to note that the 1978–1979 IISS statistics list 28 North Korean Army divisions and 15 brigades (a division has 9,000 men, and a brigade 8,000). If the 15 brigades are simply counted as

divisions, then 15 brigades can be regarded as 13 divisions, bringing the total number of divisions to 41. If, on the other hand,
there has been a genuine buildup of North Korean power, it is difficult to understand why initial reports of the new assessment put
the number of tanks at only 2,000. It is inconceivable that the
number of divisions could increase from 28 to 41 while the number of tanks declined and air power was not significantly increased.
Later reports on the reassessment have, of course, significantly
raised the estimate of North Korean tanks.

KAMIYA: I, too, feel that a certain skepticism is warranted
with respect to the new estimates. The assertion that the estimates
of North Korean strength are being drastically revised upward
because previous collection capabilities were inadequate simply
strains credulity. It is very hard to believe that U.S. intelligence
could have failed to pick up any evidence of 160,000 men. How
could the United States have been so far off? While I think it is
unwise to withdraw U.S. ground forces as President Carter proposed, I believe we must recognize that the situation in Korea is
becoming more stable and, contrary to the impression given by
these new estimates, less dangerous.

MOMOI: What can we conclude about the military balance between the two Koreas as of 1979? The overall balance seems
roughly even and likely to remain so through the mid-1980s,
unless some external power introduces sophisticated new weapons. Implementation of President Carter's plan to withdraw U.S.
ground-combat forces by 1982 probably would not have had any
effect on that balance, so long as the promised compensatory aid
was provided. It should be noted that, ignoring the U.S. presence,
the static military balance presently favors North Korea in a number of respects. But several points concerning the quantitative
measures need to be clarified if those numbers are to be properly
interpreted. (See Table 1.1.)

With respect to ground forces, South Korea has either an
overwhelming manpower superiority, if one relies on IISS statistics, or at most a slight inferiority, if the U.S. Army's high
figure of 600,000 North Korean troops is correct. There is no disputing the fact that the North Koreans have at least twice as many
tanks and armored vehicles as the South. While the North Koreans
may lack the latest Soviet tanks, as noted in the CBO report, the
quality of the North's tanks and armored vehicles is approximately

equal to that of the South. The South, however, has recently acquired its own production capabilities in this area, while the North remains dependent mainly on the Soviets for tanks and armored vehicles. North Korea's superiority in every category of surface firepower—artillery, mortar, and surface-to-surface missiles (SSMs)—is impressive; but the South recently test-fired a domestically produced SSM. Although it will be some time before South Korea's SSMs become operational, this domestic production capability could eventually prove quite significant.

WEINSTEIN: Some observers would go even farther in emphasizing the qualitative advantages possessed by the South. For example, Congressman Les Aspin notes that the South Koreans have M-60 and M-48 tanks, while North Korea's T-54 and T-34 tanks are of "a far older model and probably less reliability."[35]

SAEKI: The North Korean superiority in firepower is not decisive enough to tip the North-South power balance in favor of the North. The key questions involve the effectiveness with which the superior North Korean firepower can be mobilized to attack South Korea and the kinds of efforts the United States and South Korea are making to offset the imbalance in firepower. The largest defense problem for South Korea is, of course, the geographic proximity of Seoul to the thirty-eighth parallel.

MOMOI: Indeed, the critical issue for South Korea is not the defense of all of its territory, but its ability to stop a North Korean ground advance before it reaches Seoul. Even a temporary loss of Seoul could be fatal, because of the psychological impact on the South's leadership. If the citizenry of the capital city should panic, Seoul could collapse even if it has not been overcome militarily.

WEINSTEIN: Some U.S. military analysts are concerned that, in a surprise attack against the South, North Korea could mass its firepower in support of infantry attacks to break through South Korean forward defenses and launch a high-speed armored drive toward Seoul, only 30 miles below the DMZ. Steps are being taken to improve the Republic of Korea's (R.O.K.'s) capability to deal with this contingency. South Korea's Force Improvement Plan and the current U.S. military assistance programs seek to reduce this risk by improving South Korean firepower, antitank capabilities, mobility, and communications in order to contain North Korean penetration north of Seoul.

Moreover, some officials are dubious about the ability of the

North Koreans to stage a genuine surprise attack, even if they were irrational enough to try it. There has been general agreement that the North Korean forces have been deployed in an offensive mode, though the 1979 discovery of additional rear-echelon forces has led some to conclude that the North Korean deployment strategy is one of "defense-in-depth," rather than "forward defense."[36] In any case, one State Department official suggested that even a "forward defense" strategy probably reflected a North Korean assumption that the best defense is a good offense. The North could attack with the forces and equipment presently in place, but the chances of success would be greatly reduced. Even a modest amount of mobilization—say, over several days—would give the South Korean defenders a considerable advantage. In addition, there is some doubt whether the allies of the North Koreans would provide them with the fuel needed to sustain a large-scale invasion.

Even if the new estimates of North Korean capabilities are correct, they do not necessarily signify a major change in the overall balance, according to government officials contacted in Washington. The *Far Eastern Economic Review* reported the belief of "most observers" in both Seoul and Washington that the situation "had not changed that dramatically." That journal also cautioned against underestimating the significance of recent improvements in the South's capabilities.[37] If the major threat to the South is a surprise attack aimed at capturing Seoul, the additional North Korean troops are unlikely to have a decisive effect on the outcome because the number of troops that can usefully be deployed in such an operation is limited. As Congressman Aspin has noted, nearly all of the newly discovered North Korean forces are located in the rear areas.[38] If, on the other hand, the issue is the staying power of the two sides in a war of attrition, then the superior strength of the South—with its advantages in population, economic capabilities, and potential for resupply by the United States—is readily apparent. The addition of 60,000–160,000 North Korean ground forces and 400–500 tanks does not weigh heavily against the basic advantages possessed by the South in any protracted struggle.

MOMOI: The static military balance in naval and air forces tends to favor the North, but some qualifications are necessary. Since the North Koreans have no marines, South Korea has absolute superiority in that area. But the South's marines are geared toward fixed defense and are incapable of executing independent amphibious operations. Since the navies of both the North and the South are so limited in size, it is unlikely that North Korea's numerical superiority in naval forces would have a significant impact. North Korea's vast numerical advantage in air forces is partially offset by the superior quality of the South's aircraft; the North Koreans simply have nothing to compare with the F-4s and F-5s of the South, not to mention the F-16s that Seoul hopes to acquire. But in a combat situation, North Korea's numerical superiority in aircraft, if combined with the advantages of a first strike, could prove to be of crucial importance.

WEINSTEIN: In the past, most U.S. analysts have concurred that North Korea holds a clear lead in air power, as a result of its substantial numerical advantage. But now many analysts view the two air forces as much more evenly matched in overall capabilities. The majority of the officials interviewed in Washington viewed the North and South Korean air forces as very close, with the North possessing at most a slight overall advantage. Some felt that the R.O.K. air force had already attained a rough parity with that of North Korea. It was noted that a realistic comparison must consider not only the number of aircraft, but pilot training, maintenance capabilities, range of the aircraft, bomb load, firepower, and other performance characteristics. In most qualitative areas, the South Koreans are felt to be significantly ahead. The superior skills of South Korean pilots, excellent maintenance capabilities, and the relatively high percentage of modern aircraft were frequently cited by the U.S. officials interviewed. In contrast, the North Koreans have large numbers of obsolete airplanes (see Table 1.1), and their pilots have very low flying time.

MOMOI: Other factors raise doubts about the significance of sheer numbers—including logistical capabilities, the quality of communications systems, the "state of hardening" or damage-absorption capability, the availability of "air sanctuaries," alert status, and morale. While hard information is missing, it is fair to conclude that despite the imbalance in the numbers of combat aircraft, there is a general balance between the two Korean air forces if all factors are taken into consideration.

WEINSTEIN: Moreover, several U.S. officials noted that the trend is moving rapidly in favor of South Korea, mainly as a result of the R.O.K. force improvement plan. Even though the

North will probably continue to hold a numerical advantage, its lead is expected to shrink considerably by the mid-1980s. The South Koreans are rapidly increasing their inventories of F-4Es and F-5Es, and as already mentioned, they plan to purchase F-16s to replace the remaining F-86s.

MOMOI: In contrast, there is real doubt about the North's ability to modernize its forces. The crucial issue is whether either China or the Soviet Union can be relied on to supply sophisticated weapons prior to or immediately after the outbreak of conflict. Since the North's weapons are becoming obsolete, North Korea will become progressively inferior unless its allies assist. Although the North has long had a larger domestic arms-production industry than the South, that advantage, too, is being lost as the South Koreans rapidly increase their arms-production capabilities and the North Koreans find their development constrained by persistent economic difficulties.

Ultimately, the question of access to modern weapons may well be the key element of the Korean equation. We should view a possible Korean confrontation not as a war between existing capabilities, but as a war of supply and attrition. What counts is not the number of tanks or aircraft each side has at present, but the capability of each side to acquire such weapons, either through its own production facilities or through purchase abroad.

By 1982, the South should have greater confidence in its ability to stop a North Korean advance toward Seoul without U.S. assistance. And by that time, the South Korean force improvement plan is expected to be concluded. South Korean self-confidence is already rising rapidly. Japanese analysts are now considerably less concerned about the military balance in Korea than they were in 1977. But until 1982, the South Koreans are unlikely to feel sanguine about their ability to stop a well-planned, determined North Korean assault preceded or accompanied by an extensive air attack. In the absence of any U.S. involvement, this would quickly give the invader air supremacy, and regardless of what U.S. or Japanese analysts may conclude about the importance of the South's qualitative advantages, the North Korean leaders will continue to believe that the numerical superiority of their forces places them in a strong position. Hence, to ensure the maintenance of the military balance and to deter a North Korean attack, a U.S. ground presence in the South or a credible U.S.

threat to use nuclear weapons against the North will be essential until 1982.

Even if war seems unlikely, we must consider North Korean capabilities to initiate subversive operations against the South. With respect to overland penetration, the DMZ and the warning system to the South, together with civilian defense capabilities such as village informant networks, constitute extremely difficult barriers for infiltrators seeking to launch an extensive, synchronized, subversive campaign. South Korea remains relatively vulnerable, however, to amphibious infiltration; the R.O.K.'s long coastline affords many ideal landing sites for infiltrators and makes it hard for village informant networks to spot infiltrators quickly. On the other hand, air drops are easy to detect and can be localized. It is harder to be optimistic about internal subversion, since the potential for such subversion depends on the extent of domestic discontent, political/economic disruption, and restiveness among students. Whether these can be averted or nipped in the bud will hinge on the future course of the South Korean government's political and economic policies.

Notwithstanding all that we have said, the possibility of war cannot be ruled out. Thus, it is useful to consider the circumstances under which a conflict might break out. The most likely scenario is as follows. The first step would be rising instability in either or both of the Korean states, followed by North Korean infiltration into the South and the start of sabotage operations. This would be followed by border exchanges, which, through uncertainty or miscalculation, would quickly escalate. The next step would be an all-out North Korean air attack against all South Korean air bases, giving the North air control and opening the way for the advance of North Korean ground forces toward Seoul. As the North's FROG missiles reach Seoul, panic would ensue, followed by a limited air attack against the city. This would result in the fall of the first line of defense, bringing North Korean artillery within range of Seoul.

This scenario assumes not only that the United States has already withdrawn its ground troops and that Washington refuses to reintroduce them, but that because of indecision or pressing needs elsewhere in the world, the United States does not provide air support to Seoul. But if, after the withdrawal of U.S. troops, it is clear that U.S. tactical air forces will participate fully in the initial phases of the conflict, it is unlikely that hostilities will escalate beyond border incidents. This, in turn, suggests the importance of Japanese attitudes regarding U.S. use of air bases in Japan. U.S. air power based on a single aircraft carrier may not be sufficient to deter the North Koreans from seeking air supremacy, unless Pyongyang is convinced that the United States might use nuclear weapons. A second carrier could be deployed, of course, unless there is a serious threat of conflict elsewhere in the world.

All of this suggests that North Korea is unlikely to undertake a military adventure unless it can be certain that

1. U.S. troops have been completely withdrawn
2. U.S. air and naval power will either be withheld or sharply circumscribed in its use
3. China and/or the Soviet Union will rush hardware aid to North Korea immediately after the start of the conflict, even if they have not given advance approval of the attack
4. the domestic situation in South Korea is unstable
5. Japan will not permit the United States to use its bases for offensive operations against North Korea

The first two days of the conflict would probably be decisive in determining the outcome. Two days could be enough time for the North Koreans to capture air control in the northern part of South Korea and to break the first line of defense north of the capital. But after two days the capability of the United States to augment its own forces would increase significantly. One tactical air squadron deployed in the western Pacific could lend support immediately. Aircraft in the United States and marines based in Okinawa could reach Korea within two days. But it would take five days to bring in an additional naval task force from outside the area.

WEINSTEIN: Perhaps the deepest concern expressed by U.S. officials and legislators has to do with the possibility of irrational action by Kim Il-sung. Many voiced concern, not about the military balance created by the U.S. withdrawal plan, but about its psychological impact on Kim. Indeed, a number of liberal senators and congressmen who supported the Carter administration's Korea policy expressed uneasiness about the timing of the withdrawal plan. They preferred to wait perhaps ten years, until Kim passed from the scene and South Korea had additional time to demonstrate its strength beyond any doubt.

One official argued, however, that the announcement of the withdrawal plan had enhanced stability during the five-year withdrawal period, because the North Koreans had to be careful to avoid doing anything that might upset the situation and thus risk a reversal of the withdrawal decision. According to this official, the administration's policy had left North Korea "up a creek." He added that the "statesmanlike" reaction of the South Koreans to the withdrawal plan, emphasizing self-reliance, also served to reinforce the prospects for stability. President Park and other top Korean officials consistently took a positive approach in public, stressing the adequacy of South Korea's defense capabilities. Indeed, some argued that the South Koreans, having endured the shock of the withdrawal announcement and survived, had become stronger and more self-confident than they would have been if they had not been forced to undergo that shock.

What Are U.S. and Japanese Interests in Korea?   To What Extent Do Their Economic Interests Overlap?

HARRISON: An assessment of Japanese and U.S. interests in Korea is inevitably something of a circular exercise. The Japanese debate over Korean policy hinges to a considerable extent on divergent assumptions with respect to the future U.S. posture; conversely, the U.S. debate over whether to disengage from Korea has become, to an even greater extent, a debate over the nature of Japanese interests in the peninsula. Defenders of the U.S. presence contend that a U.S. withdrawal would lead to a militarized, possibly nuclear-armed, Japan, while advocates of disengagement respond that a withdrawal in gradual stages would not critically affect Japanese defense or foreign policies. Both Tokyo and Washington, in varying degrees, have tended to view relations with Korea as ancillary to relations with each other, though as Okimoto has suggested, the dynamic growth of South Korea's economy is gradually leading U.S. observers to see more clearly a direct interest in Korea.

When one does focus squarely on the Korean problem as such, it soon becomes clear that Japanese and U.S. interests are largely congruent. At present, the governing interest of both Japan and the United States in Korea lies in reducing North-South tensions and in preventing a renewed large-scale military conflict in which either of the two countries could become even indirectly involved. This goal is directly linked to their broader mutual interest in the preservation of regional stability and the avoidance of conflict with China or the Soviet Union. For both Japan and the United States, the danger of renewed conflict in the peninsula poses a continuing threat to their efforts to improve relations with Peking and Moscow.

As regional neighbors, Japan, China, and the Soviet Union all have an overriding interest in preempting control of Korea by any of the others. This interest is not served by the current polarization between the Japanese-backed South and the Chinese- and Soviet-backed North. On the contrary, the safest situation for all concerned would be the emergence of patterns of contact and cooperation that would enable both North and South to reduce their external dependence, to present a common front toward all outside powers, and to move toward eventual confederation or unification. Here one sees the parallel interests of the United States and Japan sharply underlined; the ultimate interest of Washington, like that of Tokyo, lies in the emergence of a strong Korean buffer state able to stand up to both of its Communist neighbors.

To some extent, it would be correct to say that Japan has a special stake in a reduction of tensions in the peninsula as a result of the psychological legacy of the colonial period in Korea. Even if Korea could be completely insulated from the involvement of other powers, Japan would still have an overriding interest in a peaceful resolution of the North-South rivalry. History makes it peculiarly important for Japan to detach itself from the North-South struggle, and to move toward harmonized relations with Seoul and Pyongyang in order to help moderate tensions in the peninsula.

Given the depth of the bitterness left over from the colonial period, the potential for future conflict between Japan and Korea would appear to be serious under the best of circumstances. Colonialism aggravated what was already an endemically difficult sociocultural encounter between Japanese and Koreans, touching off a psychological cycle of challenge and response that continues still. Translated into policy terms, this background would appear to rule out a Japanese alignment with either side that would tend to sensitize and polarize the division. To be sure, significant support in Japan for a policy designed to harden the North-South division does exist. But although this might serve certain immediate Japanese economic interests, it would be an extremely risky long-term policy.

In this connection, one is struck by the basic historical fact that the present asymmetrical Japanese involvement with the South came only after protracted and insistent U.S. pressures on both Seoul and Tokyo. Evidence indicates severe differences between Washington and Seoul during the Syngman Rhee years over South Korean policies toward Japan. Washington pressed for normalization of relations between Seoul and Tokyo, not only for military reasons but, more importantly, as an avenue for supplanting U.S. aid outlays to Korea with Japanese investment. Rhee consistently opposed normalization. But despite widespread opposition reflected in serious riots, the new Park regime proved more malleable and ultimately concluded the 1965 normalization treaty.

Though many Japanese advocated normalization, considerable prodding was necessary before the conclusion of the 1965 accord. The Japanese objective of gaining economic access to South Korea would have been satisfied by a joint declaration. That solution would have allowed Japan to avoid signing a formal treaty, which was more likely to require at least a partial bow in the direction of recognizing Seoul as the exclusive sovereign in Korea. A simple declaration would also have been less provocative to the broadly based Japanese domestic opponents of normalization, who wanted Japan to avoid involvement in the Seoul-Pyongyang rivalry. Prime Minister Hayato Ikeda, after all, had often emphasized that Japan could not disregard the de facto existence of the Pyongyang regime and had strongly suggested on many occasions that Japan would eventually deal with the North. The treaty language finally chosen was deliberately ambiguous, which led to divergent interpretations on the part of South Korea and Japan.

Ironically, the years following the 1965 treaty when the North was reaching the zenith of its long effort to maximize self-reliance, were the same years in which the Park regime opened the gates to extensive dependence on Japan. The Japanese economic role in the South has resulted in the growth of significant vested interests in the business sectors of the two countries, as well as powerful political lobbies linked to the economic groups involved. Given the size the economic stakes have reached during the past decade, it is clear that the protection of existing vested interests in the South will be a major objective affecting future Japanese policy toward Korea. This should be sharply distinguished from the larger national interests of Japan as a whole, however.

It is noteworthy that there is widespread support in Japan for a more symmetrical policy toward Korea, in which Tokyo would balance its links to Seoul with economic and, gradually, diplomatic contacts with Pyongyang. One measure of this support is the fact that the group of Diet members advocating stronger ties with the North (*Niccho Giren*) had 285 adherents in early 1978, including 31 members of the governing Liberal Democratic party, as against 252 for the Seoul-oriented group (*Nikkan Giren*). To define Japanese interests in Korea in narrowly ideological terms, therefore, would be misleading.

Most Japanese appear less fearful of an eventual Communist triumph in Korea than of two other possible outcomes. One would be a conflict entailing U.S. intervention that could in turn embroil Japan militarily, complicating relations with other powers. The other fear involves precipitate U.S. disengagement from the South that would not allow Japan time to reshape its approach to the peninsula. In particular, there is concern in Japan that a new Korean conflict could seriously strain U.S.–Japan relations. Although the United States would expect Japan to support its military operations in Korea during a renewed conflict, as an obligation under the Mutual Security Treaty, the domestic political climate in Japan would permit only very qualified support. Kei Wakaizumi, explaining why Japan fears a Korean conflict, emphasized not the danger to Japan from the North, but the "profound apprehension that such a conflict may draw Japan into a conflict with China or the Soviet Union, or that it may damage her relations with the United States."[39]

Similarly, when pressed to define the nature of the security threats that would result from a Pyongyang victory, then Foreign Minister Kiichi Miyazawa did not point to the danger of North Korean aggression against Japan. Instead, he addressed his concern to the immediate spillover effects of a Korean civil conflict, principally the flood of refugees or "routed troops" who might seek shelter in Japan as a consequence of Japan's current ties to Seoul.[40]

To be sure, such spillover effects could pose significant problems, especially relating to Japan's already sizable Korean minority. It is not surprising, therefore, that Japan would want to see peace maintained in Korea. But this is very different from saying that long-term Japanese interests would be threatened by a North Korean victory, given Pyongyang's free-wheeling, nationalist foreign policy and its desire to offset its present dependence on Moscow and Peking with non-Communist ties. As we have already observed, even if the South were to win a new Korean war, Japan would no doubt find it just as distasteful to live with a unified Korea under Southern leadership as with one dominated by the North. It is the dislocations attendant to a military resolution of the Korean conflict that would be peculiarly costly for Japan, in addition to the stresses that are likely to bedevil future Japanese-Korean relations, regardless of how the conflict is resolved.

OKIMOTO: It is important, however, to note that because the prospects for peaceful reunification seem so remote, Korean reunification and war are inextricably linked in the Japanese mind. Thus, while it may be accurate to say that the Japanese fear a conflagration on the peninsula more than they worry about the consequences of a Communist victory, in reality they do not distinguish between the two, since they cannot easily imagine the South capitulating without a struggle. Although it is conceivable that a unified Communist Korea could come into being without producing severe repercussions in Japan, it would be a serious mistake to assume that such repercussions would not occur. Of course, the impact of a Communist victory would depend on a number of circumstances, including the duration of the conflict, the role of the major powers, the nature of the regional power balance, and the attitude of the new Communist regime toward Japan. Extreme reactions on the part of Japan, though not inevitable, certainly cannot be ruled out.

HARRISON: In comparing the Japanese and U.S. stakes in Korea, one is left with the conclusion that it would be specious to draw sharp distinctions between specifically Japanese or U.S. interests on the peninsula. In one sense, Japan has a more pronounced interest in avoiding military conflict, given its proximity to Korea and the possibility of spillover effects. But, in another, the United States has far more to lose in view of its direct combat involvement. Like Japan, the United States has accumulated substantial vested interests in the South, but these do not outweigh the larger national interests that would be served by U.S. disengagement from the North-South rivalry.

The United States had cumulative direct investments totaling $434 million as of December 1977, as against $1.007 billion for Japan. Both figures are misleading, however. A more accurate measure of the extent of U.S. economic interests in the South is suggested by the fact that $2.475 billion in private credits from U.S. banks were outstanding as of December 1978; in addition, Seoul owed $1.454 billion in governmental loans to the United States.[41]

In assessing the relative importance of U.S. and Japanese investment, it is important to recognize that Japanese companies often exercise informal control over South Korean enterprises through dummy partners and technical assistance (for example, licensing agreements), as distinct from equity investment. My inquiries in Tokyo and Seoul from 1971 through 1974 indicated that Japanese parent companies controlled South Korean enterprises with combined assets of at least $1.7 billion and possibly as much as $2.1 billion. Two-way trade between Japan and South Korea reached $8.5 billion in 1978 (with a $3.3 billion surplus for Japan), much of it in the form of components and raw materials for Japanese-linked companies.

Significantly, most of the Japanese firms with investments in Korea are small and medium-sized enterprises, in marked contrast to the U.S. situation.[42] Gulf Oil Company alone sells more than $1 billion per year in crude oil to the South and has a $200 million stake in refining, fertilizer production, and petrochemical manufacturing facilities. The United States maintains a $2.3 billion military base infrastructure, which is continually being refurbished. The nature of these U.S. vested interests is such that their abandonment would represent an even greater economic loss than Japan would suffer in the event of a North Korean takeover. Most of the U.S. economic stake in the South is in the form of equity investment, whereas Japanese economic involvement is, as already noted, predominantly in the form of technical assistance and licensing arrangements. The latter would be less directly affected than equity holdings, should expropriation occur, since much of the Japanese export trade with the South consists of raw materials and components for Japanese-linked enterprises that would still be needed even if the enterprises concerned were operated by the state.

KAMIYA: Japanese and U.S. interests in Korea are essentially the same, particularly in the short run. But there are some differences. Japan tends to be more satisfied with the existing situation on the peninsula. The United States, as the Nixon Doctrine and Carter's withdrawal policy show, is unwilling to contemplate the indefinite continuation of the current U.S. military presence. It should, however, be possible to avoid a major split between Japanese and U.S. policies, since the Americans are likely to recognize that any rash change in the present situation would jeopardize the overriding U.S. interest in the maintenance of peace and the deterrence of armed conflict.

Japan's interests in Korea lie not only in peace and stability, but in preventing any power from exercising hegemony over the peninsula. The Sino-Japanese War (1894–1895) and the Russo-Japanese War (1904–1905) provide historical evidence of the long-standing Japanese perception that Korea under the paramount influence of any outside power is a threat to Japan. Although Japan's annexation of Korea was one of the greatest mistakes of Japanese foreign policy in the modern era, it, too, was motivated by this concern about an externally dominated Korea. In today's Korea, we find not only a confrontation between North and South, but a complicated set of checks and balances among four powers— the United States, China, the Soviet Union, and Japan. China and the Soviet Union are in a competitive relationship in their dealings with North Korea, which is advantageous to Japan although there are some costs as well.

The Korean peninsula is particularly important to Japan in terms of Tokyo's relationship with Peking and Moscow. It is probably in Japan's interest to seek equidistance from China and the Soviet Union, though it is not easy to achieve. The conclusion of a peace treaty with China has not affected Japan's view of the importance of maintaining a balance in Korea. Any radical change in the present situation will lead China and the Soviet Union to engage in intense competition to improve their respective positions in Korea. Each must be aware of the danger that it could lose influence in Korea. This competition would make it even harder for Japan to maintain equidistance from the two Communist powers. Furthermore, both powers attach more importance to their relations with Washington than to those with Pyongyang. So, despite what they say publicly, the Soviet Union and China are probably not unhappy to see the present situation on the peninsula maintained.

It is not hard to understand why the United States is dissatisfied with having to keep approximately 40,000 soldiers in South Korea. The United States would like to avoid the persistence of a situation in which it would be automatically involved should a military conflict erupt on the peninsula. It is also reasonable for the United States to conclude that South Korea's impressive progress in economic and military development should make it possible to reduce the U.S. military burden. But it is questionable whether the United States should try to change the situation by itself, when Japan, China, and the Soviet Union all desire the maintenance of the status quo. Although Carter's withdrawal policy was understandable from the viewpoint of U.S. domestic politics, as foreign policy it was extremely naive. It is fortunate that the withdrawal program has been suspended. This came as no great surprise to the Japanese.

Of course, it is not necessarily correct to conclude that the Carter administration was eager to bring about any major change in Korea. Carter stressed that the military balance on the peninsula would be safeguarded through U.S. compensatory aid to South Korea, as well as by the continued presence of U.S. air forces there. But without credible political arrangements to maintain stability, troop withdrawal could lead to unanticipated results, because a military balance is always subject to change. Moreover, U.S. compensatory aid and South Korea's own intensified military development could well heighten political tensions and create increased instability. In summary, though a unilateral withdrawal may seem to serve U.S. interests in the short run, this may not be the case over the long run.

WEINSTEIN: There is no consensus among the members of this working group on the merits of U.S. troop withdrawals. But we can agree that the Carter administration's withdrawal plan raised important questions about modes of consultation between the United States and Japan, the relationship between the U.S. military presence and the deterrence of conflict, the likelihood and implications of a nuclear-armed Korea, the means of avoiding a spiraling conventional arms race, and the diplomatic or economic steps that might ease tensions and lay the groundwork for a modus vivendi between North and South. These are the principal questions that will be addressed in this book.

Notes

1. Suh Sang Chul, "Development of a New Industry through Exports," in *Trade and Development in Korea*, eds. Won Tack Hong and Anne O. Krueger (Seoul: Korea Development Institute, 1975).

2. Mikio Sumiya, "Growth Economy and Unstable Society: Mechanism of the South Korean Economy" (Paper prepared for the Conference of Japanese and U.S. Parliamentarians on Korean Problems, Washington, D.C., September 19–20, 1977), pp. 21–22. See especially Table 5, p. 22, citing R.O.K. Economic Planning Board statistics. Sumiya is a professor emeritus of economics at Tokyo University.

3. Ibid., p. 28. For a sympathetic treatment of R.O.K. wage statistics, see Irma Adelman, "Growth, Income Distribution and Equity-Oriented Development Strategies," *World Development*, February–March 1975, pp. 67–76, esp. p. 71.

4. Bruce Cumings, "Political Repression and Economic Development in the Republic of Korea: A Necessary Relationship?" (Paper prepared for the Conference of Japanese and U.S. Parliamentarians on Korean Problems, Washington, D.C., September 19–20, 1977).

5. The figures are as follows:

Countries	Early 1960s	Early 1970s
India	0.47	0.48
Indonesia	n.a.	0.46
Korea	0.34	0.37
Malaysia	0.57	0.52
Philippines	0.51	0.49
Taiwan	0.47	0.28
Thailand	0.51	0.43

The source of these figures is J. Alexander Caldwell, "The Economic and Financial Outlook for Developing East Asia" (Paper prepared for Pacific Forum Conference on Future Economic and Security Cooperation in the Pacific Region, Kona, Hawaii, December 2–4, 1978), p. 13.

6. The 1977 statistics are in *Far Eastern Economic Review*, May 18, 1979, p. 70. Concerning the growing imbalance in income distribution, see the article by Sam Jameson in *Los Angeles Times*, July 22, 1979; Samuel P. S. Ho, "Rural-Urban Imbalance in South Korea in the 1970s," *Asian Survey*

19, no. 7 (July 1979), pp. 645–659; and Irma Adelman and Sherman Robinson, *Income Distribution Policy in Developing Countries: A Case Study of Korea* (Stanford: Stanford University Press, 1978).

7. *Los Angeles Times,* March 4, 1979; *Asian Wall Street Journal,* February 12, 1980.

8. *Far Eastern Economic Review,* December 29, 1978, pp. 22–24.

9. *New York Times,* January 3, 1979, and February 28, 1979; and *Asian Wall Street Journal,* October 6, 1979, October 16, 1979, and October 23, 1979.

10. *Haptong,* December 20, 1979, and *Far Eastern Economic Review,* December 21, 1979, pp. 20–21.

11. *Asian Wall Street Journal,* December 27, 1979.

12. *New York Times,* December 7, 1979, and December 13, 1979.

13. *New York Times,* December 13, 1979, December 14, 1979, and December 18, 1979.

14. *New York Times,* December 16, 1979, and December 21, 1979; *Far Eastern Economic Review,* February 22, 1980, pp. 15–16.

15. U.S., Central Intelligence Agency, National Foreign Assessment Center, *Korea: The Economic Race between the North and the South,* January 1978, pp. 1–16. The analysis that follows draws heavily on this study.

16. International Institute for Strategic Studies, *The Military Balance 1978-79,* pp. 63–64; *Korean Newsletter* (Issued by Korean Information Office, Embassy of Korea, Washington, D.C.), January 1, 1979, pp. 7–8, and December 4, 1978, pp. 1, 8; *Far Eastern Economic Review,* May 18, 1979, p. 43; and *Asian Wall Street Journal,* January 1, 1980.

17. *Far Eastern Economic Review,* May 18, 1979, p. 52.

18. *Asian Wall Street Journal,* June 12, 1979; *Far Eastern Economic Review,* August 10, 1979; *Asian Wall Street Journal,* August 21, 1979; and *Far Eastern Economic Review,* January 25, 1980.

19. *Asian Wall Street Journal,* April 18, 1979.

20. *Korean Newsletter,* January 1, 1979, p. 8.

21. *Far Eastern Economic Review,* May 18, 1979, p. 52.

22. *Asian Wall Street Journal,* May 3, 1979, December 29, 1979, January 1, 1980, and February 12, 1980; and *New York Times,* December 22, 1979, and January 12, 1980.

23. *Far Eastern Economic Review,* January 25, 1980, p. 31.

24. *Asian Wall Street Journal,* September 18, 1979, and November 15, 1979.

25. See *Los Angeles Times,* July 16, 1979, and *New York Times,* August 9, 1979.

26. U.S., Congressional Budget Office, *Force Planning and Budgetary Implications of U.S. Withdrawal from Korea,* May 1978, pp. 10–13, 33–38.

27. *New York Times,* January 4, 1979.

28. *New York Times,* January 21, 1979.

29. *Far Eastern Economic Review,* May 18, 1979, p. 49, and discussions with U.S. officials.

30. *Los Angeles Times,* July 16, 1979.

31. Ibid.

32. Representative Les Aspin, "The Korean Troop-Withdrawal Plan: A Reassessment," mimeographed, June 1979, p. 3.

33. *New York Times,* January 21, 1979.

34. Testimony of Assistant Secretary of State for East Asian and Pacific Affairs Richard Holbrooke, quoted in *Asian Wall Street Journal,* March 13, 1979.

35. Aspin, "The Korean Troop-Withdrawal Plan," p. 4.

36. Ibid., p. 3.

37. *Far Eastern Economic Review,* May 18, 1979, pp. 49–50.

38. Aspin, "The Korean Troop-Withdrawal Plan," p. 3.

39. Kei Wakaizumi, "Japan's 'Grand Experiment' and the Japanese-American Alliance," Woodrow Wilson International Center for Scholars, October 9, 1975, p. 33.

40. "Foreign Minister Refers to Inflow of Refugees and Routed Troops as Effect of 'War in R.O.K.' upon Japan's Security," *Yomiuri,* August 23, 1975, p. 1.

41. The figures on direct investments and on loans were supplied, respectively, by the Departments of Commerce and State.

42. Mikio Sumiya, "Growth Economy and Unstable Society," p. 19.

2
The Meaning of Consultation

WEINSTEIN: It would be a serious mistake to dismiss the problem of consultation as merely a procedural matter. Because Washington is well aware of Korea's importance to Japan, the Americans know that any U.S. move vis-à-vis Korea will have an important impact on Japan. Similarly, the Japanese know that any initiative they might contemplate with reference to Korea will be of the greatest interest to Washington. Thus, each side's handling of the process of consultation is an indicator of its sensitivity to the needs and concerns of the other. Form and substance cannot easily be separated, for inattention to procedure is in itself a statement about the substance of the relationship—namely, about whether the ally is taken for granted or is considered important enough to deserve careful treatment. It is through the consultation issue that policies regarding Korea often become an issue in U.S.–Japan relations. And in the final analysis, it is what a failure to carry out adequate consultations says about the overall relationship between the United States and Japan that gives the greatest cause for concern.

Among the members of this working group, there is a virtual consensus that U.S. consultations with Japan were far from adequate in connection with the Carter administration's decision in 1977 to withdraw ground-combat forces from Korea within five years. Although the administration had repeatedly asserted that any change in U.S. policy would be developed in close consultation with Tokyo, as well as with Seoul, the Korean withdrawal decision showed just how difficult it is in practice to give meaning to that assertion. After making the basic decision on its own, the United States undertook consultations with Seoul and Tokyo concerning implementation of the withdrawal plan. But many Koreans and Japanese questioned whether there remained anything significant about which to consult.

We have chosen to consider at length the consultation process accompanying the Carter administration's 1977 decision to withdraw U.S. ground-combat forces from Korea in five years because of (1) the importance of that decision for all subsequent discussions of Korean security and (2) the broader impact of that decision, and of the manner in which it was reached, on the way the Japanese view their relations with the United States. In this chapter we will attempt to clarify the problems with the consultation process in 1977, the current expectations of each side concerning the substance of consultations, and the lessons that can be drawn from the 1977 experience to facilitate future efforts at consultation.

What Went Wrong in the Carter Administration's Consultations Concerning the Troop-Withdrawal Decision?

MOMOI: There is no question that the consultations were handled badly. Both the Japanese and the South Koreans believe that consultations with the United States were very inadequate. There were no formal consultations regarding the withdrawal decision in advance of the decision. Both Tokyo and Seoul learned of the U.S. decision through the mass media and were officially "informed" of the implementation program only after it had been decided on by the United States. This did a great deal to reduce the credibility of the United States.

Essentially, the failure of consultations on the question of troop withdrawal from South Korea is rooted in three aspects of the process that was used.

1. *Timing.* The issue was initially raised in the presidential campaign. Since most Japanese assumed that the campaign slogans were not to be taken seriously, they did not know how to interpret what was being said.

2. *Inconsistency.* After Mr. Carter became president, it seemed as if there were 32 different versions of his statements on Korea. There was great confusion in Tokyo and simply no way of knowing what policy he would follow.

3. *Lack of government-level discussions.* There was no govern-

ment-level approach until Vice President Walter Mondale visited Japan at the end of January 1977. By that time the Japanese government had already decided not to take up this issue as a major point of consultation, even though as Senator Charles Percy and others have noted, it did represent a basic issue between the United States and Japan.

The central problem is that *consultation* (which *Webster's* defines as an "act of asking advice and comparing views") simply was not undertaken by Washington. In short, no advice was sought, nor were any views compared.

KAMIYA: The crux of the problem was the failure of the Carter administration to consult Japan in advance of the basic withdrawal decision. Since his campaign days, President Carter had said time and again that he would consult Japan before deciding to withdraw U.S. troops from South Korea. The Japanese assumed that the United States would consult Japan on whether or not the withdrawal was appropriate, or at least on the size of the withdrawal—whether it would be an all-out affair or a partial reduction.

Even those Japanese authorities (both in the bureaucracy and in the Diet) who had few illusions about the realities of international politics had thought until early in February 1977 that the "consultation" mentioned in previous U.S. statements referred to discussions on the basic feasibility of U.S. military withdrawal from Korea. More optimistic people thought so right up to the Fukuda-Carter summit in March 1977. In time, however, it became clear that the Carter administration's thinking was based on a unilateral outlook and that the United States had no intention of discussing the basic withdrawal decision with Japan.

The administration's decision must be viewed from the standpoint of U.S. status as a Pacific state. As such, the issue of removing U.S. troops from South Korea must be considered a diplomatic one, and one that cannot be properly settled by a unilateral U.S. decision. Even if the United States was irrevocably resolved to carry out the withdrawal no matter what its allies said, the country should have started consulting its allies early in the decision-making stage in order to give credence to its stated position of "giving consideration to our allies' circumstances." This would surely have been a wiser procedure. But the United States did not choose this step because the issue of the troop withdrawal from

Korea was, in the U.S. view, primarily a domestic problem and not a diplomatic matter.

WEINSTEIN: The inadequacy of the Carter administration's consultations with the Japanese may reflect the administration's more general deficiency in carrying out consultations. Leaders of the U.S. Congress and many members of the executive branch also felt excluded from any meaningful consultations on the withdrawal decision. Much of the criticism of the withdrawal plan stemmed from the way in which the administration developed and presented its new policy. The legislators' dissatisfaction with the lack of White House consultations on Korea resulted in a Senate vote in June 1977 to require that all future policy decisions concerning Korea be made jointly by the president and Congress.

The interviews that I conducted with members of Congress and congressional staff personnel in September 1977 gave strong evidence that, like the Japanese, congressional spokesmen were resentful at not having been included in discussions held before the withdrawal decision. Indeed, one member of Congress related the widespread sense of shock among his colleagues when they learned that the CIA had not been asked before the decision for its estimates of the military balance in Korea. (The CIA estimate differed from those put forth by the Joint Chiefs of Staff in support of the administration's withdrawal plan.) Even after the decision was announced, the administration appeared to have had only limited success in communicating its motives to Congress.

Several discussions in Washington serve to illustrate the confusion surrounding the reasons for the administration's policies. A well-informed administration official assured me in the strongest terms that members of Congress understood perfectly the reasons for the troop withdrawal. The reasons set forth were that (1) the forces were militarily superfluous and (2) they fostered and perpetuated in the South Koreans a psychologically debilitating dependence on the United States. Several days later, in an interview with a member of the House International Relations Committee, I referred in passing to those two reasons as the ones the administration had given for its withdrawal policy. The congressman stopped me in mid-sentence and asserted, "Those are not the reasons at all. The troops are being withdrawn because the American people will not tolerate another land war in Asia. That is the administration's reason." The next day Congressman Les Aspin, who was inclined to be sympathetic to the withdrawal program, asserted categorically that the administration had not given Congress any reasons whatever for the troop withdrawals. In a memorandum he had written in July 1977 following hearings on Korea in the House Armed Services Committee, Aspin noted that there had been "a lot of testimony explaining why . . . troop withdrawal [was] not a *bad* idea" and why the risks were low, "but no testimony as to why it [was] a *good* idea." In Aspin's words, "the case for withdrawal [was] not being made."

Thus, it seems fair to conclude that the Carter administration had considerable difficulty holding meaningful consultations on the issue of Korea, not only with the Japanese and Koreans, but also with members of the U.S. Congress and even, to some extent, agencies of the executive branch. This suggests that the problem is deeper than one involving merely the U.S.–Japanese relationship. But that does not diminish the feeling on the part of the Japanese that this decision was taken unilaterally, ignoring Japanese interests and sensitivities.

KOSAKA: The unilateral aspect of the U.S. decision to withdraw troops from Korea is all the more disturbing because U.S. policymakers did not even seem aware that they were acting unilaterally. At least when Nixon undertook unilateral actions, he knew he was doing so. From the Japanese standpoint, unconscious unilateralism may be even worse than conscious unilateralism.

The U.S. attitude toward consultations has not only been one of unconscious unilateralism; it has also been characterized by what must be described as ignorance and unfairness. It is unsettling to the Japanese that the United States made the troop-withdrawal decision so suddenly and with so little regard for history. After all, in 1969 Washington had insisted on the so-called Korean clause, in which Japan recognized the importance of Korea for Japanese security. Some U.S. leaders say that Japan should have spoken up if it had strong feelings about the Korean decision. Indeed, they say that Japan should have backed up those feelings by agreeing to make a contribution to the security of Korea. But this view ignores the realities of the situation and is unfair to the Japanese. The fact is that Japan cannot do anything vis-à-vis Korea. Japan's colonial past in that country inhibits any such role. Few U.S. decision makers genuinely appreciate the delicacy and complexity of Japan's relationship with Korea. Japanese feelings about Korea are marked by a high degree of ambivalence. There is a vague but strong sense of concern about Korea and a clear sense that Japan needs a nonhostile Korea. But it would be going too far to describe the Japanese as "sympathetic" to the Koreans. The whole relationship is conditioned by a strong sense of the volatility of the psychological relationship. The Japanese are also aware of the flow of Korean immigrants and the polarization in Japanese politics that would result from turmoil on the Korean peninsula. Americans do not seem to appreciate fully the extent to which these concerns— especially the fear of a psychological shock—dominate Japanese perceptions of the Korean problem.

The situation is complicated because the Japanese are concerned about Korea without being in a position to do anything directly. This, indeed, is the way we see the situation: Japan is powerless to act, and it is unfair to expect Japan to be forthright in asserting its views, much less to take direct action concerning the maintenance of security in Korea. The Japanese want to be consulted on Korea and will respond to U.S. invitations to take part in such consultations. But it is impossible for Japan to take the initiative in this area.

OKIMOTO: There was widespread frustration among Japanese leaders about the manner in which the United States handled the matter of consultations concerning the decision to withdraw U.S. troops from Korea. Even those Japanese who basically endorsed Carter's decision complained that Japan had not been properly consulted.

After their unilateral decision, U.S. policymakers maintained that the Japanese should not have been surprised by the decision. Despite Japanese complaints about the suddenness of the announcement, warning signals of U.S. intentions could have been picked up years before the Carter announcement. The possibility of withdrawing troops from Korea had been discussed in public by presidents all the way back to John F. Kennedy. The Nixon Doctrine should have been seen as a clear sign that troop withdrawals were coming. Anyone who had followed the course of policy deliberations could have anticipated that changes were in the making, especially with the mounting pressures on Capitol Hill to cut back defense expenditures and the growing public sentiment to reduce U.S. military commitments overseas. Of course, it is fair to point out, as Kamiya and Momoi have done, that the signals from Washington were mixed. Indeed, Kamiya may be right when he says that one can "find anything" in the various statements by U.S. policymakers. Nevertheless, at least part of the responsibility for the "Korea shock" must be borne by the Japanese because of their failure to anticipate the inevitability of the shift in U.S. policies. It is essential that allies like Japan keep their antennae out to pick up signals of impending changes in U.S. policy.

U.S. policymakers have maintained, moreover, that even though mistakes may have been made in the early phases of deliberations, the Japanese were in fact consulted and their views taken carefully into account by the spring and summer of 1977, when plans were being made for the implementation of the withdrawal. Secretary of Defense Harold Brown made a point of stopping in Tokyo following his trip to Seoul to explain the U.S. position. Although quid pro quos could not be secured from Pyongyang or its allies, U.S. leaders reassured the Japanese that the gradual phase-out of U.S. forces would be carried out without damaging the structure of deterrence. Evidence of this commitment could be seen in the plan to maintain indefinitely U.S. air capabilities on the peninsula. To dispel whatever doubts remained about the U.S. commitment to the region, Secretary of State Cyrus Vance reaffirmed the undiminished importance of Asia in a speech before the Japan Society in New York.

Furthermore, U.S. defenders of the withdrawal plan could point to the fact that from the start of his administration, President Carter had emphasized the importance of maintaining close ties with Japan. In keeping with this objective, he dispatched Vice President Mondale on a special mission to Japan to demonstrate, both symbolically and functionally, the commitment of the new administration to keep communications open and relations close between the two countries. Japanese leaders were fully aware that one of Vice President Mondale's ostensible missions was to determine how the Japanese felt about the proposed plan for troop withdrawals from Korea. On the eve of Mondale's arrival, the Japanese cabinet met and decided not to press him in public for the retention of troops in Korea. When asked about Japan's stand, Prime Minister Takeo Fukuda stated that the issue of U.S. troops in Korea was a matter to be settled between Washington and Seoul and that Japan would not interfere. The message seemed clear: the Japanese government would not voice any objection to the U.S. removal of ground forces from Korea.

Given the Fukuda government's "hands-off" posture, how could Japanese leaders later complain about a lack of consultation? If conservative Liberal Democratic party (LDP) leaders had grave reservations about the withdrawal, as several of them later indicated, why did the government refrain from expressing its views? The answers lie in the complexity of Japanese feelings about Korea and in the dynamics of domestic politics in Japan.

Kosaka has already mentioned the volatility of the whole Korean issue. Feelings on both sides of the Sea of Japan run strong, largely as a consequence of the enmity generated by the history of colonization and war. The problem is compounded by the existence of active lobbying groups and a highly politicized Korean minority in Japan. Any position the government takes on matters related to Korea is bound to engender a heated reaction from either the pro-Seoul or the pro-Pyongyang group. Moreover, Tokyo has sought to maintain a semblance of openness concerning Japan's relationship with North Korea. There was also a fear, as Kosaka has noted, that pleading for the retention of U.S. forces in Korea would cast Japan in the awkward role of supplicant. This, in turn, might have rendered Tokyo vulnerable to the demand that Japan make greater sacrifices for the security of Northeast Asia. Besides, the Japanese probably felt that opposition to the withdrawal plan would have been futile. It made little sense to expend valuable political capital on an issue that apparently had already been settled.

It was especially hard for the LDP to take a clear stand on the troop-withdrawal issue. Since opinions about Korea within the LDP range across the spectrum, achieving consensus on the troop-withdrawal question would have been difficult and time-consuming. More importantly, a clear call to keep U.S. troops in Korea would have antagonized several of the opposition parties and might have forced a bitter confrontation in the Diet. At the time, two important pieces of legislation—a fisheries agreement and the Japan-Korea Continental Shelf Treaty—were pending before the Diet. To pass those measures, the LDP needed some support from the opposition parties. And because Fukuda had only recently come to power, his position was such that he could not risk antagonizing those whose support he needed to govern effectively.

The Fukuda cabinet's neutral public stance (*tatemae*) contrasted sharply with its private position (*honne*), as communicated indirectly to U.S. officials. Members of the Foreign Ministry and the Defense Agency, fearful of the potentially destabilizing effects of unilateral U.S. troop withdrawals, expressed their concern. They indicated their opposition in principle to the idea of withdrawing forces without winning some kind of quid pro quo from the North or its allies. Some Japanese were also concerned about Washington's failure to relate the troop withdrawals to the overall U.S. strategy for maintaining security in Northeast Asia and wondered whether this step presaged further withdrawals.

The intense Japanese concern over the lack of consultation about the Korean troop withdrawals must be viewed against the background of the series of "shocks" they feel Washington has exposed them to since the early 1970s. The "Korean shock" was viewed as but one of a number of unilateral U.S. decisions imposed on the Japanese as faits accomplis. The earlier shocks included the double "Nixon shocks" relating to China and to monetary policy (1971), the oil shock (1973–1974), the soybean embargo (1973), the abrupt change in the U.S. position on nuclear reprocessing (1977), and the sharp criticism of Japan resulting from the trade imbalance problem (1977 and onward). It is hardly surprising that some Japanese have come to feel increasingly beleaguered and pressured by their closest ally.

It is necessary, finally, to ask whether genuine consultation on the Korean withdrawal question was possible, or even desirable, from the U.S. standpoint. Is it realistic to expect a nation to make decisions about the deployment of its own troops subject to the veto of an ally? While U.S. officials, in the last analysis, do not deny that the withdrawal decision was taken unilaterally, they see nothing improper about that.

WEINSTEIN: In this connection, a high-ranking South Korean official indicated in mid-1978 that the issue of Washington's failure to consult its allies prior to the withdrawal decision should not be taken at face value. Even though they had raised the issue, the Koreans were aware that it was unrealistic to expect the United States to give them a veto over U.S. policies. As one South Korean official stated, "We have criticized the United States for the lack of advance consultations, but to be fair we must admit it is impossible. If they gave Japan and Korea an opportunity to veto, then what would the United States gain?"

OKIMOTO: It may well have been both infeasible and undesirable for Washington to consult the Japanese before the Korean withdrawal decision. What if Japan had formally, even publicly, asked the United States not to withdraw its ground forces from Korea? If the United States had gone ahead with the decision after Japan had argued publicly against it, the Japanese government would have suffered a serious loss of face and the Americans would have looked very high-handed. Washington's decision not to deploy the neutron bomb illustrates the pitfalls of advance consultations. The West Germans were consulted and indicated that they wanted to see the neutron bomb deployed. The United States then found itself in the extremely awkward position of having to override the West German request.[1]

The apparently contradictory Japanese position of refusing to take a forthright stance and then complaining that they had not been consulted was advantageous to them. Since they were not consulted, the Japanese were free of any responsibility for the decision. Vocal complaints over not having been consulted offered an indirect way of expressing criticism of the decision. Moreover, Japanese government leaders, anxious to raise public consciousness about defense problems, have found in their criticism of Washington's failure to consult Tokyo and in their expressions of concern about the troop withdrawal a politically safe way to keep the subject of defense before the public.

What Are Japanese and U.S. Expectations Regarding Consultation? What Lessons Can Be Drawn from the Korean Experience to Facilitate More Effective Consultations in the Future?

WEINSTEIN: The United States and Japan approach the subject of consultations with fundamentally different expectations, reflecting basic differences between their respective decision-making processes. It is well known that the Japanese normally make decisions through a consensus-seeking process. This means that extensive consultations in advance of a decision are an integral part of the process. U.S. businessmen have been struck by the differences between Japanese and U.S. approaches. They note that when a U.S. firm sets a policy, the basic decision is usually made quickly by the senior executives. After that, lengthy discussions with subordinates may follow, laying the groundwork for the implementation of the decision. Many of the specific details may not be decided until the implementation of the basic decision is worked out. In a Japanese firm, the basic decision takes a long time to reach, as officials at various levels are brought into the discussion. But when the decision is made, implementation is usually very rapid, since all of those responsible for implementing the policy have already been involved in the process.

Some U.S. officials, feeling that U.S. decision makers are unlikely to be swayed by the Japanese, are inclined to regard consultations in advance of a decision as something of a charade. This ignores another important cultural difference. Two students of Japanese corporate decision making have noted that Japanese who are consulted about an impending decision will normally indicate their consent. This does not, however, imply approval, as it might in a U.S. context. The fact that the Japanese have been consulted and have been given an opportunity to express their reservations may lead them to acquiesce in a decision they might otherwise have resisted.

MOMOI: What we call "consultations" may take three forms: (1) merely informing the other party after objectives have been decided; (2) informing the other party about previously determined objectives, as well as about plans for implementation, and then soliciting comments on the plan (as in the Korean case); and (3) requesting the other party's views on both the objectives and on ways of implementing them. Many Japanese feel strongly that there should be genuine "mutual talk" (*sodan*) involving both sides, not merely a process by which one side informs the other. But we must acknowledge that the Japanese government has generally felt more comfortable merely being informed, since this enables Tokyo to avoid responsibility for the actions taken. If there is to be effective "mutual talk," it must involve an exchange of hard intelligence and information, joint analysis of the data, and a joint program for carrying out the policy.

ROWEN: Part of the misunderstanding about consultation stems from our use of an excessively narrow and formal concept of the term. We need to remember that foreign policy is not determined by the president or even by the executive branch alone. There is a much larger set of players, including the Congress and various interest groups. Effective consultation requires the development of an extensive network of ties to all of these groups, not just a series of meetings with responsible executive-branch officials.

OKIMOTO: We need to take a broad view of consultation, from the standpoint of the functions it can be expected to fulfill and the diversity of mechanisms that might be used. Effective consultations may fulfill the following functions:

1. keeping lines of communication open and transmitting important information on a regular basis
2. anticipating problems and undertaking basic spadework before the problems reach crisis proportions
3. providing a setting for the resolution of disagreements and conflicts
4. legitimizing policies that have been worked out by the two countries
5. standardizing processes of negotiation, so that every administration does not have to start from the beginning

A variety of mechanisms can be used to perform these functions: high-level meetings between elected leaders; regular conferences between officials of parallel agencies; interagency gatherings; legislative exchanges; meetings involving business, labor, and other private-sector interest groups; and seminars for scholars and journalists.

Successful consultations require a common understanding of what the two countries mean by *consultation* and what each expects to achieve by the process. Certain fundamental differences between Japanese and U.S. concepts of consultation have already been noted. For Americans, the term has a range of meanings from informing an ally about U.S. policies to full, cooperative deliberation on problems of mutual interest. For the Japanese, the term normally implies a frank exchange of views and an effort to reach solutions that adequately take into account their views. Misunderstandings can arise, therefore, if Washington assumes, as it sometimes has, that consultation requires only that the Japanese be kept informed.

There are, of course, certain issues that preclude a full and equal exchange of views. For example, the Japanese do not expect their views to be reflected in U.S. policies on strategic arms limitation and European force reductions. The Japanese view such issues as being beyond the scope of Japanese influence and, to some extent, interest. For instance, progress reports are probably sufficient for the Strategic Arms Limitation Talks (SALT) and the Mutual Balanced Force Reduction (MBFR) negotiations. But where vital Japanese interests are clearly at stake—for example, in U.S. energy policies, measures to protect the dollar, and, for some Japanese, the future of the U.S. military presence in Korea— the Japanese expect their views to be solicited and taken fully into account. Of course, it is important that the two sides reach an understanding about which issues require full-fledged consultations.

Experience has shown that the effectiveness of consultations is diminished when issues become highly politicized and participation in the policymaking process extends beyond the executive branch of government to include legislators, interest groups, and the mass media. Since the early 1970s, the U.S. Congress has placed pressure on the administration by playing an increasingly interventionist role in U.S.-Japan relations. Similarly, a weakened conservative majority in the Japanese Diet has found it necessary to compromise in order to gain a certain amount of support from the opposition parties. Legislative bodies, often the focus of intense lobbyist activities and representing parochial interests, do not always act in ways that solidify bilateral relations. The Congress has been a breeding ground for protectionist sentiments, threats of trade sanctions, and efforts to curb expenditures for overseas activities and commitments.

The growing assertiveness of Congress means that the Japanese have a greater stake in learning about its operations, its membership, its moods, and the cluster of lobbyist groups associated with it. Thus far, the Japanese have not been very effective in bringing their case before the U.S. Congress. It will serve both Japanese and U.S. interests for the Japanese to bring information to the attention of U.S. legislators to balance the selective interest-group lobbying that now dominates. To play a constructive role in the formulation of U.S. policies on matters of interest to Japan, the Japanese will need a better understanding of how the U.S. policymaking process works. They will need to learn how to influence the process without, of course, overstepping the bounds of responsible behavior.

The same, of course, applies to U.S. efforts to influence the Japanese policymaking process. U.S. leaders must be able to comprehend how factions interact within the LDP, the political constraints that inhibit Japanese prime ministers and cabinets, the ways ministries make decisions and relate to one another, and the reasons for certain practices in the Diet. The United States particularly needs to understand the ways the Japanese national press influences the policymaking process and the course of bilateral consultations. By giving wide and sustained coverage to bilateral problems, the press can raise the political stakes, rapidly creating a tense atmosphere for negotiation. The leading Japanese newspapers are truly national in circulation and influence; the top five each have a circulation exceeding one million, and the two leading dailies—the *Asahi* and the *Yomiuri*—have circulations over six million each for their morning editions alone. When the Japanese press decides to play up an issue, which the three leading dailies tend to do in concert, the resolution of bilateral problems can become exceedingly difficult.

There are numerous cases in which the Japanese press has affected the course of international negotiations. For example, the negotiations leading to a Treaty of Amity and Friendship between Japan and China were slowed down and complicated enormously by the extensive attention that the press gave to the antihegemony clause. Similarly, the sustained press coverage of trade issues between the United States and Japan has helped create an atmosphere of confrontation, making it harder to reach a settlement acceptable to politicians, bureaucrats, and interest groups. Of course, the press sometimes takes strong, nationalistic positions, fully conscious that this may strengthen the government's hand in the negotiations. Examples of this include demands for the reversion of Okinawa and for the return of the Northern Territories from the Soviet Union. Some Japanese feel that, by creating a sense of crisis surrounding an issue, the press helps to speed the sometimes cumbersome process of consensus building (though the search for consensus may be impeded if the debate becomes overheated). On occasion, foreign pressures dramatically portrayed in the press are cited by certain groups to buttress their positions in domestic deliberations. This tactic may backfire, however, if those groups are perceived as inviting external interference in Japan's affairs.

Because the press plays such a pivotal role in Japan, the United States should give some thought to ways of capitalizing on its influence or neutralizing its impact when it acts to impede effective consultations. One constructive step might be to make efforts to facilitate the work of Japanese correspondents in Washington by inviting them to regular meetings with members of both the executive and legislative branches. Such discussions should be aimed at explaining U.S. perspectives and policies, not just when crises arise but on a regular basis. Then the Japanese will be less likely to be caught by surprise; there will be fewer shocks and crises; and Japanese understanding of the United States may improve.

If the United States and Japan, with overriding common interests and a large reservoir of goodwill, have had problems communicating with one another, a long history of stormy relations has made dialogue between Tokyo and Seoul much more difficult. The Japanese government, cautious in its dealings with nations like the United States and China, has demonstrated a willingness to employ sanctions against Korea for failing to comply with certain demands. In 1974, Tokyo cut back economic aid in protest against Seoul's refusal to settle matters relating to the abduction of Kim Dae-jung. At the same time, Korea has applied its own pressure against Japan. This has included stirring up anti-Japanese demonstrations, arresting Japanese nationals in Korea, expelling Japanese journalists, and capturing Japanese fishing vessels that strayed too close to Korea's territorial waters. The two countries came close to breaking diplomatic relations during the tense period from 1973 to 1975 when the Kim Dae-jung affair was the focal point of controversy.

Although South Korea's dynamic economic growth presents new opportunities for cooperation with Japan, it may also produce new conflicts. The two countries are likely to become increasingly competitive for natural resources and markets. The trade imbalance is already a serious problem, with Japan holding a surplus of more than $3.3 billion as of 1978. As the comparative advantage shifts from Japan to Korea in certain industries, the Japanese will need to make structural adjustments in their economy; these are never easy.

These trends make it increasingly important that Japan and Korea work to establish better channels for consultation in both the public and private sectors. The United States may have a special role to play here; because it is uniquely important to each

nation—politically, economically and, with U.S. defense commitments to both nations, militarily—Washington may be in a position
to help Japan and South Korea resolve their differences when
problems arise.

Trilateral consultations among the United States, Japan, and
South Korea should be undertaken to the extent that the political
milieu in each of the three countries permits. At present, political
sensitivities may be too delicate to facilitate such consultations,
especially over questions of military security. In order to become
accustomed to the idea of regular communication, the three
countries might begin discussing, at least semiofficially, the economic issues (trade, resource development, fishery problems, and
energy) in which each has a high stake and over which conflicts
could arise. Trilateral consultations on those issues may help to
relieve some of the sources of friction. It may be possible, as
several of the Japanese members of the working group have suggested, to hold consultations concerning intelligence data and the
"definition of a crisis." In time, the three countries may move
gradually toward more far-reaching joint discussions of the military
security of Northeast Asia.

Notes

1. Okimoto is indebted to Morton Halperin for the neutron bomb
analogy.

3
The Withdrawal of U.S. Forces
and the Deterrence of Conflict

WEINSTEIN: From 1977 to 1979, Japanese and U.S. concerns about the security of Korea focused on the implications of the Carter administration's announced plan to withdraw U.S. ground-combat forces from South Korea by 1982. In early 1979, the withdrawal program was suspended, and in July the suspension was extended at least until 1981. The real impact of the suspension is unclear, since, under the Carter administration's withdrawal program, most of the troops were not to be taken out until 1981 and 1982 anyway. Furthermore, many observers had noted that President Carter's ability to implement his withdrawal policy was contingent on his winning reelection in 1980. One may safely assume that the troop-withdrawal question will reemerge as an important issue for the 1980s.

The Carter administration's troop-withdrawal plan stimulated a debate that raised some important questions about the long-term security of Northeast Asia. There is no consensus among the members of the working group on the merits of troop with-drawals. But there is general agreement on several points, in-cluding the view, already discussed at length, that the Carter plan was formulated and announced in a way that revealed the inadequacy of the consultation process. In this chapter, we will assess the reactions to the Carter withdrawal plan of the major parties concerned—the two Koreas, the Soviet Union, China, and Japan. In addition, we will consider the future of the U.S. commitment, the implications of troop withdrawals for Japanese security, and Japan's potential role in the deterrence of conflict in Korea.

How Did the South Koreans Adapt to President Carter's Announcement That American Ground-Combat Forces Would Be Withdrawn Within Five Years?

MOMOI: The South Koreans adapted extremely well to the withdrawal decision. The decision had actually been anticipated for some time, though the manner of its announcement came as a surprise. The Seoul government responded to the withdrawal plan by moving to consolidate the populace behind President Park and, as noted in the discussion of the military balance in Chapter 1, by taking steps to accelerate the modernization of the Korean armed forces. Not only was the R.O.K.'s Force Improvement Program stepped up, but there was a more rapid development of South Korean defense production capabilities, including substantial improvements in the capabilities for production of sophisticated arms. Equally important, the South Korean people demonstrated an increased willingness to bear sacrifice. Even opposition groups rallied to support the president on this issue. This left the South Koreans feeling stronger and more self-confident than before. Of course, the knowledge that U.S. troops were to be gradually phased out over five years, rather than immediately pulled out, as had previously been feared, allayed feelings of uneasiness and resentment among the South Koreans.

Assuming that withdrawals of the sort envisaged by President Carter were carried out, the military impact on the South would not necessarily be significant. It is not mandatory that the withdrawn forces be replaced by an enlarged R.O.K. army, because the Second Division's manpower contribution has not been significant. The strategic importance of U.S. ground-combat forces has been mainly psychological. From a tactical standpoint, the Second Division's most important contributions have been firepower, tactical nuclear weapons, and reassurance to South Korea of logistical support from the United States. The United States should be able to transfer this firepower to the R.O.K. army. The Koreans will not be hurt by the removal of U.S. nuclear weapons, if Washington avoids making this public. It will be more difficult, however, to maintain secure supply lines once the Second Division has been withdrawn, and it is hard to reestablish lines that have been cut. Thus, in the absence of the Second Division, there will be a need for special measures to protect supply lines.

It is fair to say that by 1978 the South Koreans had come to accept the Carter administration's withdrawal plan. By then, it had essentially become a closed issue, though it was reopened in 1979 when new U.S. Army intelligence estimates of North Korean strength led to suspension of the withdrawal. Overall, the South Koreans took the withdrawal decision very calmly and there is little reason for concern about future South Korean reactions should the withdrawal plan be revived. Nevertheless, even though they had accepted the withdrawal policy, the Koreans continued to have reservations about it and they certainly welcomed the suspension. Some Koreans doubt whether U.S. air and naval forces would really constitute a sufficient deterrent. The Koreans who voice these concerns often refer to the inadequacy of U.S. air and naval power in Vietnam. These Koreans forget that the R.O.K. army, already the best army in Northeast Asia, is being substantially strengthened. The key, of course, is morale. There have been some reports of declining morale among South Korean soldiers stationed at the DMZ, perhaps a subtle result of the withdrawal decision. But since we know virtually nothing about the morale of North Korean soldiers, comparisons are difficult. The demonstration of a firm U.S. commitment, through regular exercises that bring U.S. forces across the Pacific, is the best means of assuring high morale among R.O.K. soldiers.

The question of civilian morale is also a matter of some concern. As noted in Chapter 1, there is a good deal of doubt how the morale of civilians in Seoul would hold out in the event of hostilities. If the R.O.K.'s first line of defense holds, the civilians will stay in the city. But from the second line of defense, North Korean artillery can reach Seoul. So, if the first line of defense falls, there could be panic among the civilian population. Even so, the Seoul government has voiced confidence that civilians will remain in the city if the second line of defense is maintained.

WHITING: In considering the question of South Korean morale, the United States should be careful not to let concern about Korean morale unnecessarily constrain policy options. One element of the Carter administration's Korea policy that certainly deserves support is the effort to build the self-confidence of the South Koreans. If by 1982 the South Koreans lack confidence and are plagued by low morale, the United States will have a serious problem. But Washington should not be limited in policy decisions by worries about the reactions of South Koreans. This was a mistake the United States made during the Vietnam War. For example, in 1964 U Thant obtained Hanoi's agreement to meet secretly with the United States in Rangoon, but Secretary Rusk vetoed this for fear Hanoi would leak word of the meeting and Saigon would lose confidence in the United States. Another possible initiative was vetoed on the same grounds in May 1965. Although it would be a mistake to disregard the wishes of the South Koreans, the United States should make its own judgment concerning the merits of its Korea policies.

HARRISON: There may in fact be a basis for South Korean morale problems more profound than their uneasiness at the possible withdrawal of U.S. troops. The South's psychological malaise basically results from an angry ambivalence with respect to its dependence on the United States and its U.S.–promoted dependence on Japan. On the one hand, the U.S. presence is a constant irritant to nationalist sensitivities. On the other, there is a deep feeling that as one of those responsible for dividing the country, Washington has a responsibility to support Seoul until the country is reunited on terms favorable to the South. Similarly, while the Japanese presence arouses bitter memories of the colonial period, there is a feeling that it is an unavoidable expedient in the South's contest with the North.

Given this ambivalence, the South has been able to rationalize an economically comfortable dependence that would otherwise have been difficult to bear. Nevertheless, the psychological burden of dependence has been considerable, and it has been tolerable only to the extent that continuance of the status quo has seemed assured. The prospect of U.S. force withdrawals has brought to the surface the malaise in the South, compelling Seoul to reappraise its long-term options. In my view, this reappraisal is a healthy and long-overdue process. The ultimate result will be greater self-confidence on the part of the South, reflected in increased readiness to seek accommodation with the North.

Until now, the combined economic subsidy represented by U.S. forces, U.S. bases, U.S. military aid, and such ancillary economic aid as Food for Peace has enabled the South to have a maximum of security with a minimum of sacrifice. The upper- and middle-income minority, in particular, has acquired a vested interest in the status quo. So long as the South has the U.S. presence as an economic cushion, it is under no compulsion to explore the mutual force reductions proposed by the North. In fact, until now the South has been moving in the opposite direction, expanding its defense-related industries.

Opponents of disengagement have argued that the South will react to U.S. withdrawal by accelerating its defense buildup and that the accompanying anxieties will foreclose any peaceful dialogue with the North. Only the U.S. presence, it is argued, infuses the confidence and sense of security needed to promote a North-South dialogue. The latter contention, however, is not borne out by the manner in which the South has approached the North-South dialogue in recent years. On the contrary, it is only in the absence of U.S. forces that Seoul, for the first time, would have to make hard choices between the sacrifices required to match the level of defense strength now provided by the United States and an approach to the North that more accurately reflects the complex mixture of anti-Communist and prounification sentiment in the South. Although the South initially reacted to the U.S. withdrawal plan by expanding its defense buildup, this will impose economic burdens that will ultimately force a painful reappraisal of long-term options. Since the objective of U.S. policy should be to promote such a reappraisal, it is therefore self-defeating to accompany withdrawal of U.S. forces with the huge amounts of compensatory military aid the administration is pledged to provide to the South Koreans.

It would be an exaggeration to say, as some maintain, that the South feels "psychologically inferior" to the North. Recent reports of the North's foreign-payments defaults and possibly deeper economic problems have bolstered the South. However, there is a widespread fear in the South of the North's ideological discipline and nationalist fervor, as well as a sense that the South's dependence has eroded its will and its capacity for disciplined resistance. Scholars maintain that economic policies based on dependence produce an "international demonstration effect," in which privileged elites with foreign links acquire an appetite for living standards that cannot be achieved by the majority of the population. As disparities in wealth grow, it is argued, the nationalist spirit erodes.[1] Significantly, Kim Hyung-wook, the former KCIA director, echoed this analysis in his 1977 congressional testimony:

The North Korean people do not suffer from a high degree of inter-national demonstration effect. The international demonstration effect in South Korea is extremely high. There are no visible gaps between the haves and the have-nots in North Korea. Therefore, I feel that the North Korean population most likely feel less relatively deprived than their southern counterparts. I estimate that the stan-dard of living of the ordinary people in North Korea is higher than in South Korea. Even though the average standard of living in North Korea may be lower than the standard of living of South Koreans, I believe that the people of North Korea live with a greater sense of satisfaction. . . . The discipline and ideological zeal of the North Korean Communists is much stronger than that of the South Koreans. In fact, I feel that there is no comparison; the will of the North Koreans is almost 100 times stronger than the will of the South Koreans.[2]

In the long run, the psychological malaise in the South can only be overcome by reducing its dependence, establishing more egalitarian economic policies, and developing a nationalist ethos. The Park regime intermittently attempted to fill the nationalist vacuum by xenophobic, anti-Japanese appeals and nativistic cul-tural policies; but xenophobia and nativism are not the same as nationalism.[3] In the Korean context, nationalist feeling can only be evoked by allowing expression of the desire for reunification and by achieving a maximum Korean identity in world affairs. Syngman Rhee recognized this in his pledge to "march North," while Kim Dae-jung does so in another way with his pledge to seek peaceful unification on the basis of coequality. The initiatives of early 1979 notwithstanding, Park, by contrast, failed to make a credible effort to seek peaceful unification. Nor did he believe that the South was strong enough to attempt a militarily enforced unification. His initiative of early 1979 to reopen contacts with Pyongyang indicated a desire to escape from a defensive posture on the unification issue. It remains to be seen whether his succes-sors will show greater flexibility on substantive North-South issues.

To appreciate the depth of resentment shown by Seoul in its dealings with Washington over the withdrawal issue and over the Tong-sun Park affair, it is necessary to understand the background of built-in tension between the two capitals over the unification issue. In an unpublished interview with the John Foster Dulles Oral History Project, one of Rhee's prime ministers, Paik Too-chin, has recounted the impasse over unification between Washington and Seoul following the Korean War. President Eisenhower, seeking to resolve the issue, invited Rhee to Washington in July 1954. But he soon found that the Korean leader was adamant in his insistence on language in the minutes of the talks that pledged support for unification "by all means" as against a U.S. draft of the minutes specifying "peaceful means." Rhee "wanted very much to reserve the sovereign right to unify Korea" and had come to Washington with a plan for a 1955 offensive against the North that he never presented because "the atmosphere at that time didn't allow him to do so."[4] For six months, Rhee refused to sign the minutes, which led to a virtual paralysis in Seoul-Washington relations and a U.S. cutoff of civilian oil supplies.[5] He finally agreed to abandon his language on unification only under pressure from South Korean military leaders eager to complete a major arms aid agreement.[6] As former Prime Minister Chung Il-kwon has said, Rhee's insistence on the unification issue signified the South's "desire to get an assurance from the United States that she would stay with us until *we could reunify the country*" [emphasis added] .[7]

SAEKI: Whatever evaluation one may make with respect to the morale and self-confidence of the South Koreans, the fact remains that even after U.S. ground forces are withdrawn, the economy and per capita GNP of South Korea will continue to grow faster than those of North Korea. Since the population of the South is more than twice as large as that of the North, it should not be impossible to achieve in time a military equilibrium and a state of peaceful coexistence between the two Koreas. It should not be too difficult to convince the North Koreans that the possibility of establishing military superiority over the South or achieving reunification of Korea through military force is diminishing with the passage of time. Eventually, the North will also accept the view that the only feasible solution is to establish a framework for the maintenance of peaceful North-South coexistence.

The problems relate to the geographical proximity of Seoul to the thirty-eighth parallel and to the possible decline in the credibility of the U.S. defense commitment to South Korea. If effective measures are taken to deal with these problems, the security of the Korean peninsula will be assured even after U.S. ground forces are withdrawn.

How Did the North Koreans, the Soviets, and the Chinese React to the U.S. Troop-Withdrawal Plan, and What Are They Likely to Do If Withdrawals Take Place?

SAEKI: The North Koreans were careful not to make any moves that might bring the U.S. withdrawal plan to a halt, and they made an all-out effort to learn the true objectives of the policy. During the period that any withdrawal of U.S. ground forces is in progress, the North Koreans can be counted on to avoid taking actions that might check the continuation of the withdrawal.

WEINSTEIN: Although North Korean commentary on the withdrawal plan was mixed, there were some encouraging signs that the announcement of the plan had produced a softening of Pyongyang's attitude toward the United States. Kim Il-sung told a Japanese correspondent in July 1977 that the U.S. ground-force withdrawal plan was "a very good thing." While he emphasized that air forces must withdraw as well, he spoke of the United States in a moderate tone.[8] Even the South Koreans unofficially observed that Pyongyang had noticeably softened its anti–U.S. line. A high ranking official in Seoul noted that the North Koreans were now more inclined to refer to the United States without using some epithet, such as "imperialist." Moreover, since the announcement of the troop-withdrawal policy, Pyongyang has displayed eagerness to establish a dialogue with Washington. Of course, the North Koreans expressed displeasure, too, not only with the partial nature of the withdrawal, but also with the plan to augment U.S. military assistance to Seoul. Similarly, we can assume that Pyongyang's increased flexibility concerning talks with Seoul, which began in early 1979, was linked to a desire to encourage the implementation of the U.S. troop-withdrawal plan. Needless to say, Pyongyang reacted with extreme hostility to the suspension, which it denounced as "a criminal act."

WHITING: Even though the North Koreans had an interest in avoiding statements or actions that would cause the United States to reconsider its withdrawal policy, some of the North Korean commentary on the plan was as vociferous and extreme as might have been expected. Some Pyongyang commentators attacked the withdrawal as a deceit because it did not meet North Korea's demand for the immediate and total withdrawal of the U.S.

military presence in the South.

MOMOI: As for the Soviet and Chinese reactions, both Moscow and Peking indicated to Japanese visitors that they were opposed to the "hasty" reduction of U.S. forces in Korea. They were not opposed to withdrawal in principle, but they did not genuinely desire the sort of immediate and total withdrawal demanded by Pyongyang.

SAEKI: This does not, however, indicate that the Soviets and Chinese opposed the Carter administration's withdrawal plan. Though some might dismiss this as *tatemae* ("public posturing," rather than actual views), high-level Soviet leaders have in fact argued privately with foreign visitors for a rapid U.S. withdrawal from Korea, and the Chinese expressed no concern about the withdrawal program when Secretary of State Cyrus Vance visited Peking. Furthermore, the Soviets, like the North Koreans, would avoid any actions that might jeopardize a U.S. withdrawal program. The Chinese, who assume that there is little possibility of North Korea's staging armed aggression against the South, would probably merely observe the situation.

WHITING: The tone of Peking's initial reaction to the withdrawal plan was considerably more muted than that of Pyongyang, but not the content. Peking's media treatment of Korea in 1977 showed a consistent effort to maintain some distance from Pyongyang, while providing sufficient support to compete with Moscow as a reliable ally. Pyongyang's statements were printed selectively, if at all. North Korean news agency releases appeared belatedly in the New China News Agency and considerably later in *People's Daily*. The more strident the anti-U.S. tone of the statements, the more likely they were to be specifically identified by source in the headline. Virtually none of Pyongyang's accusations linking the U.S. military presence with Japan appeared in Chinese media. Only five authoritative articles on this subject, in the form of editorials, commentaries, or analyses, appeared in *People's Daily* between January 1 and September 30, 1977.

In substance, however, Peking's reaction paralleled that of Pyongyang, terming the withdrawal "a gesture" in response to "the firm opposition of the entire Korean people and the pressure of public opinion at home and abroad."[9] The Chinese media accused the United States of planning to remain in the South "to obstruct the Korean people's independent and peaceful reunification . . . and create 'two Koreas' so as to perpetuate the division of Korea." Peking increased its demand for "the *immediate* and complete withdrawal of all U.S. forces" from the South (emphasis added). This was in line with Pyongyang's reaction to the Carter announcement, but with the addition of the more imperative time dimension.

It appears that opinion was divided in Peking, particularly regarding the gains versus costs of relying on the U.S. détente. A careful content analysis of the Chinese media revealed a heavier and more strident emphasis on the Taiwan issue in 1977 than in 1976. In addition, it showed the United States in a more unfavorable light than previously, vis-à-vis the Soviet Union in the power balance. Finally, there was a startling willingness to recall long-forgotten instances of alleged U.S. misbehavior, in particular reviving charges of germ warfare associated with the Korean conflict.

The ambivalence with which the United States was portrayed as a quasi-ally emerged bluntly and authoritatively in Chairman Hua Kuo-feng's report of August 12, 1977, to the Eleventh Congress of the Chinese Communist party. Citing Lenin on defeating "the most powerful enemy" by "skillfully making use *without fail* of every, even the smallest 'rift' among the enemies," Hua stressed "taking advantage of every, even the smallest, opportunity of gaining a mass ally, even though this ally be *temporary, vacillating, unstable, unreliable, and conditional*" (emphasis added). Although the words were Lenin's, their applicability to Mao's policy toward the United States could not be missed.

It is impossible to say whether these shadows on the China–U.S. relationship stemmed from frustration and anger over the dilatory handling of normalization and the question of Taiwan or from genuine doubt about the U.S. will and capacity to confront the Soviet Union. But, contrary to conventional wisdom, the fall of the "gang of four" did not lead immediately to a better press for the United States. On the contrary, in terms of sensitive indicators measured both quantitatively and qualitatively, the public image of the United States was worse just after the death of Mao than it had been before.

Subsequent developments were more encouraging. During Premier Hua Kuo-feng's May 1978 visit to Pyongyang, China's new leader dropped the demand for an "immediate" withdrawal of U.S. forces, contrary to the previous summer's posture and

Kim Il-sung's continuing position. This may partially explain the absence of a joint communiqué during Hua's first official visit abroad as chairman and premier. His new position suggests how uninhibited Peking feels about differing with Pyongyang, even at the risk of increasing Moscow's influence in North Korea. It also may show the degree to which Peking is willing to accommodate Washington in developing détente toward a joint stance against Moscow. Whatever the reason, the result was a significant signal of Chinese moderation and flexibility.

WEINSTEIN: The task of ascertaining China's "real" position on the troop-withdrawal question is further complicated by a temptation to which many commentators have succumbed. They suggest that Peking is playing a two-faced game, lending verbal support to Pyongyang while privately winking at Washington's continued military presence on the peninsula. Indeed, Chinese diplomats in various countries around the world reportedly have dropped hints that they have no objection to a continued U.S. military presence in Korea. But, according to a high-ranking South Korean official interviewed in the latter half of 1978, the Chinese had ceased to hint at acquiescence in the U.S. military presence. For some time, this official said, the Chinese had expressed their unequivocal opposition, in private as well as in public, to the presence of U.S. troops in South Korea.

How Did the Japanese Adapt to the Troop-Withdrawal Plan?

KOSAKA: It is necessary to begin by pointing out that the majority view among the Japanese was either one of indifference or one of accommodation to the Carter administration's policy concerning troop withdrawals from Korea. While many Japanese view U.S. forces as unnecessary, they were unimpressed by the troop-withdrawal plan, which they generally regarded as too little too late. As for Japanese officials, they will always accommodate. They may be disappointed, but they see no alternative to continued cooperation with the United States. This means going along with Washington's troop-withdrawal policies.

I am personally more critical of the U.S. policy. U.S. ground forces perform a very important role in Korea at minimal cost. They fill a gap of strength between North and South Korea. Although improved South Korean forces can easily fill that gap, the presence of U.S. forces makes the military balance in Northeast Asia multilateral—and this is the most important function of the U.S. presence in Korea. If the balance is just between the two Koreas, one side or the other might feel that it can gain the advantage. With the United States as one factor in the balance, it is harder for the North Koreans to hope that they might gain a superior position. Furthermore, U.S. ground troops are a symbol of a serious U.S. interest in the tripolar military balance. If the United States can do all of this with one division, the price is cheap. It is hard to avoid the conclusion that a withdrawal would mean that Asia is no longer important to the United States. At the very least, it is hard for me to see what purpose would be served by the withdrawal.

MOMOI: One can also question whether some of the basic assumptions underlying the U.S. decision to withdraw ground forces from Korea are likely to hold up. The withdrawal decision seems to be based on five assumptions.

1. The Soviet Union, China, and North Korea will refrain from taking any hostile action toward South Korea in the near future.
2. The North-South climate might improve as a result of the withdrawal decision.
3. The domestic and diplomatic behavior of South Korea may improve.
4. After force reductions, Japan will remain calm.
5. The United States will not be automatically involved in any future conflict but will remain firmly committed to a residual role.

The only assumption that can be made with a high degree of confidence is that Japan will remain calm in the face of U.S. troop withdrawals from Korea so long as necessary steps are taken to ensure that the residual U.S. commitment to Seoul remains credible.

We cannot assume that the North Koreans rule out hostile actions toward the South. It is possible that the North Koreans will calculate that they can get away with limited and relatively nonprovocative actions aimed at creating internal problems in South Korea. Pyongyang might have an extra incentive to take hostile action against the South after the succession to Kim Il-sung, since a limited external venture could help Kim's successor establish himself. This need not mean an all-out invasion but merely probing actions near the DMZ. These might be intended merely to see what the South Korean reaction would be or to provoke the R.O.K. to some rash action that would give the North Koreans a pretext for escalating to a limited armed conflict. In this case, the North Koreans might stop short of taking Seoul; their aim might be simply to create havoc in the capital and then to seek a political détente. The only way to prevent such a situation is through the maintenance of a firm assurance that the United States will immediately make whatever response is necessary, including the reintroduction of U.S. forces.

WEINSTEIN: While many Japanese continue to hold these and other reservations about the withdrawal policy, Tokyo, like Seoul, has demonstrated its ability to adjust to such a policy. Responsible U.S. officials are convinced that by late 1977 Tokyo had come to understand and accept the Carter administration's decision, though there remained a notable lack of enthusiasm for it and a good deal of continuing resentment at the manner in which it was made. The Japanese continued to attach great importance to the maintenance of a U.S. presence in Korea. But the emphasis was not on undoing the withdrawal decision but on finding ways to enhance the credibility of the residual U.S. commitment. There seemed to be a reasonable degree of optimism in Japan that this could be done. According to officials in Washington, the initial Japanese apprehension about the administration's troop-withdrawal policy was based on fear that Washington might withdraw all of its forces from Korea in a few years without any adjustment in the form of military aid or continued air support. These U.S. officials felt that the "statesmanlike" reaction of the South Koreans had helped the Japanese overcome their fears.

What Were the Carter Administration's Reasons for Deciding to Withdraw Ground-Combat Forces from Korea?

WEINSTEIN: There is no doubt that the decision to withdraw U.S. ground-combat forces from South Korea was taken at the initiative of President Carter himself. His decision dates back at least to January 1975, when his presidential campaign was still in its earliest stages. Some of those who discussed Korea with Carter in late 1974 and early 1975 believe that his main concern was with the "tripwire" effect of U.S. ground forces stationed just below the DMZ, which might automatically involve the United States in any new Korean conflict. Carter was said to have told a group of editorial writers for the *Washington Post* in January 1975 that he would remove U.S. troops from Korea as a money-saving measure aimed at bringing about better defense management. It seems evident that Carter originally envisaged withdrawing all U.S. forces from Korea. But by mid-1975 he had begun to move toward the conclusion that the withdrawal should be limited to ground forces, lest a strengthened R.O.K. air force feel tempted to under-take a preemptive strike against the North.[10] By early 1976 Carter was publicly committed to a withdrawal of U.S. troops over five years, but as the campaign progressed his commitment became hazier. Shortly after being designated as secretary of state, Cyrus Vance described the new administration's Korea policy as a commitment to troop withdrawal, but he did not mention how long that process would take.

Studies ordered after Carter became president were apparently based on the premise that U.S. ground forces would be withdrawn from Korea. The question was not whether, but how, they should be withdrawn. Because the troop withdrawal had been pledged by Carter during the course of the campaign, some observers assumed that the withdrawal decision was primarily a product of U.S. domestic politics—that Carter had made a promise to withdraw U.S. troops from Korea in order to win votes during the campaign and that as president he felt obligated to fulfill his campaign prom-ise. Although it is possible to argue for such an interpretation, it fails to account adequately for the fact that his position had grown hazy enough by December 1976 to permit him considerable flexibility after assuming office. It would not have been difficult for the new president to announce that the withdrawal would be stretched over a time longer than five years or, indeed, that it would be started without any terminal date set in advance. The hasty and almost offhand manner in which the troop-withdrawal decision was announced, together with the administration's failure to explain fully the assumptions and goals underlying the decision, have reinforced the impression that the president was merely intent on fulfilling a campaign promise. But this does not mean that good reasons for the decision did not exist.

Part of the problem may stem from differing views about where the burden of proof resides. The president reportedly is inclined, as a matter of principle, to question the stationing of U.S. troops overseas, believing that keeping U.S. forces abroad "is something you need a good reason to do." Carter is said to have added that he had not yet seen a convincing argument for keeping U.S. troops in Korea indefinitely.[11] In essence, the president felt that the burden of proof lay with those who would keep U.S. forces in Korea. Thus, he felt he needed only to show why it would not be dangerous to remove them. From his standpoint, therefore, the central question was not what would be gained by withdrawing U.S. forces, but whether there were any compelling reasons for keeping them in Korea.

It would have been preferable if the administration had elaborated in a systematic way on this view of the role of U.S. forces, rather than merely relaying it through the president's press secretary in response to a question. I believe that a strong case for the withdrawal decision can be made, based on the view that the burden of proof must rest with those who would keep U.S. forces overseas, not on those who would bring them home. Elsewhere, I have set forth in some detail reasons why the withdrawal policy is reasonable.[12] The principal reasons relate to the following:

1. the growing military capability of the R.O.K. armed forces to deter an attack from the North without U.S. ground forces
2. the important advantages enjoyed by the South in geography (specifically, terrain), economic vitality, and population
3. the psychological, political, and diplomatic costs for South Korea of perpetuating an unnecessary dependence
4. the lack of any justification for automatic U.S. involvement in a potential conflict when the South Koreans are capable of handling the situation without any U.S. ground forces
5. the likelihood that the withdrawal of U.S. forces will gradually help create a basis for a modus vivendi between the two Koreas and thus provide a more meaningful stability than one based on the perpetual presence of U.S. forces

How Do Troop Withdrawals Relate to the Broader Strategic Context in Asia?   What Can Be Done to Enhance the Credibility of the Residual U.S. Commitment?

ROWEN: There is no need to discuss at length all of the arguments that support or oppose troop withdrawals, but several points should be made. One can be reasonably confident concerning the Carter administration's assertion that South Korea is growing strong enough to defend itself against a North Korean attack. The excellent defensive terrain enjoyed by the South helps to offset some of the R.O.K.'s inadequacies in antitank capabilities, artillery, and logistics. Although Seoul is close to the DMZ, it is not easy for either side to attack the other with the expectation of an early, sweeping tactical success. (In this respect, it is very different from the Arab-Israeli confrontation, which is highly unstable.) The mountainous South Korean terrain and the existence of few north-south valleys foster defense against invasion. But the main point is that Seoul's present military deficiencies exist because of earlier decisions that South Korea would rely on the United States in these areas. So long as a decision has been made to develop R.O.K. capabilities in these areas, it should not be difficult to overcome these weaknesses.

There are, of course, uncertainties about the impact of a U.S. troop withdrawal on the stability and character of the two Koreas. The fact that South Korea is growing so strong economically (and in other areas) may be regarded as a plus for the South; but Pyongyang's recognition that its situation is worsening vis-à-vis the South may suggest a fundamental instability. There is also some question as to how much repression is needed to preserve the position of the Seoul government. The withdrawal of U.S. forces could lead to a heightened sense of threat to the government, and therefore an increase in repressiveness. Conversely, the withdrawal could produce a greater sense of self-confidence and national unity, which might open the way for some easing of controls on dissidents. Although it seems clear that withdrawals would create added incentives for North Korea to remain relatively quiescent during the period of the withdrawal, one cannot be certain about the stability of the North Korean regime. Another area of uncertainty about a troop withdrawal is the possibility that it might cause the South Koreans to consider the nuclear option more seriously. This will be discussed in the next chapter.

But the fundamental concern raised by a decision to withdraw U.S. ground-combat forces from Korea relates to the broader international context. The issue is much larger than the defense of Korea. The Carter administration's 1977 decision was merely one in a series of U.S. troop reductions raising in the minds of the Koreans, Japanese, and other U.S. Asian allies the question of where U.S. policy is leading. Public opinion in the United States concerning the role of U.S. forces in Asia is not so easy to fathom. It is not accurate to say that the Carter decision was taken in response to popular pressure for a withdrawal from Asia. The issue was mentioned in the campaign, but Carter brought it up. It is now evident that there was little political gain for Carter in the Korean withdrawal policy. There may still be something of a mood of retrenchment in the United States as an aftereffect of the Vietnam debacle, but this is cast within broader feelings of ambivalence and indecision. The neoisolationism that some predicted after the end of the Vietnam War has not materialized. Still, the central question that needs to be clarified is how the withdrawal of U.S. troops from Korea relates to the broader, long-term purposes of the United States in Asia.

There seem to be several alternatives for the United States. It may be possible to continue the suspension indefinitely. Or the administration might decide in 1981 to carry out ground-force withdrawals and to undertake no further unilateral retrenchment. Either of these options would carry few risks. On the other hand, the United States could opt for the removal of all U.S. forces from Korea and could even pull back the marines from Okinawa. But such a move could well jeopardize the credibility of the remaining U.S. commitments. Another possibility is that the United States might attempt to negotiate with North Korea in an effort to persuade Pyongyang to agree to force reductions that would maintain an equitable balance. But the prospects for doing this are not favorable. There may also be initiatives elsewhere that could make Korea less of a central concern. For example, normalized relations with the P.R.C. already have begun to change our notion of what the Korean problem is all about.

WEINSTEIN: There is general agreement among the working-group members that the central issue here is the relationship of the troop-withdrawal decision to the broader strategic context in

Asia. If we accept that the two are related, then a major obstacle
to a credible U.S. posture is the lack of any clear conceptual framework underlying U.S. policy in Asia. What does the U.S. withdrawal of ground forces from Korea imply about the future of the
U.S. commitment to Seoul, the willingness of the United States
to defend Japan, and the readiness of the United States to maintain
a military presence in Southeast Asia? Administration spokesmen
asserted in 1978 that planning for Korea did not extend beyond
the five-year period during which the ground force withdrawals
were supposed to take place. It was deemed "irrelevant" to plan
beyond that point; after the five years had passed, then the situation could be reviewed and subsequent steps considered. While
such a procedure made good sense from a bureaucratic standpoint,
it tended to convey the impression that the withdrawal process
might be inexorable. Since the principal concerns of U.S. allies
relate to the long-term implications of troop withdrawals, the U.S.
view about the longer term may, indeed, be central to the maintenance of a stable relationship with our allies.

This is hardly the place to set forth a long-term framework for
U.S. policies in Asia.[13] But there are two points to consider.
First, while there is considerable apprehension among U.S. allies
about the long-term role of the United States in Asia, the degree
of concern about Korean troop withdrawals per se is not so great.
As indicated, the Koreans and the Japanese were able to accept
the Carter administration's withdrawal policy; it is quite accurate
to describe the reaction of the South Koreans as "statesmanlike."
Far from panic, the South Koreans showed more self-confidence
than previously. Rather than emphasizing their weakness, they
placed more stress on their growing strength.

There were some reports in the press of Southeast Asian fears
that the troop withdrawal decision was additional evidence that
the United States was turning its back on Asia.[14] Senate Foreign
Relations Committee staff members who toured Southeast Asia in
June 1977 found that in Thailand and Indonesia, as well as in the
Philippines, Japan, and Taiwan, the leaders wanted the United
States to keep its forces in South Korea. A key executive-branch
official also indicated that there had initially been considerable
concern in Southeast Asia about U.S. policy toward Korea. In
Singapore and Malaysia leaders tended to draw analogies to the
earlier withdrawal of the British, who, at each stage, pledged that

the withdrawal would go no further. But the official observed that by September 1977 the fears of the Southeast Asians had largely subsided.

In October and November 1977, I interviewed military and civilian leaders in the Philippines, Indonesia, Singapore, Malaysia, and Thailand. Reactions to the Carter administration's Korean policy varied, of course, but overall there was only a modest degree of concern. In the Philippines, U.S. embassy officials indicated that the Filipinos did not seem concerned about Korea and seemed to take the administration's stated explanations at face value. Filipino foreign ministry officials said that Korea was not of direct concern to the Philippines, though there was some apprehension that a U.S. withdrawal from Korea might lead to accelerated Japanese rearmament. One well-informed Filipino claimed that most officials actually welcomed the withdrawal, because it would increase the importance of U.S. bases in the Philippines and thus strengthen Manila's bargaining position in the then ongoing base negotiations.

Indonesian leaders wondered about the possible implications for their country of any move that seemed to indicate diminished U.S. interest in Asia. But the military leaders interviewed, noting that Korea was "so far away," indicated that they did not pay much attention to the situation there. Several top military officers in Indonesia actually appeared to welcome the move. According to a senior foreign ministry official who was also a military officer, the Koreans in Jakarta already seemed to be "more self-confident as a result of the U.S. withdrawal decision." Other officers stated that the move would strengthen Seoul by reducing feelings of dependence on the United States. So long as the withdrawal was gradual, they felt, there would be no problems. A senior defense ministry official noted that the United States still had the capacity to intervene in Korea if necessary.

Malaysian officials, in an assessment confirmed by U.S. embassy sources, said they had given little thought to Korea and that there was not much concern about the U.S. withdrawal. In Singapore there was some evidence of unhappiness about the withdrawal. A foreign ministry official summarized his government's feeling this way: "We are like the Japanese. We prefer you to stay, but we can live with the policy." It was noted, however, that Lee Kuan Yew had cited the Korea withdrawal decision as evidence of the general unreliability of the United States.

There was more evidence of concern in Thailand than any-where else in Southeast Asia. General Kriangsak, who took office as prime minister in October 1977, had fought on Pork Chop Hill during the Korean War, as had other influential Thai generals. One of these generals stated that Thailand's concern was enhanced by the fact that North Korean technicians were operating in Laos and Cambodia. It was suggested that a successful North Korean attack on the South could encourage the Indochina Communists. The Thais felt that if the United States was correct in its estimate of Seoul's strength, then the policy was acceptable. But they still expressed some concern that the withdrawals were part of a larger pattern of U.S. actions indicating a retreat from Asia.

It seems clear, then, that the concern of U.S. allies has not been excessive and has focused on the longer-term implications of troop withdrawals from Korea. Secondly, a number of steps can be taken to ensure that such withdrawals do not jeopardize sta-bility. To begin with, it is necessary for the United States to spell out its long-term goals. Is it a long-term U.S. goal to help the South Koreans attain the capability to defend themselves against a purely North Korean attack without any direct participation by U.S. forces? In my judgment, this ought to be a goal of U.S. policy. Is it a long-term goal of U.S. policy to encourage Japan to develop its military capabilities so that it can defend itself without U.S. assistance? In my judgment, this should *not* be a goal of the United States. The distinctions between Korea, Southeast Asia, and Japan need to be made explicit, so that our allies can be con-fident that the withdrawal process will not be endless. A clear understanding of the limits of withdrawal and the ideas under-lying these limits will provide the best assurance that U.S. commit-ments will not be dissolved incrementally.

MOMOI: The United States can take a number of specific steps relating to Korea to minimize the potential destabilizing effects of a withdrawal of U.S. forces. First, the withdrawal should be gradual, subject to the condition that if North Korea becomes hostile, the United States will immediately respond by sending in a small force—at least a brigade—to show that the U.S. has not abandoned South Korea. In other words, if the United States is intent on withdrawing its forces, it should view its possible rein-volvement in terms akin to a "yo-yo." If even a minor crisis is detected, there must be a firm response from the United States in order to sustain the confidence of the South Koreans. Relatively frequent joint exercises involving U.S. and Korean forces would also be useful confidence-building measures and would remind the North that the United States remains willing and able to come to Seoul's defense.

If the United States wishes to remove its nuclear weapons from Korea, this should be done quietly. Washington should let the press write that the weapons have been withdrawn but should say nothing officially. This ambiguity would minimize the psychological impact of the move and would limit the damage to the credibility of the U.S. commitment. Removing nuclear weapons in this manner would be less destabilizing; it would avoid giving the Soviets any excuse to give more aid to North Korea and, at the same time, would discourage South Korea from seeking nuclear weapons. In short, the best way to remove the nuclear weapons is simply to pull out the weapons and defuse the nuclear mines without saying openly that this is being done.

It would also be desirable for the United States and Japan to take some initiatives vis-à-vis North Korea that might have a moderating effect on Pyongyang. Specifically, Japan could offer North Korea economic aid, while the United States could offer diplomatic assistance, i.e., recognition. In any such endeavor, coordination between the United States and Japan is of the utmost importance. If the United States takes unilateral action vis-à-vis Pyongyang, this will be a repetition of the "Nixon shock" experience. Finally, Japan may be able to make a number of additional contributions to help create the political and military climate necessary for a credible residual U.S. commitment. These will be spelled out later in the discussion of Japan's potential role in the maintenance of Northeast Asian security.

How Do Americans View the Future of the U.S. Commitment to South Korea? Is Air Power a Meaningful Deterrent? What Are the Prospects for the Withdrawal of U.S. Air Forces? Could the U.S. Commitment Be Maintained in the Absence of a U.S. Military Presence on the Peninsula? How Does the United States Perceive the Relationship Between the Defense of Korea and the Security of Japan?

WHITING: A complete U.S. withdrawal of military forces from

South Korea, even if it left the formal treaty commitment intact, would contradict the withdrawal policy President Carter pursued until 1979. This could only be interpreted in Moscow and Peking as signaling a decisive turn in U.S. policy, aiming for conflict avoidance, if not simple isolationism. Only a truly credible U.S. offshore posture, demonstrated through intermittent exercises staged from nearby bases, would enable either Communist power to argue convincingly that the North should refrain from eventually taking offensive action. Moscow and Peking might compete to supply the North with a superior capability against the South, perhaps warning that they would not intervene directly unless the United States acted first. This could lead to serious destabilization of the balance of forces on the peninsula and sharply increase the likelihood of war.

WEINSTEIN: Members of Congress and the executive branch who were interviewed in September 1977 saw, for the most part, no real alternative to a continuation of at least some U.S. military presence in Korea until the North Koreans change their basic attitudes. The predominant view is that North Korean recalcitrance prevents any real accommodation in Korea. It is generally felt that the withdrawal process should not be completed until North Korea agrees to peaceful coexistence with the South. The U.S. officials interviewed believed that the South Koreans were justified in feeling threatened by the North. As indicators of Pyongyang's true intentions they cited North Korea's claims of being the only sovereign government on the peninsula, its efforts to have Seoul treated as an international pariah, the impressive development of the North's military capabilities, the concentration of its forces near the DMZ, the construction of secret tunnels beneath the DMZ, and frequent provocative incidents. The only persuasive demonstration of North Korea's desire for peaceful coexistence, it was said, would be its willingness to talk with the South Korean government and to work toward a modus vivendi. Even among some liberal Democratic members of Congress there was a belief that Kim Il-sung's top priority is the reunification of Korea under Communist auspices and that he must be prepared to use force, since there is no other way to achieve this goal. An interesting exchange took place at a Japanese–U.S. conference of parliamentarians held in Washington in September 1977. While Japanese Diet members Yohei Kono and Hideo Den questioned whether

North Korea poses any real threat to the South, even the liberal U.S. congressmen viewed such a threat as a given.

There were, however, other views expressed. One State Department official specializing in Korea argued that Seoul's recalcitrance, not Pyongyang's, stands in the way of negotiations that might yield an accommodation. He believes that the U.S. military presence should be made contingent on Seoul's willingness to negotiate "seriously" with the North in order to reduce tensions. Also, he added, he had seen no evidence of North Korean intentions to attack the South, at least since 1970. Pyongyang has for some time viewed itself as being relatively weak, he continued. This is not only because of its foreign debt problem, but is due to its lack of support from its Communist allies and its preoccupation with the problems of political succession and the maintenance of revolutionary momentum. An attack by the North would be futile, he felt, in the absence of a strong political foundation in the South and a more secure base in the North. His views, he acknowledged, are shared by only a small minority within the U.S. government.

The most troublesome aspect of the situation to members of Congress was their inability to grasp the basic assumptions and operating methods of the Carter administration. There was a sense that Jimmy Carter was an unknown quantity, still feeling his way through unfamiliar terrain. A major source of congressional uneasiness about the administration's policy was, as one House staff member put it, the "lack of any clear intellectual core" to the administration's foreign policy. "At least we knew where Kissinger stood, what his basic assumptions were," he observed. "Carter's and Brzezinski's assumptions—their longterm views—are not so clear." Was the withdrawal merely cosmetic? How important a factor was human rights in the administration's thinking about a U.S. troop withdrawal? The purposes of the troop withdrawals and their relationship to a longer-term perspective on how the Korean situation might be stabilized simply were not made clear. This concern overlaps, of course, the widespread dissatisfaction at the way the administration handled consultations with Congress and with members of the executive branch. But there was also a strong suspicion that the problem ran deeper—that the administration had not worked out a coherent conceptual framework for its Asian policies.

Members of Congress seemed to assume that the principal

reason for the troop-withdrawal decision was a desire to make U.S. involvement less "automatic" in the event of hostilities. But many officials had serious doubts that the withdrawal of the Second Division would, in fact, have this effect. Some questioned whether the U.S. commitment is really automatic even with the Second Division astride the principal invasion route. According to a State Department official, it is automatic only in the sense that the president would have to make an immediate decision in the event of an attack. One should not assume that the death of a U.S. soldier would make a U.S. response inevitable. A Senate source took the same position, drawing a distinction between an attack on Japan, which would elicit an automatic U.S. response because of the manifest importance of Japan to the United States, and a challenge to South Korea, the importance of which is not so clearly established. But all of those interviewed acknowledged that U.S. casualties would make some sort of U.S. response very likely.

Though one congressman strongly disagreed, most of those interviewed felt that the withdrawal of ground forces would not significantly diminish the likelihood of a U.S. response to a North Korean attack. Few were inclined to go along with the oft-quoted observation that "airplanes are like geese—they can honk and fly away." For one thing, it was generally agreed that air forces are almost as effective as ground forces as instruments for deterrence. Any credible North Korean attack would involve immediate strikes on U.S. air bases. According to State Department officials, there would "certainly" be U.S. casualties, both in aircraft and airmen, in the first hour of a war. The North Koreans would have to take out the U.S. F-4s at the outset, since it would be too risky for them to stage an invasion without doing so.

Despite the growing strength of the R.O.K. air forces, few officials contemplated a withdrawal of U.S. air forces. Indeed, it was noted that the U.S. air presence in South Korea was being augmented, not reduced. Even if South Korea's air forces were judged equal to those of the North, withdrawal of U.S. aircraft was ruled out because, as one official stated, "we could never prove that they are equal, so why take the risk." This argument, he was confident, would prove compelling for Washington. Furthermore, he added, air forces are important as a bargaining lever. If the North Koreans were convinced that the United States intended to keep its aircraft in Korea for a long time, then Pyongyang might decide that the only way to get the U.S. forces out was by reaching an accommodation with Seoul. Why couldn't the same logic that led to the decision to withdraw ground forces (they were "superfluous" and "psychologically debilitating") be applied to air forces at some later date? His answer lay in "the international dimension." Even ten years hence it would be necessary to keep U.S. air forces in Korea to maintain the "general structure of stability in the region." This, he said, also involved serving as an "honest broker" to restrain the Koreans from undertaking actions the Japanese might find threatening. The last thing the Japanese would want is "two heavily armed Koreas without [the United States] there as a moderating force."

Another official asserted that the U.S. air forces would remain in Korea far into the future for two reasons: (1) Seoul's proximity to the DMZ, which makes it especially important to maintain control of the air in the early stages of hostilities; and (2) the desirability of using U.S. air power to compensate for possible deficiencies in South Korea's ground and naval forces. Besides, he noted, it is difficult to contemplate South Korean self-sufficiency, because one cannot assume that North Korea's air power will remain static. Indeed, the North Korean air force is said to be "due" for some modernization. He felt, however, that by 1982 it might be possible to set a target date for the withdrawal of U.S. air forces.

In the Congress, supporters of the Carter administration's withdrawal of ground forces indicated that no one was thinking about pulling out air forces. Air support was described as "politically tolerable" for a long time into the future; a long-term U.S. air presence in Korea was thus viewed as feasible. There was "no political payoff" in announcing a withdrawal of air forces. The broader Asian context was mentioned here, too, and it was asserted that no other location was available to station U.S. air forces needed for the defense of Japan, Taiwan, and other U.S. interests in Asia. (A reinforcement of U.S. air forces in Japan was infeasible, because facilities in Okinawa and other Japanese islands were already overcrowded.)

Several of those interviewed noted, however, that a withdrawal of air forces could well be "sold" to the Congress and even to the military by the mid-1980s if international tensions eased and South Korea seemed strong. The replacement of Kim Il-sung by a more moderate leader could have a major impact on this decision. Clearly, the general preference is to withdraw ground forces first, and to contemplate the future of U.S. air forces only after the "results are in" on the ground-force withdrawals.

One U.S. official with military expertise indicated that some people in the government were thinking about the subsequent withdrawal of air forces, but it was not being formally discussed because of concern about the reaction of the South Koreans. Several officials indicated that they would support the withdrawal of U.S. air forces if they were convinced that the U.S. presence was no longer needed to deter the North Koreans. "No one really wants to stay indefinitely," it was stated, although some military men might be reluctant to abandon "our last outpost on the Asian mainland." The secretary of defense, responding to a question in a public forum, stated that it was "conceivable" we would help the South Koreans build a substantial air force capability to make them clearly self-sufficient but that this was "not our present intention." He stated that the United States plans to leave air force units in Korea beyond 1982, because of the financial burden withdrawal would place on the Koreans. He also indicated that these forces would be needed to serve the broader interests of the United States in Asia. But a knowledgeable Washington official claimed that, in fact, it is U.S. policy to build up the R.O.K. air force toward ultimate self-sufficiency, although the secretary of defense could not state this publicly.

Could U.S. air forces stationed offshore serve any significant deterrent role following the withdrawal of those forces from Korea? Some military experts felt that U.S. aircraft based in Japan, Okinawa, and the Philippines and at sea could still perform a meaningful role in support of South Korea. But others sharply disagreed, stating that U.S. air support, to be of any value, must be physically located on the Korean peninsula. They asserted that aircraft could not reach the DMZ from anyplace outside of Korea with a full load of bombs. Furthermore, in order to maintain air control, which is the critical requirement, the aircraft would have to carry out several sorties a day, which means that they would have to be based in Korea. The problem with carrier-based aircraft is that it is impossible to maintain a sufficient volume of munitions on a carrier. Nor will B-52s suffice, since the requirement is for close air support and for fighters capable of knocking enemy planes out of the air, not for heavy bombers.

But couldn't the necessary aircraft be flown to Korean bases, from which they could then operate locally? Military experts expressed confidence in the ability of the United States to move a massive number of aircraft to Korea in a short time. The problem, it is asserted, lies in supporting the aircraft after they arrive, not just in bringing them in. At the time of the August 1976 DMZ incident, airplanes brought in as reinforcements used bases that had been in caretaker status to see how this procedure would work out.

The long-term U.S. strategy, as Whiting notes, should probably be viewed as one of residual, not optional, involvement. This means, presumably, that the United States would be involved to the extent needed, rather than responding with an automaticity implied by the presence of U.S. forces. Matters could become complicated, of course, if the circumstances surrounding the outbreak of hostilities were ambiguous. But there is no doubt that so long as the formal commitment remains in force, the United States would have to make some response, whether or not U.S. forces remain in the country. A strong case can be made for retaining a virtually open-ended commitment to defend South Korea against an attack in which the Soviets or Chinese are directly involved. If there is clear evidence of Soviet involvement on behalf of North Korea, then, as Harrison has observed, there would be broad support in the United States for action to meet this challenge.

As for the relationship between Korea's defense and the security of Japan, most U.S. policymakers believe that Japan considers a U.S. presence in Korea essential to Japan's security, and this belief plays a vital role in sustaining U.S. support for Seoul. As a State Department official stated, a Japanese statement to the effect that they were not opposed to further U.S. withdrawals from Korea would have a "very strong influence" on many people in the executive and legislative branches. Congressional sources tend to agree with that assessment. One Democratic congressman said, "We would not be in Korea if it were not for Japan. The Japanese connection is central to our commitment. South Korea is of no great strategic importance to us. But it is to the Japanese, because the Japanese say it is." Other legislators, however, including some "moderate" Democrats like Senator John Glenn, would probably argue for a continued U.S. commitment in Korea to maintain regional stability even if the Japanese felt it unnecessary.

What would be the likely impact of a second Korean war on Japan? There was surprisingly little fear among those interviewed in Washington that even a Communist South Korea would lead Japan either to move drastically toward the left or to seek nuclear weapons. There was concern, however, that Japan would undertake some further rearmament and that an inflow of Korean refugees could significantly destabilize the political situation in Japan. A congressional staff expert predicted that the only impact of a Communist South Korea on Japan would be to make Japan less reliable as a democracy and as a trading partner.

How Important to Japan Is the U.S. Military Presence in and the Commitment to South Korea?   What Would Be the Impact on Japan of a Complete Withdrawal of U.S. Forces from South Korea?   Do the Japanese Fear the Outbreak of Hostilities as Such, or Merely the Likelihood That Japan Would Become Involved?   If the Security of South Korea Is Indeed Vital to That of Japan, What Can the Japanese Do to Contribute to the R.O.K.'s Security?

SAEKI: The U.S. defense commitment to South Korea is vital for the security of the Korean peninsula. Therefore, a continued U.S. commitment is desirable until a system of peaceful North-South coexistence is established, i.e., until mutual recognition of North Korea by the United States and Japan and of South Korea by the Soviet Union and China takes place, and until the two Koreas are admitted simultaneously to the United Nations.

The impact on Japan of a complete withdrawal of U.S. forces would vary according to the process and timing of the withdrawal and the international environment in which the withdrawal was carried out. Complete withdrawal of U.S. forces from South Korea would not seriously damage Japanese security interests, provided that

1. there was a good prospect for progress toward the establishment of a system of peaceful coexistence between the North and the South
2. there had been sufficient consultations with South Korea and Japan on the timing and steps of the withdrawal

3. the withdrawal was carried out in stages under conditions that facilitate South Korean confidence in its capability to maintain the North-South military equilibrium

If these conditions were met, a complete withdrawal of U.S. forces could have a positive impact on the security of the Korean peninsula. The withdrawal would not hurt the credibility of the U.S. commitment to the defense of Japan. On the other hand, if these conditions were not met sufficiently, complete withdrawal of U.S. forces would seriously and rapidly damage the credibility of the U.S. defense commitment.

The reaction of the Soviets and Chinese to a complete U.S. withdrawal would, of course, be very important. The Soviets and the Chinese would assess a complete withdrawal of U.S. forces from South Korea from the viewpoint of the U.S. global military posture and the U.S. military presence in the entire western Pacific region. If there were no other significant change in the U.S. military presence in the western Pacific, the Soviets and Chinese would assume that the United States had withdrawn its military forces from the perimeter of the Asian continent and that it was shifting its policy to an island chain strategy.

If the United States reduced its military presence in the western Pacific (including Japan), the Soviets and Chinese would assume that the United States was shifting its military interest and efforts from the Asia-Pacific region to other areas. In that case, the Chinese would question the effectiveness of using the United States as a countervailing power against Soviet threats. The Soviets, on the other hand, would assume that conditions in the Asia-Pacific area were moving in a direction that would permit the expansion of Soviet influence there. If, however, U.S. global strategy and the U.S. military presence in the western Pacific are appropriate, the Soviets and Chinese may think that a complete withdrawal of U.S. forces from South Korea will help lay the groundwork for a system of peaceful coexistence on the Korean peninsula.

It appears that although they are aware of the possibility, the Japanese do not seriously fear the outbreak of hostilities on the peninsula. They do not seem to be seriously considering the extent to which Japan would become involved. Nor is the Japanese government preparing for the crisis management that would be required by the outbreak of hostilities on the peninsula.

In the opinion of most Japanese, if there is an outbreak of hostilities, Tokyo should seek to minimize the impact on Japan by refraining from any military involvement beyond cooperation in the use of U.S. military bases on Japanese territory in accordance with existing obligations. Japan should minimize its nonmilitary involvement as well. It may be selfish of Japan to minimize its involvement while assuming that U.S. military involvement will be both inevitable and effective. But the history of complex relations between Japan and Korea indicates that South Korea will not expect more from Japan than what the Japanese now intend to do.

If the North initiates armed aggression, it may be necessary for the United States to attack boldly in the enemy heartland at the initial stage of the conflict to localize and limit the hostilities. It is not clear whether the United States now has the readiness to take such action or whether Japan would cooperate with such an action.

In summary, Japan is ready to cooperate with the United States in the execution of the U.S. defense commitment to South Korea through the U.S. use of its military bases in Japan. But this means only that Japan is ready to fulfill faithfully its duties and obligations promised under the Mutual Security Treaty with the United States. Japan is not ready to accept new duties and obligations in exchange for the continuation of the U.S. defense commitment to South Korea or for the continuing presence of U.S. air forces there. Accordingly, Japan is not in a position to request the United States to continue indefinitely its defense commitment to South Korea. But Japan can suggest to the United States that for the security of the Korean peninsula and the surrounding area, including Japan, and for U.S. global security interests, it would be wise for the United States to continue its defense commitment to South Korea until a system of peaceful coexistence is established between North and South Korea.

MOMOI: Indeed, the importance of the U.S. commitment to South Korea can only be appreciated if the question is considered within a global context. In the Japanese view, the U.S. military presence in South Korea is important because it serves three functions.

1. It represents an unmistakable strategic signal to the other side that the United States remains firmly committed

to the security of Northeast Asia.
2. It acts as a restraint on the R.O.K.
3. It serves to reassure foreign investors, on whom South
    Korea depends for an increasing inflow of capital in order
    to maintain domestic stability and to implement the mili-
    tary force improvement plan.

The U.S. commitment is vital because, coupled with a military
presence on the peninsula, it functions as a deterrent to the Soviet
Union, the real source of insecurity in the region.

From the Japanese perspective, given the increasing deployment of Soviet naval and air forces in the northern Pacific, the
absence of U.S. military forces on the peninsula would provide
the Soviets with two strategic options—expansion to the Yellow
Sea through the peninsula, and the development of a major strategic base complex northeastward toward Kamchatka. Thus, if
the United States is to remain a Pacific power, it should contemplate keeping at least some U.S. forces indefinitely stationed on
the Korean peninsula. In the event of a complete withdrawal,
understood as a total disengagement, Tokyo would immediately
ask how this would be interpreted by the USSR and China. The
danger is that a complete withdrawal may lead to a misunderstanding on the part of the Soviets that the United States has abandoned
not only its commitment to Northeast Asia but its posture as a
Pacific power. Tokyo would then have to face the possibility of a
complete about-face in the global strategic picture, and it is most
likely that Japan would have to make some accommodation to
these changes.

The question of what Japan is prepared to do to contribute to
the R.O.K.'s security reveals a basic perceptual difference between
Japanese and others concerning the whole issue of Korean security.
The oft-quoted statement that the security of Korea is essential to
Japan's security is less strategic than political. Japan's prime stra-
tegic concern is the future course of action of the Soviets. If the
Soviets are not directly involved in the Korean developments, the
security of Korea is a matter of only secondary importance to
Japan, at least in a strict strategic sense. If the USSR is involved,
then there is little that Japan can contribute to Korea's security.
Either way, the question has to be considered in a global context.
This means that Japan does not necessarily fear the outbreak of

hostilities on the Korean peninsula unless external powers are involved in the fighting.

It is, of course, inevitable that any major armed conflict on the peninsula would involve Japan indirectly. At the very least, Japan would have to accommodate refugees, deal with violations of territorial air or sea space, and perhaps counter certain diplomatic bluffs. Whatever scenario unfolds in Korea, it is very unlikely that Japanese volunteers would be involved in any kind of direct military role. Japan's response might be limited to logistic assistance and cooperation with U.S. forces if those forces are acting as an element of the United Nations Command or under other specific directives of the United Nations. It would be vitally important for the Japanese public to be fully informed about the nature of the conflict on the peninsula. The Japanese public might not support the U.S. use of bases in Japan for Korean operations unless they were convinced that the Soviets were involved on the side of North Korea.

Could U.S. bases in Japan be used in a Korean conflict if the United States had already withdrawn its forces from the peninsula and no longer maintained any bases in Korea? If the United States withdrew from its Korean bases and asserted that any future U.S. air operations in Korea would be undertaken from bases in Japan, this would probably be viewed as a political expedient and, hence, would not be very believable. The central fact would be the withdrawal itself, which would be viewed as a sign of declining U.S. interest in the security of the region. One can assume that neither the Soviets, the Chinese, nor the North Koreans would believe that the United States would fight in Korea from bases in Japan. In any case, Japan's decision whether or not to permit the bases to be used in such a crisis would depend on first convincing Tokyo of the military utility of using these bases for combat operations. There would also have to be ample evidence that the United States was seriously committed to the conflict.

To be sure, there are some areas in which cooperation between Japan and South Korea would be useful, even in the military field. But the domestic political climate in both countries makes it difficult to do anything along those lines at this time. Although the Korean government has not been anxious for Japanese military assistance, there are some signs that R.O.K. military circles are willing to develop such a relationship. Specifically, it might be useful for Japan and South Korea to exchange intelligence and undertake some division of labor with respect to surveillance, even in peacetime. Japan could transfer technology that would indirectly aid the Korean defense effort, including know-how and, to a limited extent, certain components of military-related equipment. One can even imagine joint production of certain kinds of equipment. Standardization of weapons systems among the United States, Japan, and South Korea might also be useful.

Japan could contribute to Korea's security by giving the United States improved logistic facilities, especially with respect to stocks of fuel and ammunition. In any conflict, the R.O.K.'s supply of TOW and Maverick missiles would be quickly expended, and resupply capabilities would be an important part of the military equation. Tokyo could indicate that staging areas would be made available in case of an overt attack on South Korea. But this could be done only if Japan had strong confidence that the U.S. was willing and able to recommit its forces quickly to Korea. Rowen notes that a decision to recommit U.S. forces would take less than five days if the attack were unambiguous. A U.S. return to Korea within a week would be fast enough; but if it took two weeks, it would be too late. Finally, Japan could deny North Korea and its allies any Japanese industrial and economic facilities, and pro-North Korean elements could be barred entry into Japan. But, as indicated, for the present these are all merely theoretical possibilities.

WEINSTEIN: As for U.S. views of the contribution Japan might make to Korea's security, there is little evidence of effort on the part of the United States to prod Japan to play a military role in Korea, or to link arguments for the buildup of the Self-Defense Forces (SDF) with the U.S. withdrawal from Korea. Defense Secretary Harold Brown clearly stated in July 1977 that Japan's contributions to Korea's security should be exclusively in the non-military sphere. According to U.S. officials, there is a "tacit understanding" that Japanese bases could be used in the event of a Korean emergency, even though such use is not considered likely.[15] Some U.S. officials in Korea suggested privately in 1976 that they would like to see Japanese aircraft flying patrols over the Sea of Japan in the vicinity of Korea. Individuals associated with SRI International are said to have proposed that Japan should be prepared to send an expeditionary force to Korea if needed. The Government Accounting Office (GAO) reportedly once suggested that Japan pay the costs of maintaining U.S. troops in Korea, but a State Department official stated that the idea had been dismissed because "we knew it wouldn't work." In any case, the official added, the idea died with the Carter administration's withdrawal decision and Japan was "let off the hook."

Of the individuals interviewed in Washington, not one argued for a Japanese military role in Korea. As stated by a key official: "It is clear that no one on either side, Japanese or Korean, wants any kind of military liaison between Japan and Korea." Most U.S. officials stated a lack of interest in any Japanese military role and alluded to the intense animosity between Japanese and Koreans.

On the other hand, a number of officials did propose that Japan be asked to make certain contributions if U.S. troops were withdrawn. If South Korea had to pay more for its own defense as a result of the U.S. withdrawals, then Japan might be expected to lend greater support to Korea's economic growth so that Seoul could afford the additional military expenditures. The following four specific contributions were cited by officials in the executive branch:

1. liberalized Korean access to Japanese markets, in particular an easing of Japanese importer association "restraint agreements" and other trade restrictions on such items as silk and textiles, which have contributed to the substantial deficit in Korea's trade with Japan
2. increased Official Development Assistance (ODA) to Korea
3. increased Japanese investment in certain key Korean industries
4. greater sensitivity to South Korea's needs on the part of Japanese who carry out unofficial relations with North Korea

Officials acknowledged that it has long been the "general view" in the Pentagon and, to some extent, in the State Department that Japan ought to do more to provide for its own defense. But these officials did not tie this to the Korean situation and even expressed some concern that the Japanese might go too far in developing their military capabilities. Among members of the Congress, the general feeling seems to be that burden sharing is not now a major issue, though it could well become one.

Certain influential members of Congress, like Senator John Glenn, who chairs the Foreign Relations Committee's Subcommittee on East Asian Affairs, are said to be dubious about the notion of an arbitrary ceiling on Japanese defense spending at 1 percent of GNP (or any other set figure). If demands for greater Japanese defense efforts were presented properly, most U.S. legislators probably would go along with them, according to sources knowledgeable about the Congress. Many members of Congress feel that Japan should at least make a greater contribution to the cost of keeping U.S. troops in Japan. The burden-sharing issue could become very lively if there is any direct linkage of Japan's "free ride" on defense and several of the major economic issues dividing the two countries.

Of course, it should be noted that certain Japanese defense officials may privately welcome U.S. withdrawals from Korea as a new basis on which to justify the gradual expansion of the Self-Defense Forces. According to Pyongyang, Washington has been urging Japan to assume a military role in Korea. Furthermore, a former chief of the Japanese Maritime Self-Defense Forces is said to have declared in Seoul that Japan and South Korea would have to work together in the event of hostilities on the peninsula. The Japanese spokesman reportedly stated that Japan would conduct naval operations in the vicinity of Korea.[16]

WHITING: The key point is that, over the long run, neither the United States nor Japan can be regarded as crucial to the stability of Korea. While both the United States and Japan may play a certain role, this is essentially something extra. The Koreans themselves are the key. Furthermore, we must recognize that it is politically impossible for the United States to withdraw its forces and then later to return in a kind of yo-yo fashion. The Congress would never permit such an arrangement. If it suddenly became necessary for the United States to send U.S. troops back to meet a North Korean challenge, the Congress would conclude that this signified the failure of South Korea's military modernization plan. It would evoke a very emotional response. It is even more apparent that the United States would be unable to respond to a minor or ambiguous challenge. If, for example, North Korea put the squeeze on the western islands, no U.S. ground involvement would be possible. The United States might move its ships around, but, if pressed, Washington would have to concede that the islands are not locked into the U.S. commitment and are not vital to the defense of South Korea. Similarly, if the security of South Korea is viewed as having been weakened by Seoul's repressive domestic policies, Americans will ask why they should become involved. Indeed, it may well be that Kim Il-sung, while recognizing that it is becoming increasingly difficult for North Korea to compete on economic and military grounds, will be saved from despair by his hope that the repressiveness of the Seoul government will reopen divisions and will bring about a repeat of the kind of events that led to the overthrow of Rhee in 1960. Kim may also hope that disunity among Park's successors, particularly intra-army conflict, will lead to a protracted period of instability that will weaken the South and force the United States to reconsider its commitment.

It may be true, as Kosaka has pointed out, that if the U.S. goal is to avoid automatic involvement in a Korean conflict, then the United States should withdraw both ground and air forces. The political reality, however, is that an air involvement is much easier to sustain over a long period of time. There is a great difference in the U.S. public image of air versus ground involvement. We recognize that many Japanese would like to have U.S. ground forces in Korea in order to reduce U.S. options and make U.S. involvement in Seoul's defense more likely. I personally disagree with the policy of unilateral withdrawal aimed at increasing U.S. flexibility. I don't think we should try to keep our options open. It would have been preferable to seek some quid pro quo from Pyongyang in exchange for the promise to withdraw U.S. ground forces.

WEINSTEIN: In my view, it is essential to understand the reasons why the United States may wish to reduce the likelihood of automatic involvement in a new Korean conflict. If the withdrawal of U.S. ground forces and possible future withdrawals of air forces are related to a desire to avoid automatic involvement in a Korean war, this does not necessarily indicate that the U.S. no longer cares about the fate of Korea, much less the rest of East Asia. The central point is that there is no reason for the United States to become automatically involved when U.S. forces are not needed to deter or to repel aggression. The growing capabilities of the South Koreans, not increasing doubts about Seoul, are the key.

This, too, explains why it would not be reasonable to expect a quid pro quo from Pyongyang. The withdrawal of U.S. forces need not be regarded as a concession but may be seen as a sign that South Korea no longer needs these forces. The withdrawal is a concession to North Korea only in the narrowest sense of the term, i.e., we are doing something that they have long asked us to do. But if it is done because we believe the South Koreans are able to defend themselves, then it represents no real concession to Pyongyang. Rather, it is a move undertaken because it serves the interests of both Washington and Seoul. An important corollary to the U.S. withdrawal would be a continued readiness to intervene on Seoul's behalf in the unlikely event of Chinese or Soviet involvement. Nor should we forget that the treaty remains in effect whether or not U.S. forces are stationed in Korea. As Whiting has observed, the costs to Pyongyang of the 1950 invasion, when there was no treaty, were very high. It seems unlikely that Kim or his Communist allies would want to risk another invasion with the treaty still in effect.

The more difficult problem stemming from withdrawals undertaken because of Seoul's growing strength is twofold. First, as South Korea grows more independent and comes to take greater responsibility for its own defense, Seoul may feel it desirable to seek, as the ultimate trump card in deterring Pyongyang, a nuclear weapons capability. Secondly, the North Koreans, faced with an adversary armed with increasingly sophisticated weaponry, may pressure their Soviet and Chinese allies for accelerated military assistance, thus intensifying the arms race between the two Koreas. These concerns are the subject of the next two chapters.

Notes

1. Ch'a Ki-byok, "Han'guk minjokchuuie ui tojon kwa siryon" [Trials and challenges of Korean nationalism], in *Han'guk ui minjokchuui Seminar* [Seminar on Korean nationalism] (Report of the Korean Association of International Relations, Seoul, 1967), p. 13. For a partial English summary of this symposium, see *Korea Journal*, Korean National Commission for UNESCO, December 1966. See also Yi Yong-hui, "Kijo Nonmun: Han'guk kundaehwa ui kibon munje" [Keynote address: fundamental problems in the modernization of Korea], in *Han'guk kundaehwa e issosoe kaldunggwa chohwa* [Conflict and harmony: report of conference on modernization], publication no. 8, April 20, 1968 (Seoul: Korean Association of International Relations, 1969), pp. 10–15.

2. Testimony by Kim Hyung Wook, U.S., Congress, House, Subcommittee on International Organizations, *Investigation of Korean-American Relations,* 95th Cong., 1st sess., June 22, 1977, pt. 1, p. 21.

3. This is discussed further in Selig S. Harrison, *The Widening Gulf: Asian Nationalism and American Policy* (New York: Free Press, 1978).

4. Transcript of an interview with Paik Too-chin, Seoul, September 28, 1965, John Foster Dulles Oral History Project, Princeton University Library, pp. 11, 15.

5. Transcript of an interview with Son Won-il, Seoul, September 29, 1964, Dulles Oral History Project, pp. 14–15.

6. Transcript of an interview with Chung Il-kwon, Seoul, September 29, 1964, Dulles Oral History Project, p. 35.

7. Ibid., p. 33.

8. The Kim Il-sung interview is recounted in Tokyo JOAK television, July 13, 1977; on the softer North Korean line resulting from the troop withdrawal plan, see the *New York Times,* June 5, 1977, and the *Washington Post,* July 14, 1977.

9. *People's Daily,* August 7, 1977.

10. This account is based on the *Washington Post,* June 12, 1977.

11. Ibid.

12. See Franklin B. Weinstein, "The United States, Japan, and the Security of Korea," *International Security* 2, no. 2 (autumn 1977), pp. 68–89; and "The Korean Debate, Continued," *International Security* 2, no. 3 (winter 1978), pp. 160–167.

13. See Franklin B. Weinstein, "U.S.–Vietnam Relations and the Security of Southeast Asia," *Foreign Affairs* 56, no. 4 (July 1978), pp. 843–846; and Franklin B. Weinstein and John W. Lewis, "The Post-Vietnam Strategic Context in Asia," in *U.S.-Japan Relations and the Security of East Asia: The Next Decade,* ed. Franklin B. Weinstein (Boulder, Colo.: Westview Press, 1978), pp. 127–160.

14. *Los Angeles Times,* June 8, 1977.

15. *Asahi,* June 24, 1977.

16. Pyongyang Domestic Service, July 8, 1977, and Voice of the Revolutionary Party for Reunification, clandestine, July 7, 1977.

4
The Nuclear Dimension

WEINSTEIN: There is no doubt that the withdrawal of U.S. ground-combat forces from South Korea and the implied possibility of further withdrawals subsequently would increase in some measure the possibility that Seoul will seek a nuclear weapons capability. Even more to the point, the South Koreans may feel that the removal of U.S. nuclear weapons from the peninsula would justify development of their own nuclear force as a replacement. But much of the argument on this point has been characterized by oversimplification and exaggerated fears about the likelihood and the consequences of a nuclear Korea.

To gain a better understanding of the nuclear dimension of the Korean security problem, it is necessary to understand the role of nuclear weapons in the defense of South Korea and the implications of a withdrawal of U.S. tactical nuclear weapons. We must consider Seoul's incentives and disincentives for going nuclear, the kind of nuclear capability the Koreans might seek, their ability to satisfy the technical requirements for such a capability, and the leverage that might be exerted on Seoul in response to signs that the Koreans were moving toward nuclear weapons. We must also make a sober assessment of the consequences should the Koreans acquire nuclear weapons. How would this development affect Japanese attitudes toward their own defense, U.S. views of the U.S. commitment to Seoul, and prospects for war on the peninsula?

What Is the Role of Nuclear Weapons in Deterring Conflict in Korea?   Do U.S. Tactical Nuclear Weapons in South Korea Have a Military or Political Role That Cannot Be Filled by Other

Weapons?   What Are the Implications of a Withdrawal of U.S. Tactical Nuclear Weapons from Korea?

WEINSTEIN: There is inevitably a certain amount of ambiguity surrounding the role of U.S. nuclear weapons in Korea's defense, because Washington maintains a policy of not commenting specifically on the location of U.S. nuclear weapons. There have, however, been some government statements alluding to the use of nuclear weapons in the Korean context. In the summer of 1975, then Secretary of Defense James Schlesinger, seeking to bolster the South Koreans in the wake of the Vietnam debacle, referred to the possibility of using nuclear weapons against North Korea. On May 29, 1977, President Carter declared that the United States might use nuclear weapons in case of a North Korean attack. This was reaffirmed in Secretary of Defense Harold Brown's press conference in Seoul in late July 1977. Secretary Brown added, however, that the United States did not contemplate using these weapons, since conventional forces should be adequate to deter North Korea. Brown indicated that South Korea would continue to enjoy the protection of the U.S. nuclear umbrella, although he was not specific as to whether the nuclear weapons would remain in South Korea.

According to press reports, the Carter administration had informed Seoul by June 1977 of a decision to remove all of the approximately one thousand tactical nuclear weapons assigned to U.S. ground and air forces in South Korea.[1] The House International Relations Committee was said to have heard testimony to the same effect. Committee Chairman Clement Zablocki stated that it would be a matter of concern if U.S. nuclear weapons were left in South Korea after U.S. ground troops had been withdrawn. Presumably, this concern focused on the inability to protect these weapons in the absence of U.S. ground forces.[2] But by mid-July 1977, it was reported in the press that the president was reconsidering his decision to withdraw all U.S. tactical nuclear weapons from Korea. In response to pleas from Seoul, Washington was now said to be considering the possibility of leaving, as a "token," a small number of tactical nuclear weapons with U.S. F-4 fighter-bomber squadrons at Usan and Kunsom airfields.[3] Government officials whom I interviewed in Washington in late September 1977 gave conflicting accounts of the administration's decision.

One official indicated that the United States would leave behind "a very few tactical nuclear weapons under tight U.S. control." But another official stated his understanding that all of the nuclear weapons would be withdrawn along with U.S. ground forces. The discrepancy may be explained by a report that the nuclear weapons at Usan and Kunsom airfields are not scheduled for removal until late in the withdrawal cycle, and that some may be left in place if it appears in 1982 that North Korea is contemplating an assault on the South.[4]

In terms of the calculus of deterrence, the removal of U.S. tactical nuclear weapons presently stationed in Korea should be the least controversial element of any U.S. withdrawal plan. To begin with, most Japanese and U.S. specialists agree that the weapons are not needed for the defense of South Korea. Although military planners undoubtedly have contingency plans indicating how nuclear weapons might be used in the defense of South Korea, several government officials reiterated in interviews the oft-stated view that no one in a position of importance in the government can realistically imagine the use of such weapons.

One knowledgeable official noted that certain Japanese defense officials have stated on occasion that nuclear weapons are needed in Korea, not only for the defense of South Korea, but to maintain the strategic balance in Northeast Asia. This, he said, was a strange argument for the Japanese to make, given their attitude toward nuclear weapons and their refusal to allow such weapons in Japan. Besides, he asserted, it is hard to see why keeping these weapons in Korea should be so decisive, since they are "merely symbolic" and are significant only in the context of other things we do.

To be sure, a State Department official who closely follows Korean affairs observed that even though the U.S. does not consider nuclear weapons to be an important deterrent in Korea because it is difficult to contemplate their use, "for some reason the North Koreans don't seem to know that." North Korea's media strongly suggest that the North Koreans are in fact deterred by U.S. nuclear weapons. Some Senate leaders worry about the impact of withdrawing nuclear weapons on Kim Il-sung, whom they are inclined to regard as a madman. Of course, it is possible that the North Koreans talk so much about U.S. nuclear weapons not because they view them as an effective deterrent to an attack on

the South but because this is a convenient issue on which to criticize both Washington and Seoul. In any case, most U.S. policymakers agree that the capacity of U.S. nuclear weapons to deter
conflict in Korea is not contingent on stationing those weapons in
Korea. In the event it is needed, the U.S. nuclear deterrent remains
available from offshore, just as it does for the defense of Japan.

Some have proposed that U.S. nuclear weapons be secretly
withdrawn from Korea. The South Koreans would be unlikely to
breach the secret because it is in their interest to make Pyongyang
think the weapons are still there and to preserve an appearance of
cooperation with the United States. Others have argued publicly
that there is no way a total withdrawal of nuclear weapons—which
are stored in specially patrolled barbed-wire enclosures—could be
kept secret from the North Koreans.[5] But, presumably, the
specially patrolled enclosures could be maintained even in the
absence of the weapons. Members of the working group, however,
generally doubted that the removal of U.S. nuclear weapons could
be kept secret.

In Congress, interest in the nuclear weapons aspect of the
Korean problem seems low. But staff specialists agree that only
a few of the most adamant backers of Seoul in Congress would oppose the withdrawal of those weapons, so long as it is made clear
that South Korea still enjoys the protection of the U.S. nuclear
umbrella.

MOMOI: Notwithstanding these U.S. perspectives, it is essential to recognize that the South Koreans may have a different view
of the role of nuclear weapons. They may be interested in both
the deterrent and combat functions of tactical nuclear weapons.
In their defense strategy, South Koreans may attach some importance to the tactical use of nuclear weapons, including the ones
that would be withdrawn along with the Second Division's combat
troops. For example, nuclear land mines (ADMs) placed at critical
choke points could play an important antitank role. Nuclear weapons may be used as terrain-changing devices. They may be especially effective against underground facilities in North Korea.
According to some reports, most of the North Korean headquarters
and supply depots are now underground. From the standpoint of
deterrence, nuclear weapons pose a uniquely awesome psychological threat to North Korean cities.

The U.S. tactical nuclear weapons presumably based in Korea

serve three important roles. Politically, they dramatically symbolize the U.S. commitment. Psychologically, they force North Korea to consider the possibility that aggression against the South would bring about massive destruction of Pyongyang. And at least theoretically, they are likely to keep Seoul from undertaking the development of its own nuclear weapons. If U.S. nuclear weapons are not stationed in South Korea, their deterrent capabilities are likely to disappear, not only in Seoul's eyes but in those of Pyongyang and Tokyo as well.

Kamiya asks why the South Koreans wish to rely so heavily on tactical nuclear weapons, while Saeki and Rowen state that these weapons are unimportant for South Korea's defense. Rowen argues that the Koreans do not need nuclear weapons for an effective defense as long as modern nonnuclear substitutes are available to them. But the United States has already done so much to play up the role of tactical nuclear weapons that it will be difficult, if not impossible, to persuade Korean planners to abandon a nuclear-oriented defensive strategy. The Koreans believe a massive land invasion from the North cannot be stopped by conventional means alone. In their view, there is no substitute for the military and political roles assigned to nuclear weapons. Precision-guided munitions (PGMs) have not yet received much attention in expositions of South Korean strategy, although both Maverick and TOW missiles are, in practice, already part of their operational thinking. But the South Koreans will probably find it hard to conceive of PGMs as a substitute for nuclear weapons, because PGMs are not normally associated with the concept of deterrence and because Korean planners are attracted only to certain kinds of PGMs. Given the characteristics of Korea's terrain, the expectation of saturation attacks, and memories of the last war, the South Koreans' interest in PGMs is focused on antitank weapons, antiaircraft missiles, and interdiction land mines.

The South Koreans do not need nuclear weapons as long as they have enough antitank missiles and other sophisticated weaponry. But it will probably take until 1982 or 1983 for them to accumulate enough of these weapons. Until they are able to produce their own TOW missiles, they will probably still want to rely too much on nuclear weapons. In any case, as I have already indicated, if the United States is determined to remove its nuclear weapons from South Korea, it is important that Washington avoid saying anything definitive on the subject. It may well be that the weapons cannot be taken out secretly, but a lack of explicitness on Washington's part would leave at least some ambiguity.

WHITING: If it is merely rumored in the press that the weapons have been removed, the North Koreans will have to exercise a degree of caution. Even if the North Koreans are aware that the nuclear weapons have been removed, Pyongyang will still have to consider the possible use of U.S. nuclear weapons from offshore. Thus, even with the removal of nuclear weapons from South Korea, there is still some deterrent potential. As Rowen has noted, U.S. nuclear weapons stationed offshore have less deterrent potential than weapons kept in Korea, but their deterrent capability is not eliminated.

The withdrawal of U.S. tactical nuclear weapons from the South is unlikely to increase the likelihood of aggression by the North so long as U.S. military forces remain in the South to confirm Washington's treaty commitment. Under these circumstances, the rapid introduction of nuclear-capable forces by air and sea remains a serious risk to the North. Pyongyang took ten years to recover from its 1950 miscalculation. The next one could invite even worse destruction. The North will avoid the high-risk option so long as it remains confident that a revolution will eventually occur in the South and aware of a possible U.S. response to open attack.

Neither Peking nor Moscow would be likely to comment publicly on, much less approve, the withdrawal of U.S. tactical nuclear weapons. Privately, however, they might have somewhat mixed reactions. On one hand, neither Communist regime wants Pyongyang to provoke a major conflict on the peninsula. To a limited extent, the more evidence that emerges of a U.S. disengagement, the more difficult it will be to dissuade Pyongyang from launching an attack on the South. On the other hand, the basic deterrence lies in the U.S. military presence in Northeast Asia to back a treaty commitment to Seoul. Even though neither factor was present in 1950, the U.S. response then proved devastating to the North. Therefore, on balance, the nuclear withdrawal might evoke relief in Moscow and Peking that, should war break out, it is unlikely that nuclear weapons would be involved. More significant, from the vantage points of both Moscow and Peking, would be the political and military context surrounding the withdrawal.

SAEKI: The last point needs emphasis. The Communist powers would not judge the strength of the U.S. defense commitment solely on the basis of the withdrawal of U.S. tactical nuclear weapons from South Korea. They would judge the credibility of the U.S. commitment and assess the U.S. capability to defend South Korea by examining the overall U.S. military posture toward the defense of the R.O.K. The Communist powers will almost certainly recall the valuable lesson they learned from the Korean hostilities and thus are likely to avoid reckless behavior. If, however, the United States fails to demonstrate sufficiently the credibility of its defense commitment to South Korea, the withdrawal of tactical nuclear weapons could further diminish the credibility of that commitment.

What Is the Likelihood That South Korea Will Seek an Independent Nuclear Capability? From the Perspective of South Korea, What Are the Incentives and Disincentives for Acquiring Nuclear Weapons?

WEINSTEIN: There is no consensus among U.S. officials as to the likelihood that South Korea will seek nuclear weapons of its own. Those in the executive branch tend to downplay the danger. They find "no evidence" that South Korea is presently considering the nuclear option, although "all indications" are that Seoul was seriously considering such a move in 1975, until the United States acted to prevent the sale by France of reprocessing facilities to South Korea. A high-ranking Korean government official reportedly told U.S. congressional investigators that a military advisory group to President Park voted in the early 1970s to proceed with nuclear-weapons development. According to one U.S. government analyst, in 1975 the Koreans were "running all over the world picking up material and equipment" for a nuclear-weapons program. The reprocessing plant, in his words, was "practically the last thing on the list of things they needed, from special machine tools to the non-nuclear components of weapons." To stop the Korean effort, the Ford administration threatened, in effect, to bring South Korea's civilian nuclear-power program to a halt by blocking the sale of reactors ordered from Westinghouse and by persuading Canada to suspend negotiations for a similar sale.[6]

Since early 1976, U.S. officials assert, the South Koreans have not been thinking seriously about nuclear weapons, despite some "intellectual discussion." Several U.S. officials dismissed as a poor indicator of Korean thinking the South Korean foreign minister's June 1977 statement that Seoul could decide to develop nuclear weapons if this were deemed necessary to preserve the country's security.[7] They saw no need to take that statement at face value because it was made in the broader context of a discussion of the nuclear umbrella and it was extracted in response to a parliamentary query. Besides, the foreign minister claimed that he had been misquoted and regretted the statement. No one would rule out the possibility that the Koreans might decide to acquire nuclear weapons in five or ten years. But according to a State Department official, in the current climate, the South Koreans "would have to be crazy" to give the impression that they were thinking of going nuclear. Furthermore, the South Koreans have given no indication of a revived interest in reprocessing facilities, although they have expressed an interest in participating in joint reprocessing projects under international auspices.[8] Even if they did decide to seek their own reprocessing facilities, the South Koreans would have a hard time obtaining them, according to one official. The French, this official said, probably were no longer prepared to sell Seoul such facilities; indeed, France seemed "to be getting out of the business."

On Capitol Hill there was somewhat greater concern about the danger of a South Korean move toward nuclear weapons. One senior congressman, who is highly sympathetic to Seoul, declared it "understandable" for the Koreans to desire nuclear weapons "after what we have done to them" and observed that "if these weapons are OK for Israel, why not for South Korea?" But his view did not appear to be widely shared. This same congressman also expressed his belief that Japan would acquire nuclear weapons. A number of influential senators, as well as the U.S. ambassador in Seoul, were said to be intensely worried that the South Koreans might seek nuclear weapons. According to a Senate staff member, the desire for nuclear weapons was rapidly growing in Seoul following the 1977 withdrawal decision, and this could not be dismissed as mere "intellectual talk." Some Koreans were clearly urging that the nuclear option be pursued, and individuals in the Korean nuclear industry reportedly asserted that the U.S. should realize that nuclear weapons were again being discussed in Seoul as a real option. Whether South Korea ought to seek assistance—from such sources as Taiwan, South Africa, and Israel—or attempt to develop the weapons on their own was described as an open question.[9]

It is worth noting that Korean discussion of a nuclear-weapons capability has been explicitly linked to the U.S. troop-withdrawal plan. For example, a set of "research reports" by experts from Koryo and Hanyang universities publicized by the National Unification Board called for the development of a small-scale nuclear weapons capability. One report saw the acquisition of such weapons as "a natural political requirement," given the political uses of nuclear weapons. Another asserted that the R.O.K.'s "will to arm itself with nuclear weapons" would depend on the extent of U.S. assistance in the reinforcement of South Korea's independent defense capabilities.[10]

Discussion of Korea's nuclear option clearly intensified during 1978, and foreign participants in a seminar held in Korea in January 1979 were impressed by the openness with which some Koreans made the case for nuclear weapons. To be sure, a well-placed Korean official with whom I spoke in August 1978 dismissed the idea of a South Korean nuclear capability as "appealing only to those who disdain complexities." He argued that a careful examination of a variety of scenarios showed that the nuclear option simply would not work in South Korea. But one could not help being impressed by the increasing attention paid to the nuclear issue in Seoul.

MOMOI: How do we evaluate the conflicting interpretations about whether the South Koreans are likely to seek a nuclear capability? On the basis of the data available, one can conclude that the South Korean government, like the leadership of many other potential nuclear powers, refuses to rule out the nuclear option. This position of the Seoul government is believed to have general support from the opposition parties. The nuclear option is usually aired with reference to a number of conditions under which it might be exercised: (1) "if and when U.S. tactical nuclear weapons have been withdrawn" (Foreign Minister Park, May 26, 1977); (2) "if nuclear weapons are required for national safety and the people's survival, or if under special conditions international treaties are not observed" (Foreign Minister Park, June 25,

1977); or (3) if the government feels that the United States has abandoned South Korea by tacitly or overtly ignoring its security treaty commitment or by failing, in Seoul's view, to respond to a crisis situation.

While the limited information available makes it hard to draw any firm conclusions, the possibility of developing nuclear weapons seems to have been raised not so much as a serious option, but as a political bargaining ploy, perhaps a bluff, aimed at the United States. But this bluff could turn into a serious possibility if U.S. tactical nuclear weapons are publicly withdrawn or if the other conditions previously described have been met.

WEINSTEIN: Even if the conditions described were met, we cannot assume that the South Korean bluff would become a reality. It seems especially risky to conclude that the withdrawal of tactical nuclear weapons alone would be sufficient to propel Seoul into a nuclear-weapons program. Faced with a U.S. decision to remove those weapons, the South Koreans might accept the U.S. view that adequate nuclear deterrence can be provided by U.S. weapons stationed offshore. In the present situation, it may be rational in bargaining with Washington for the South Koreans to talk as if they would go nuclear if the United States does not provide adequate support. But it may well be irrational for them to carry out that threat in the event that U.S. support is actually reduced. The outcome will depend on South Korea's degree of confidence, at the time U.S. nuclear weapons are removed, in its own ability to deter a North Korean attack without nuclear weapons, and on its estimation of the political costs of a move to develop nuclear weapons.

ROWEN: It is important, moreover, that we adopt a balanced perspective on the matter of incentives and disincentives for acquiring nuclear weapons. The most important incentive the South Korean government has for at least shortening the lead time to acquiring nuclear explosives is the possibility, which many people in Seoul take seriously, that U.S. support may critically weaken or may even disappear. Even though the continued U.S. commitment and the backing provided by the U.S. air presence remain of vital importance, there is a perceived difference between a guarantee plus a small (and possibly transient) presence and a guarantee backed up by a large ground presence. The latter offers a good deal more assurance. Looking north from the southern edge of the

DMZ, it is not difficult to imagine a sudden attack taking place. An important question then is whether R.O.K. forces, equipped with modern nonnuclear arms, backed up by U.S. air support—and reinforced if necessary by U.S. ground forces, but with an inevitable lag—would be adequate to defend the R.O.K. and, in particular, to hold Seoul. Estimates can reasonably differ on this. Risk-averse occupants of the "Blue House" might think the prospects unpromising. Other observers might estimate that the prospects are quite good that better equipped R.O.K. forces can successfully defend Seoul.

The view from Seoul carries particular weight concerning the incentives for a move toward nuclear armaments. Nonetheless, it would be simplistic and erroneous to hold that Korean incentives work only for acquiring such explosives; some powerful disincentives also exist. For instance, the R.O.K. has benefited greatly from the relatively stable set of relations among the four outside powers on the peninsula. This stability could be upset by South Korea's acquisition of nuclear weapons, or by major steps toward it. Visible development of nuclear explosives by South Korea would create great concern, in both Japan and the United States, about the possibility of being drawn into a nuclear conflict. Presumably, the regime in Pyongyang would be even more alarmed. The response that Pyongyang would make is unclear, but in time, presumably, it too could acquire nuclear explosives. China and the Soviet Union would also be concerned. They would feel a danger to themselves both because of the existence of an independent power in the region equipped with nuclear weapons and because this move might increase the chances of war on the peninsula with potentially serious consequences for their own security.

It is especially important to avoid the common assumption that the nuclear posture of the two Koreas will be asymmetric. It is unrealistic to think that this asymmetry can persist for long or that nuclear weapons could be used in a one-sided manner. To be sure, unilateral use of nuclear weapons by the South against invading North Korean forces would be highly effective, given the narrowness of the few main invasion corridors and the need to concentrate forces for invasion. But, as previously noted, an effective defense is also possible solely through the use of modern nonnuclear weapons. While nuclear attack on North Korean airfields would do great damage, the destruction of sheltered aircraft would depend on the distribution of the D.P.R.K.'s aircraft among various airfields, the adequacy of the shelters, and the yield and accuracy of the South Korean nuclear weapons. If the R.O.K. possessed adequate target acquisition capabilities, an attack on North Korean forces in rear assembly areas could also be highly effective. Nuclear attacks on population centers could, of course, produce a large number of casualties. For instance, the casualties resulting from the use of a single 10-kiloton weapon against each of the six largest cities in North Korea would be approximately 330,000 to 500,000. If six 40-kiloton weapons were used, casualties would mount to upwards of 1 million, out of a population of 16 million.[11] Civilian casualties would, of course, be greatly reduced if substantial efforts were made to evacuate or shelter the populace. The extent to which a nuclear attack at this level would damage war-supporting industries, or the economy in general, is uncertain.

But it should not be forgotten that the R.O.K. is also vulnerable to nuclear attack. South Korean defenses along the approaches to Seoul, airfields, ports, and, of course, cities could be severely damaged by nuclear weapons. Seoul, with a population of more than 8 million only 35 kilometers from the DMZ, is especially exposed. A single 20-kiloton weapon delivered against Seoul would produce between 200,000 and 300,000 casualties. And larger-yield weapons might be used; if a single 1-megaton bomb were delivered (say, in a Soviet riposte to an R.O.K. nuclear attack on the North), the fatalities and casualties in Seoul would be between 1 and 1.5 million.

In any case, it would be imprudent for Seoul to ignore how acquisition of nuclear weapons would affect existing relationships and how allies and adversaries might each respond. As we shall see when we discuss the likely U.S. and Japanese reactions to a South Korean nuclear-weapons program, the costs to Seoul's relations with its allies are likely to be quite substantial.

What Does It Mean to Speak of a South Korean Nuclear Capability?
What Are the Various Levels of Nuclear Capability the Koreans
Might Seek?   What Are the Technical Requirements, and How
Close Are the Koreans to Meeting Them?   Under What Circum-
stances Might the South Koreans Pursue Various Scenarios Leading
to a Nuclear Capability?

ROWEN: One can imagine four broadly different types of South Korean nuclear programs. First, the South Koreans might do nothing deliberate to move toward the acquisition of nuclear explosives. South Korea's acquisition of civilian nuclear technology will in any case shorten the lead time in creating a bomb. Such a policy of "doing nothing extra" could, of course, be pursued for a time and then be abandoned.

A second approach might involve taking additional steps to shorten the critical time needed to create a bomb. One important step might be to stockpile readily fissionable material, most obviously plutonium in the case of Korea. Another step would be to work on the nonnuclear components of bombs. This course of action would stop short of assembling and testing weapons and of developing or buying delivery systems specifically designed to carry nuclear weapons. If applicable international rules permitted the stockpiling of plutonium, the South Korean government would have a plausible civilian "cover" for an effort to shorten substantially the time-to-possession of bombs, perhaps to a matter of weeks or even days.

A third program might involve a covert effort to build weapons. This alternative would encompass the one just described, but it would go beyond it to include the development and assembly of weapons and, conceivably, underground testing of low-yield bombs. If international safeguards were altered to prohibit possession of fissionable material in readily separable form, then a greater number of activities, including reprocessing facilities, would have to be kept hidden than is the case under the existing international rules.

The fourth approach would be to openly build an arsenal of nuclear weapons. This might be justified by the need to block an anticipated invasion. Such a force might include atomic demolition mines and warheads deliverable by short-range missiles or by aircraft. Seoul could also seek a capability to launch a nuclear attack against deep military targets and population centers, especially Pyongyang itself.

IMAI: In efforts to define in operational terms what it means for South Korea to "go nuclear," it is necessary to distinguish several levels of nuclear capability. These levels represent stages in the process of becoming a nuclear power, because a nation does not become a nuclear power in a single step. The five levels of nuclear capability are:

1. a few crude nuclear explosive devices unfit for delivery
2. a number of devices that may be more refined and more dependable but are still too large for air delivery
3. a limited number of warheads small enough to be delivered by the normal capabilities of the R.O.K. air force
4. a tactically meaningful arsenal of nuclear warheads with appropriate delivery systems and
5. a strategic nuclear arsenal

The last category—a strategic nuclear arsenal—need not concern us here. Strategic capabilities, however small in scale, would require long-range delivery systems, early warning capabilities, and a force with some degree of survivability. In South Korea's case, this is not likely in the near term. It is safe to assume that long before the country could ever acquire such strategic capabilities, if Seoul appeared to be moving in that direction, South Korea's neighbors would probably take some drastic action. Indeed, any discussion of the nuclear-weapons capabilities that might be acquired by developing countries, however advanced they may be, must be limited to the analysis of their impact on the local or regional balance and the global implications of this balance. It would even be inappropriate to consider the fourth alternative— a tactically meaningful nuclear arsenal—were it not for the possibility that U.S. nuclear warheads stationed in South Korea might someday be seized by the Koreans. We cannot afford to ignore this possibility, for it could, under certain circumstances, be the most cost-effective way for the Koreans to proceed.

The probability of South Korea's pursuing any of the above first four alternatives depends to a large extent on political-military conditions as well as on the availability of necessary technology and materials. One must also consider the possible preventive actions, as well as the likely reactions, that can be expected from Korea's neighbors. It should be clear that one cannot refer to a "nuclear South Korea" as if there were only a single pattern of action and reaction.

If one assumes that the South Koreans will follow the expected steps in developing the various levels of nuclear capability mentioned above, the effort would take a relatively predictable amount of time. There would be a variety of direct and indirect indications to provide warning. This presupposes, like most analyses of this subject, that the Koreans would employ standard encyclopedia-type techniques and designs in building their bombs. But should new techniques and designs be developed that allow the South Koreans to overcome certain constraints imposed by the need for unavailable materials and large amounts of time, the results of the analysis would be significantly altered. Judging from the history of weapons development in the United States and the Soviet Union, it is conceivable that even a newcomer like South Korea might achieve a technological breakthrough to make it possible to produce small, efficient warheads within a short period of time, with less than optimal materials. Once the initial breakthrough has been made the process is replicable without requiring the same amount of experience.

With these possibilities in mind, let us analyze several scenarios from the standpoint of both technical capabilities and the particular circumstances that might lead the South Koreans to follow a particular scenario. The simplest route to a nuclear-weapons capability would be the seizure of the U.S. tactical nuclear weapons stationed in Korea. The weapons are known to be there, and they are known to be efficient and deliverable by aircraft or missiles. Despite the existence of strict command-and-control measures that can be used to disarm the weapons, so long as the warheads are physically present it is possible to devise methods to make them work. Rowen notes that there is now a provision for the instant destruction of the warheads and that the task of reassembling them would be like putting an egg together again. Still, this may be technically easier than manufacturing comparable Korean weapons from scratch.

There are a variety of circumstances under which the South Korean government might feel justified in seizing U.S. nuclear weapons. The first would be after an invasion from the North had already occurred. In the initial moments of confusion, if it appeared that sufficient U.S. support could not be expected, Seoul might feel that the seizure would be justified. This scenario is not subject to simple analysis because one has to make a number of assumptions about the conditions leading to the North Korean invasion and the effectiveness of the South Korean government in responding to the situation.

A second situation in which Seoul might consider the seizure of U.S. nuclear weapons would be its belief that an invasion was imminent. Then, the South Koreans might conclude that the immediate possession of nuclear warheads, even at the cost of estranging the United States and alarming Moscow and Peking, was the only reliable countermeasure.

If South Korea attempted to manufacture crude nuclear explosive devices, its first task would be to acquire the necessary material—either plutonium or highly enriched uranium. The acquisition of fissionable material from nuclear power reactors is the most remote and inefficient method, as we shall discuss later. The most suitable material would be either U-235 or plutonium with a concentration of at least 93 percent PU-239. It is generally understood that plutonium with a lower percentage of PU-239 requires greater sophistication in implosion techniques.[12] It is considered easier to achieve an explosion using U-235. If there is a choice, the bomb builder would obviously prefer to use the simpler materials.

The easiest way to obtain the needed material is to buy it or to steal it. The expanding global network of export control and physical protection of such materials makes such a scenario less likely but not impossible. Once such material is in hand, the South Koreans would be in possession of the technical capabilities to manufacture an explosive device, possibly within a year. If they cannot buy or steal it, the South Koreans are within range of acquiring the capability of producing weapons-grade material, though they now lack an immediate means of carrying this out. They would need either a medium-sized research reactor fueled with metallic natural uranium, plus a small-scale reprocessing facility for plutonium, or ultracentrifuge machines for the enrichment of uranium. None of these facilities is currently in the possession of the South Koreans.

ROWEN: The least costly and most direct source of fissionable material would be a plutonium production reactor, which could, within several years, produce a significant stockpile of plutonium. But the reasons for not embarking on this path are strong. Such a reactor would be hard to conceal. The Israelis attempted for a time to call their Dimona reactor a textile plant, but that cover rapidly became transparent. The Koreans might try to build a production reactor in the guise of a large research reactor. For example, a 100-megawatt thermal reactor could produce about 7 kilograms of plutonium a year, about enough to produce a bomb. The government's ability to separate the plutonium and to use it for weapons purposes would depend on either the absence of any international agreements preventing such use or on Seoul's willingness to violate such agreements. The latter was the case with India, which violated at least the spirit of its understanding with Canada and the United States when it extracted plutonium from its CIRUS reactor to build an explosive device.

IMAI: While there is no secret about either the technology of building research reactors or the basic science of reprocessing and centrifuge enrichment, there is secrecy with respect to engineering know-how. The degree of secrecy increases progressively as one moves from a research reactor to reprocessing to centrifuge enrichment. Of the two approaches—research reactor plus reprocessing, and centrifuge enrichment—the latter would be more efficient, though its cost would be high. The design and manufacture of high-speed rotating machines is not beyond the scope of a country possessing an automobile industry.[13] The time required to develop and deploy via either the plutonium or the enriched uranium scenario may be something on the order of three to five years.

Obtaining the necessary natural uranium might be a problem. An efficient research reactor might take tens of tons of uranium to achieve the critical mass. The centrifuge approach might require some 5 tons of uranium to produce 25 kilograms of 93 percent material. South Korea has not been believed to possess an appreciable amount of natural uranium, but major new discoveries were reported in early 1979, and there is uranium, although of very low grade, in many places around the world.[14] The ocean is known to contain 3 parts per billion (ppb) of uranium, and it is possible to obtain several tons of uranium from this source if one can bear the high cost. Another possibility would be diversion from CANDU reactor fuel, which is natural uranium. The WOELSUNG-1 plant now under construction has a 678-megawatt CANDU pressurized heavy water reactor, scheduled to begin operation in April 1982. The latter method would require finding some way to evade International Atomic Energy Agency (IAEA) safeguards.

Of the two methods, ultracentrifuge requires a smaller amount of natural uranium and may be less conspicuous. An inefficient centrifuge enrichment plant requires approximately 10,000 machines to produce 25 kilograms of 93 percent material a year. To produce 8 kilograms of high-grade plutonium, a reprocessing plant would have to handle some 8 tons of irradiated fuel a year.

Neither approach is a simple backyard operation, and each may be visible to reconnaissance satellites. The transportation of irradiated fuel in heavy lead containers may be even more easily observed by satellites.

The South Koreans could opt for an "Israeli strategy," leaving in doubt the question of whether or not the country actually possesses nuclear weapons and using this uncertainty as a deterrent. This approach would be especially feasible if weapons-grade material were obtained through purchase or theft. Production of fissionable materials in South Korea would require a longer period of time and a degree of visibility that would provide an opportunity for other states to react. One cannot rule out the possibility of a preemptive attack on South Korea. But even though the international atmosphere is very different from what it was when the Israelis accomplished their objective, it is conceivable that the South Koreans could find a way of producing fissionable materials without incurring too strong a reaction from neighboring countries. The high level of technology achieved by the Koreans would be an asset. Moreover, even if there were physical evidence of covert production activities in South Korea, it is not at all clear what effective sanctions might be exercised by the international community. Besides, as Rowen has noted, a country can go a long way toward production of nuclear weapons without having an unambiguous weapons program or violating IAEA safeguards. This last problem relates to questions about the effectiveness of international safeguards in general.

With respect to the Israeli scenario, the credibility issue is concerned not with the existence of a capability to manufacture a crude explosive device, but with the degree of sophistication one can achieve in a bomb without actually testing it. Since the detailed art of bomb making is a closely guarded secret, it is difficult to analyze this point further.

If the Koreans were to pursue an overt nuclear-weapons program, they would probably find it difficult to test their explosive devices, given the nature of South Korea's terrain. The test would have to be conducted either on the high seas or underground on small islands in the Sea of Japan. From the standpoint of South Korea, this would involve many serious risks, which will be discussed later. Since the test would have to be conducted at a fairly early stage of bomb development in order to be technically meaningful, the country would then possess only one or two extra devices; these would be too bulky and unreliable for retaliatory bombing of the North.

ROWEN: Another problem the Koreans would encounter in an effort to develop usable nuclear weapons relates to delivery systems. The most primitive designs of nuclear weapons are usually heavy in weight. This is not, however, an insurmountable problem for such uses as preemplaced Atomic Demolition Mines (ADMs). Heavy weapons can be delivered by certain aircraft capable of carrying heavy loads. In time, designs capable of delivery by aircraft such as the F-4 or medium-sized rockets would be feasible. Design improvements occur most rapidly with testing; progress would presumably be slow under the constraints of a covert program.

IMAI: Gradual progress toward a nuclear-weapons capability through the buildup of nuclear industrial capabilities for peaceful purposes is a scenario completely different from the ones we have considered so far. Unlike the more direct weapons-oriented activities we have been discussing, this is merely a matter of acquiring long-term potential capabilities. But unless South Korea sets out to use nuclear electric power as a means of obtaining the material or facilities needed to make weapons, industrial activities directly connected to electric-power generation will not in themselves provide any shortcut to a bomb.

In 1976, total electric power generated in South Korea was about 23 billion kilowatt hours, of which only about 5 percent came from hydroelectric power. The rest was provided by burning either coal or oil. Installed generating capacity was about 5.5 million kilowatts, which is about 5 percent of that of Japan. South Korea's booming economy is presently supporting something like a 15 percent annual growth rate in electric-power generation. This is partly due to the fact that electric power has in the past accounted for a relatively minor part of Korea's energy. Of the 16 million tons of coal produced in 1976, only about 1 million were used for electric-power generation. While the North has an abundant supply of hydroelectric power (about 60 percent of total electricity) and almost two-and-one-half times as much coal as the South, the South depends heavily on imported oil. There is no oil production in the South, and almost all of the 18.5 million kiloliters (320,000 barrels per day) of oil used in 1976 was imported from

Saudi Arabia and Kuwait through the distribution facilities of three of the major U.S. oil companies. Within South Korea's electric power industry, oil consumption is about four times that of coal.

The above figures give a picture of nuclear power needs in South Korea. Given the world's oil supply situation and the fast-growing demand for power, it seems unfair to deny South Korea the opportunity to develop nuclear power. On the other hand, the capacity of South Korea's national grid is so small that it cannot quickly accommodate many large nuclear plants. Table 4.1 shows the current program of the Korea Electric Company in the nuclear sector. Even this schedule seems too optimistic in light of the prevailing atmosphere in the nuclear industry around the world. On the other hand, the anticipated scale of nuclear-power generation in South Korea is far too small to justify an independent nuclear industry or a complete fuel cycle. A commercial reprocessing plant requires about 50 1-million-kilowatt nuclear power plants to justify the investment. Based on the current state of technical and economic development, South Korea would find it extremely difficult to justify an independent reactor industry, enrichment or reprocessing facilities, or any fast breeder reactor research.

ROWEN: Furthermore, although reactor-grade plutonium is usable in making explosives, it is possible to do better. Because power reactors do not operate all the time, it may be possible to remove weapons-grade plutonium from the reactor during a shut-down period. Thus a significant amount of weapons-grade

TABLE 4.1
South Korean Nuclear Power Plant Projections

Reactor	Power (mw.)	Type	Year on Line
KORI-1	595	PWR[a]	1978
KORI-2	650	PWR	1983
WOELSUNG-1	678	CANDU	1982
WOELSUNG-2	600	CANDU	1983
Unspecified	900	--	1984
Unspecified	900	--	1985

a. Pressurized water reactor

plutonium could be produced by the early 1980s without greatly reducing the efficiency of the reactors in electricity production or clearly signaling an intent to assemble a stock of PU-239 for weapons purposes. To be sure, the amount of plutonium likely to be produced over the next decade is impressive. Assuming that present schedules for nuclear power development hold and no serious operating problems develop with the reactors—clearly optimistic assumptions—the R.O.K.'s stockpile of separable plutonium should accumulate roughly as follows:

Year	Plutonium (Kg.)
1978	60
1979	140
1980	250
1985	1,600
1990	3,600

These amounts of plutonium may be impressively large, but what do they really mean? Left in spent fuel, the plutonium is not usable in weapons; in any case, spent fuel would be safeguarded. There are, however, several other possibilities. One is that South Korea might obtain a national reprocessing plant. Plans to acquire such a plant, abandoned earlier, might be revived, despite the fact that recycling plutonium from spent fuel would be uneconomical for Korea, as it seems to be even for large-scale nuclear systems. Because reprocessing is uneconomical for most states, it is not clear whether, as Imai suggests, an uneconomical fuel cycle is really an indication of a weapons program—this is a large gray area. In any case, a reprocessing plant would enable Korea to have large stocks of separated plutonium immediately usable for bombs. Even if this material were safeguarded and not legally usable in explosives, it would physically be in a form that could be put into weapons within a matter of days or less. In a crisis, considerations of "supreme national interest" might override international safeguard constraints.

Another possibility is that Korea might arrange to have plutonium separated for it by others, perhaps France, Britain, or Japan (as Japan is contemplating with France and Britain). In this case, South Korea would receive back either separated plutonium or plutonium in the form of mixed oxides (MOX), from which the plutonium could be quickly separated chemically. The result would be essentially the same as if Korea had its own reprocessing plant.

If an effort were made to keep preparations secret, a covert reprocessing facility could remain on standby for an emergency or it might be used to reprocess small amounts of diverted material. (Monitoring to detect this last possibility has been the principal preoccupation of the IAEA inspection system.) If a standby reprocessing facility were maintained, it might be able to acquire enough material for an explosive in some weeks, depending on the size of the plant, the experience of the operators, and the extent of prior preparation. Unforeseen problems could extend this time considerably.

IMAI: In any case, given the difficulty of designing effective nuclear weapons based on reactor-grade plutonium, manufacture of bombs using material derived from a nuclear power industry need not be regarded as an imminent threat. Rather, it is a subject that needs to be evaluated and resolved together with similar problems existing elsewhere in the world.

What Kinds of Leverage Might Be Exerted on Seoul in Response to Signs That the Koreans Were Moving Toward Nuclear Weapons? How Is the Acquisition of Nuclear Weapons by South Korea Likely to Affect Japanese Attitudes Toward Their Own Defense, U.S. Views of the U.S. Commitment to Seoul, and Prospects of War on the Peninsula?

IMAI: It should be apparent, from the variety of circumstances considered in the foregoing discussion of incentives and capabilities, that one cannot speak meaningfully of a single pattern of reactions to a South Korean move toward nuclear weapons. Much will depend on the prevailing political and military circumstances, as well as on the particular approach selected. One can say that the state of relations between the two Koreas and between Seoul and Washington will probably be of decisive importance in determining reactions. The reaction of other Asian countries is less important, although Korea's acquisition of nuclear arms, if unchallenged, will certainly encourage other aspiring nuclear powers throughout the world.

Two important general points should be made here. One concerns the role of nuclear safeguards. It should be apparent that safeguards cannot be expected to involve a detailed watch over nuclear power stations and related activities. But it is most important to have at all times a good understanding of the proper balance within South Korea's nuclear industry, so that any indication of commercially or industrially irregular activities will quickly come to the notice of the safeguarding authority. In addition, there is need for strenuous efforts to detect covert activities aimed at producing weapons-grade material. In this connection, satellites will play an important role, as was partially demonstrated in the case of South Africa. Finally, procedures for effective counteractions should be carefully thought out in advance. In this regard, it is more useful to plan political and other actions on a case-by-case basis than it is to rely on applying universal sanctions whenever weapons-oriented activities are detected. The last point is essential if international safeguards are to be applied effectively in the future.

The other general point is that the best way to keep South Korea from going nuclear is to create a political/military situation in which Seoul feels little need to seek such weapons. Arrangements to maintain stability on the peninsula are most important, since depriving a nation of its incentive to acquire nuclear weapons is a much more meaningful nonproliferation measure than a simple technological fix. One specific possibility is the establishment of a nuclear free zone, which will be discussed in the next chapter.

The response to Seoul's postulated seizure of U.S. nuclear weapons stationed in Korea would depend both on whether the South Koreans were justified in judging that an attack from the North was imminent and on the character of the government in power at the time. If the government is very different from the one in Seoul today and if the imminence of an invasion from the North is unclear, then the outcome would depend on the ability of the United States to recover the warheads and take measures to restore stability. Japanese reactions to such a sudden occurrence are difficult to predict, but it is unlikely that Japan would have enough time to take any meaningful action. In any case, the Soviet and Chinese reactions are of greater importance: will they feel impelled to take preemptive action against South Korea?

The best way of dealing with the weapons-seizure scenario is either to make U.S. command and control more credible to third parties like Japan or to remove the U.S. tactical nuclear weapons from the peninsula. The latter, of course, relates directly to the broader issue of the withdrawal of U.S. forces. The United States could withdraw its forces completely if it gave assurances of intervention, with nuclear weapons if necessary, in case of invasion from the North. The United States could leave a token tripwire force, with or without nuclear weapons, in the area north of Seoul. It may well be undesirable to leave a small force with nuclear weapons, however, since it would be more vulnerable to physical takeover. The core of the problem, then, is the credibility of U.S. assurances.

If the Israeli scenario were followed, the possibility that the South Koreans might be in possession of nuclear weapons would lead to vocal demands for Japan to go nuclear. It is, however, highly questionable whether either the Japanese public or the government in Tokyo would regard the possibility of a nuclear Korea as a sufficient reason for taking the necessary first steps toward a Japanese nuclear-weapons capability. In order to initiate a nuclear-weapons program, it would be necessary to gain funding through budget decisions in the National Diet and then to recruit scientists and engineers from the industrial and research communities. Barring drastic changes in the nature of the Japanese political system, this would be a practical impossibility. In addition, any overt move by Japan will risk straining relations with the United States and with other Asian countries. For a country as dependent on foreign markets and resources as Japan, this would be an unbearable price. More likely steps that Japan could take in response to the Israeli scenario in Korea would involve strengthening conventional defense capabilities, especially air defense against strike aircraft that might be armed with nuclear weapons. Japan could also make efforts to enhance the stability of the Korean peninsula, working through third countries such as the United States, the Soviet Union, and China.

A South Korean nuclear test could lead to some rather drastic reactions. North Korea, knowing that Seoul is likely to possess only one or two extra nuclear devices that would probably be unsuitable for use against the North, could decide to use the nuclear test to justify an invasion of the South and the occupation of Seoul. Under such circumstances, it is questionable whether the United States could effectively intervene, with or without nuclear weapons. Any restraining influence the Soviets or Chinese might have previously exercised on the North could well disappear if the North's action were viewed as defensive. The USSR might well decide to launch a preemptive nuclear strike on South Korea's nuclear-weapons complex, if the Soviets consider this necessary to prevent conditions on the peninsula from getting out of hand. But the Soviets would need to obtain prior assurances that this would not trigger a general nuclear exchange with the United States.

A South Korean nuclear test would be viewed by the Japanese as very dangerous. A visible event of this sort could trigger the strongest psychological reaction. If, despite all the risks, South Korea proceeded with a nuclear test and was able to ride out the initial confusion, the Japanese reaction would follow a pattern similar to that described in the Israeli scenario. But because the restraints, both domestic and international, would be fewer, the Japanese reaction would be more violent. The outcome is difficult to predict because it would be strongly influenced by the broader political/military atmosphere in East Asia. A Japanese decision to go nuclear, which by definition cannot stop at the tactical level, would not be solely a function of events on the Korean peninsula.

SAEKI: It is worth emphasizing that one should not draw hasty conclusions about what Japan might do in the event that South Korea acquires nuclear weapons. I do not believe that Japan is so sensitive concerning a possible nuclear South Korea. In the first place, if South Korea obtained its own nuclear weapons, it would be isolated. Nuclear weapons cannot be used to defend Seoul, and nuclear land mines will not play such an important role. Because an isolated South Korea would find it hard to protect itself even with an independent nuclear capability, I cannot imagine circumstances under which Seoul would have a strong incentive to seek nuclear weapons—except as a desperate act in a situation of dire emergency.

If South Korea acquired an independent nuclear capability, the Japanese government would have to consider the following: (1) the motives behind South Korea's acquisition of nuclear capability, (2) the positive as well as the negative political and military effects of South Korea's action, and (3) the potential threat to Japan resulting from South Korea's acquisition of a nuclear capability and the effectiveness of the U.S. nuclear umbrella as a deterrent to the exercise of that capability. Before deciding on its own response, Japan would have to consider these factors carefully and try to judge accurately the reactions of other nations—especially those of the USSR, China, North Korea, and the United States.

It is unlikely that Japanese leaders would believe that South Korea's acquisition of nuclear weapons was aimed at Japan. They would realize that a nuclear South Korea might have to bear risks and costs that would outweigh any benefit those weapons might bring. They would expect South Korea to face a less hospitable international environment as a result of its move to acquire nuclear weapons. Although there would be some pressures within Japan to consider developing a nuclear-weapons capability, a few low-yield nuclear weapons in the hands of the South Koreans would not pose a threat to Japan. Most reasonable Japanese would reach this conclusion. Japanese leaders would also have confidence in the effectiveness of the U.S. nuclear umbrella as a deterrent to the use of South Korean nuclear weapons against Japan. They would not consider themselves in a position where they would have to react immediately to the Korean move. Japanese leaders would feel that Japan could afford to take the time to observe the developing situation carefully and to consider its reaction in a deliberate manner. Japan would not hastily select the road to nuclear armament.

WHITING: One problem, however, is that both Japan and Taiwan would probably assume, regardless of official statements to the contrary, that South Korea had acquired nuclear weapons with the tacit agreement of Washington. It could not be credibly argued in either country that the United States was unable to deter or halt a process requiring so much time and resources. In Taiwan, the result would probably be to initiate a parallel program or to accelerate a previously existing one. In Japan, the consequences would be less dramatic and immediate. South Korea's acquisition of nuclear power would reopen a debate on Japan's nuclear option that would probably end in a reaffirmation of the status quo. But it would also call into question the credibility of U.S. policy, both on the question of nonproliferation in general and on the implications of acquiescence in Seoul's action in particular. This would reduce Japan's confidence in the predictability of U.S. support for the defense of South Korea and, therefore, of Japan.

MOMOI: Indeed, what might prove most disturbing to the

Japanese government would not be Korea's decision to go nuclear but the circumstances that had led Seoul to such a decision. It is likely that Seoul would take so drastic a step only if it perceived a basic change in the U.S. assessment of its strategic interests in the region. This would, of course, raise some question about the credibility of the U.S. commitment to Japan. Hence, Korea's decision would be viewed by Japan as a sign that the United States had abandoned its commitment to Seoul and to the region in general, unless Washington stated that it had a selective nuclear commitment to Japan. The latter would be impractical, since it could further alienate Seoul and lead to a more militant South Korean posture vis-à-vis both the United States and Japan. Among the general public, there would also be a good deal of resentment at what would be regarded as a kind of one-upmanship on the part of Korea vis-à-vis a nonnuclear Japan.

These reactions, however, do not necessarily mean that Japan would decide to seek nuclear weapons of its own. In the first place, given the differences in terrain and strategic environment, Japan sees no strategic utility in a primitive nuclear device similar to that which India detonated in 1974. Second, the acquisition of nuclear weapons by South Korea might not in itself alter the military situation significantly, unless Seoul-Tokyo relations also deteriorated and the South Koreans acquired effective strategic delivery systems. From a technological standpoint, Japan can afford to wait until it observes that the Koreans possess such delivery systems. On the other hand, public sentiment regarding nuclear weapons could undergo a major change if, for example, Japan suffered a diplomatic disgrace over some emotional issue, such as that of Takeshima Island. The public might blame such a failure on Japan's lack of nuclear status and might eventually force the government to alter its longstanding nonnuclear policy— especially by requesting that the United States introduce defensive nuclear weapons into Japan. The likelihood of such a public reaction would, of course, depend on the attitudes of future generations and on the strategic environment at the time. If the United States was unwilling to comply with this request, Japan might then seek to convey the impression that it was seriously considering the development of an independent nuclear capability. But Tokyo's decision in this regard would depend on many other factors that cannot be known at this time.

OKIMOTO: The foregoing discussion indicates how difficult it is to draw any clear conclusion about how Japan would react to a nuclear South Korea. It is clear that it would be a mistake to assume that Japan would automatically follow Korea's example. Japan's reaction to a South Korean decision to acquire nuclear weapons would depend on the particular circumstances surrounding the event. While we should not rule out the possibility that Japan might respond by going nuclear, it is easy to envisage other reactions. I would like to consider here the range of possible Japanese responses and then to indicate the ones that seem most likely.

At one extreme, the Japanese might not feel much affected by Korea's acquisition of nuclear weapons; if so, their response would accordingly be minimal. If Seoul's postulated move to develop nuclear weapons was to unfold over a long period of time, the Japanese might have already made adjustments. And if Seoul's action was a clear response to threatening behavior by Pyongyang and was sanctioned, explicitly or tacitly, by the United States, the Japanese might feel little need to respond. The Japanese might feel that Seoul's nuclear weapons would pose no threat to Japan's security, that there was nothing that Japan could do to affect the situation, and that the domestic and international costs of Japan's going nuclear would outweigh any potential benefits. Conceivably, then, Seoul's acquisition of nuclear weapons could, in itself, produce little or no change in Japan's foreign and defense policies.

Japan's reaction to the Chinese nuclear detonation in 1964 is an example of minimal response. Tokyo's defense policies were scarcely affected at all. The main effect of the Chinese move was to increase public discussion of defense questions and to partially lift the old taboo on nuclear matters. Although that was a significant step in the development of Japanese attitudes toward national security, it was hardly the dramatic reaction anticipated by some experts, such as Pierre Gallois, who had predicted that Japan would feel compelled to seek its own nuclear weapons.

There are several reasons for Japan's calm reaction to the Chinese detonation.

1. China's crude nuclear capability did not appear to add significantly to the threat already posed by Soviet weapons.
2. Japan had little reason to question the ability of U.S.

     nuclear forces, which then enjoyed overwhelming superior-
     ity, to deter Chinese nuclear blackmail or a Chinese attack
     on Japan. This was felt to be the case, at least until the
     Chinese gained the capability to strike the U.S. continent.

3. Most Japanese saw the Chinese nuclear capability as defen-
     sive, intended not to threaten Japan but to deter a U.S. or
     Soviet challenge.

4. Some Japanese, especially left-wing intellectuals, were im-
     pressed by Peking's no-first-use pledge and by its insistence
     that China's aim was to break the superpowers' nuclear
     monopoly and to force them into serious disarmament
     negotiations.

5. The backwardness of the Chinese economy raised doubts
     about China's potential to become a nuclear superpower,
     even within a decade or two.

6. There was not much reason to be concerned that China's
     action would trigger further nuclear proliferation, because
     no other nation in the region was then close to possessing
     the required nuclear infrastructure.

Subsequently, of course, the Japanese have come to see China's
nuclear potential as directed mainly against the Soviet Union. This
has further eased Tokyo's concern. Indeed, some Japanese have
even been able to see positive consequences in China's acquisition
of nuclear weapons, because, in their view, China's emergence as
part of a tripolar balance of power allows Japan greater diplomatic
latitude.

What is the relevance of the 1964 experience to South Korea's
possible acquisition of nuclear weapons in the future? There are
some similarities, but there are also striking differences between
the Chinese and Korean situations. As with China, a South Korean
nuclear capability would probably be viewed as primarily defensive, posing little threat to Japan or to the credibility of the U.S.
deterrent. But a Korean nuclear capability could be worrisome because of its destabilizing effect on the military balance on the
peninsula, producing a heightening of tensions and stimulating
countermeasures by Pyongyang and its allies. If undertaken in the
face of opposition from the United States, a Korean nuclear-
weapons program could tear apart the Washington-Seoul relationship. Seoul would certainly refuse to follow China's lead in

renouncing the option of first use, since the weapons are intended to deter a conventional threat. And South Korea's move toward nuclear weapons could be viewed by Taiwan as legitimizing a similar move on its part. Add to that the volatility of Japanese-Korean relations, and there emerges a situation far more troublesome than the one confronted by the Japanese in 1964. Even if they saw no direct military threat, the Japanese might fear that Korea would use its nuclear status to gain political leverage with Japan. In any case, the specter of a defiant, isolated, and possibly desperate Korea would probably be deeply unsettling to the Japanese. Thus, a Korean nuclear capability is likely to produce a stronger Japanese reaction than did the Chinese detonation.

It is conceivable that these concerns could lead to an upsurge of militant nationalism in Japan and a dramatic acceleration of the country's rearmament, including a decision to develop nuclear weapons. A rallying of parties and public opinion around a new consensus supporting militant nationalism could usher in a period of authoritarian rule, in which political opposition and personal liberties are curtailed. Or political life could become so highly polarized between left and right that the government would be thrown into paralysis. Clearly, such an extreme reaction to a Korean nuclear capability would have very high costs, both domestically and internationally. It is hard to imagine that Japan would take such drastic measures unless a whole series of events occurred in quick succession, creating a sense of general crisis. These events could include, among other things, a rupture of U.S.–South Korean relations, a dramatic sharpening of tensions between Tokyo and Seoul, a general loss of confidence in the U.S. commitment, further nuclear proliferation in the region, and serious economic and political dislocations within Japan. Even then, strong arguments could still be raised against Japan's building a nuclear capability.

If South Korea acquired nuclear weapons under circumstances similar to those prevailing today, the Japanese response would most likely be moderate. The current trend in Japan toward a more assertive foreign policy and an increased defense role would probably be accelerated. Japan would probably modestly increase its defense expenditures and might even consider assuming some military responsibilities beyond the defense of the home islands. Tokyo could be expected to intensify its defense cooperation with the United States, with greater coordination in planning and more

joint exercises. At the same time, efforts would be made to improve Tokyo's relations with Peking, Moscow, and perhaps Pyongyang. Détente with North Korea, however, would have to be
weighed against Japan's desire to protect its large stake in South
Korea, with which relations would surely be strained. The question of a Japanese nuclear-weapons capability would certainly
be reexamined— probably in an emotional debate—but there is not
likely to be any change in policy.

WEINSTEIN: In sum, it is unlikely that South Korea's acquisition of nuclear weapons would produce the nuclearization of
Japan or any other dramatically destabilizing reactions on the part
of the Japanese. There might even be some positive effects. But
Seoul's rise to nuclear status would stimulate so many uncertainties that even the most extreme scenarios cannot be ruled out.
Thus, most Japanese leaders would consider it very important that
everything possible be done to discourage Seoul from seeking an
independent nuclear-weapons capability.

SAEKI: The most effective means of discouraging the South
Koreans from seeking nuclear weapons is for the United States and
Japan to communicate unequivocally that if Seoul decides to go
nuclear, the United States will abrogate its defense commitment to
South Korea, while Japan will discontinue its economic cooperation and assistance to that country. If South Korea becomes
serious about nuclear weapons, there are many levers the United
States, Japan, and other countries can use, at least in peacetime,
to dissuade the Koreans from following that course. Japan has
very strong influence in South Korea; the most prominent com-
ponent of this influence may be the Koreans' large accumulated
debt. Japan could easily stop the money flow, which could lead
South Korea to bankruptcy. Besides these sanctions, efforts could
also be made to persuade the South Koreans that precision-guided
munitions can be as effective as tactical nuclear weapons.

If the United States annulled its defense commitment to South
Korea because of Korea's acquisition of a nuclear capability in the
face of U.S. opposition, this would not affect Japanese trust and
confidence in the U.S. defense commitment to Japan. The Japanese would continue to believe in the reliability of the deterrent
effect of the U.S. nuclear umbrella. If the situation on the Korean
peninsula should become unstable, the Japanese would become
more concerned about their security interests than they are now.

At the same time, they would strengthen their posture of military nonintervention in the affairs of the Korean peninsula. In any case, it is highly unlikely that South Korea's acquisition of nuclear weapons would weaken the U.S. defense commitment to Japan. If that commitment is so weak that it could be shaken by South Korea's nuclearization, then it has little value vis-à-vis the threats from the Soviet Union and China.

WEINSTEIN: How, in fact, is the United States likely to react to signs that South Korea is moving toward a nuclear-weapons capability? What leverage might be brought to bear? From the interviews I conducted in Washington in late 1977, there is no doubt that an independent South Korean nuclear capability would, in the words of a State Department official, make it "extremely difficult" to sustain any U.S. commitment to Korea. Indeed, the strength of statements from a variety of officials indicating the readiness of the United States to use "the most drastic kinds of measures" to keep South Korea from going nuclear is impressive. A knowledgeable official said there is "no question that a Korean decision to go nuclear would risk abrogation of the security treaty and the withdrawal of any remaining U.S. presence." Previous arguments for the U.S. commitment as an essential factor in the maintenance of the strategic balance would be vitiated by the fact that the South Koreans would bear the responsibility for having "changed the equation." According to U.S. officials, Japan would view the South Koreans as the ones who had "disrupted the security of Northeast Asia." Certain officials asserted that the United States would do "whatever is necessary" to keep Seoul from exercising the nuclear option; this could "easily" extend to a declaration abrogating the U.S. commitment. A policymaker who represents a military viewpoint expressed his confidence that we would certainly "cut the Koreans off without another rifle" if they moved toward nuclear weapons.

There was some disagreement among those interviewed in the legislative branch regarding the likelihood that the commitment would be abrogated. But there was a consensus that it would, at least, cause a "very serious crisis" in U.S.–Korean relations. Some of those knowledgeable about the views of Senate Democrats felt that Korean nuclear weapons "could well" lead to termination of the commitment and a cutoff of all U.S. aid. Republican sources in the House predicted that this would be the majority response. In fact, these sources said, even most of the congressmen who strongly support the R.O.K. would be deeply disturbed by a Korean move toward nuclear weapons. They would view that as a serious tactical error on the part of Seoul. While congressional supporters of the R.O.K. might not support abrogation of the commitment, they would probably "go along with or not oppose" a move to reduce or even cut off aid. Some Republicans and "moderate" Democrats might try to salvage the aid relationship, in the hope that the United States could develop enough leverage to back the Koreans away from the nuclear option or at least to discourage them from using it.

The strength of the U.S. reaction to a decision by Seoul to go nuclear would, of course, depend on the specific circumstances surrounding the move. As Rowen has noted, Seoul's hypothetical acquisition of nuclear weapons would tend to lead to two arguments against continued U.S. support of Seoul: (1) the situation would become too dangerous for U.S. involvement, and (2) South Korea, armed with nuclear weapons, would no longer need U.S. backing. The consensus among those interviewed was that the administration might then decide to scrap the entire commitment, with the probable support of the majority of Congress.

There was little disagreement that a Korean effort to acquire reprocessing facilities would be viewed as the "functional equivalent" of a decision to seek nuclear weapons—at least as long as there is no credible commercial justification for such facilities. A State Department official asserted that the Koreans "understand completely that in our minds, reprocessing equals nuclear weapons." It seems evident that many members of Congress share this view.

What instruments might the United States bring into play in order to discourage Seoul from pursuing the nuclear option? If the United States is to do anything at all, it must first learn of the South Koreans' intentions. It seems likely, but not certain, that the United States would be aware of any Korean effort to produce nuclear weapons. A well-placed official ruled out any possibility that the acquisition of nuclear weapons would be presented to the United States as a fait accompli. U.S. intelligence is such that Washington would certainly know in advance if the Koreans were moving toward nuclear weapons. During that period of development "it would simply be too dangerous for [the South Koreans] to risk a North Korean attack with neither the U.S. commitment nor nuclear weapons to defend themselves." But CIA Director Stansfield Turner has noted that although a Korean effort to obtain weapons-grade uranium from the bulky gaseous diffusion process would be relatively easy to discover, this would not be the case if more advanced technologies, such as the centrifuge process, were used.[15]

The means available to the United States to influence South Korea would range along a "virtually unlimited spectrum of relationships, nuclear and non-nuclear," from minor economic moves to the suspension of nuclear fuel and the abrogation of the security treaty. An Arms Control and Disarmament Agency official cited the U.S. reaction to the South African plan to develop nuclear weapons as evidence of the administration's willingness and ability to act in order to prevent a state from going nuclear. If Mr. Carter had been president when India detonated its nuclear device, he added, the U.S. reaction would have been far different from what it was in 1974.

There was a general belief that, as a minimal first step to dissuade the Koreans from going nuclear, the United States would suspend the supply of enriched uranium. This, officials asserted, would be easy to do, because the U.S. agreement with South Korea on nuclear cooperation gives Washington this kind of control. There are other economic levers, including credits from the Export-Import Bank and other U.S. government credits in a variety of fields. A State Department official noted that we would have used these levers under the Ford administration, and it is even clearer that the Carter administration would do so. Of course, the effectiveness of these levers depends on the importance that the Koreans attach to such credits. In the case of the leverage offered by a suspension of nuclear fuel supplies, it is assumed that South Korea will remain dependent on the United States for the bulk of its nuclear fuel. In this connection, it is worth noting that Seoul is making efforts to develop new suppliers of uranium and to attain domestic capabilities to fabricate nuclear fuel. But this is likely to be a long-term process.[16]

ROWEN: One cannot assume that the United States will actually apply the leverage at its disposal to restrain South Korea in the event that Seoul gives evidence of moving toward a nuclear-weapons capability. There will be many counterarguments against the use of sanctions, and the use of any particular sanction will be viewed by some as prejudicing some other set of interests. On the other hand, it is worth noting that sanctions relating to nuclear fuel and a range of economic transactions can be quite powerful during a noncrisis period. It is, incidentally, important here to distinguish between a crisis situation and an incremental, noncrisis situation. It would be a good deal more difficult to use such instruments of leverage effectively if the Koreans saw themselves as being in an emergency situation. In any case, the potential leverage of Japan and the United States (even in the absence of a U.S. military presence) is such that a degree of acquiescence on the part of both countries is assumed to be a precondition to any South Korean nuclear-weapons program.

In the long run, the best way of ensuring a nonnuclear South Korea is to preserve the present set of forces that work for stability on the peninsula. The U.S. troop presence is central to this stability, because it not only provides a guarantee against an attack from the North but also provides assurance against dangerous actions, nuclear or nonnuclear, by the South. Improvements in the South's ability to block a North Korean attack also will help. The United States should do all it can to facilitate better cooperation between Japan and South Korea. And, although the prospects are not promising, efforts to reduce differences between the two Koreas should not be ignored. All of these measures may help to persuade South Korea to refrain from developing a nuclear-weapons capability.

OKIMOTO: As Rowen observed, potential sources of leverage may prove difficult to exercise effectively, especially in a crisis. This is particularly applicable to the actions Japan might consider taking to dissuade South Korea from going nuclear. Discussions of potential Japanese leverage are likely to exaggerate what Japan can do unless adequate weight is given to countermeasures the Koreans may take against Japan. Economic sanctions could do great damage to South Korea's economy, which, in turn, could impose serious economic costs on Japan as well. Timing also presents a major problem, because there may be no obvious point at which leverage should be applied. That is, there may be no completely unambiguous indication of a Korean intention to develop nuclear weapons until the bombs have come into existence. Let us examine the potential levers at Japan's disposal.

Japan's most important sources of potential leverage are, of course, economic. Since 1965, when diplomatic relations were established between the two countries, Japan has provided South Korea with substantial economic aid. But with the termination of Japan's ten-year $800 million aid program in 1976, Tokyo's large-scale aid commitments to Seoul came to an end. The remaining government-to-government aid programs are scheduled to end as South Korea's rapid economic growth removes the country from the "developing nation" category. By the time South Korea decides to go nuclear, if it should do so, official development aid from Japan will almost certainly have been phased out. Thus, it is doubtful that such aid could be used as leverage to discourage Seoul from going nuclear.

Japan is the leading source of foreign investment in South Korea. Japanese investments accounted for 61 percent of the $873 million invested as of the start of 1979; the United States, in contrast, accounted for only 19 percent. Together, Japan and the United States were responsible for 80 percent of all cumulative investments.[17] But, as in the case of foreign aid, there is real doubt about the utility of foreign investment as a lever. The annual amount of new investment is not that high, and the investments are dispersed among so many companies that it would be hard for them to act in a concerted manner. Moreover, the large amount of cumulative Japanese investment in South Korea could be, in some measure, a Korean hostage; the Japanese companies are vulnerable to countermeasures that Seoul might take against them.

Despite South Korea's booming economic growth and rising exports, the country remains dependent on heavy capital inflows to meet its ambitious economic goals. South Korea's cumulative capital debt as of early 1978 was a substantial $8.6 billion, the bulk of which was owed to Japan and the United States. That dependence is likely to diminish, however. And one cannot assume that a private Japanese bank, operating on the basis of financial considerations, would readily agree to withhold loans for political purposes unless ordered to do so by the Japanese government. Also, even if Japanese and U.S. banks complied with such orders, the Koreans might find other sources. Similarly, although Japan provides 35 percent of South Korea's imports and takes 25 percent of its exports, it would be difficult to manipulate established trade relationships to serve political ends. If its past record is any indication, the Japanese government would be exceedingly reluctant to exercise trade sanctions. Japan is deeply committed to the free flow of trade, and incentives to retain and expand markets remain very strong.

There is another important factor inhibiting any Japanese move to apply sanctions to South Korea. The "Korea lobby" in Tokyo is large, well organized, and well funded. While there are both pro-Pyongyang and pro-Seoul groups and there has been no reticence on the part of the national press or the intellectual community to criticize Seoul, those aligned with South Korea tend to be more influential in government policymaking circles. A number of pro-Seoul lobbyist groups enjoy close ties with some of the most powerful LDP leaders. Some 237 Diet members now belong to the Japan–R.O.K. Parliamentarians League. Except for Prime Minister Ohira and former Prime Minister Takeo Miki, most of the LDP faction leaders belong to the league. The human nexus is vital here. By consciously cultivating close ties with key conservative leaders in Japan, Seoul has gained considerable influence in Japanese political circles. The result is that, even if they genuinely oppose certain of Seoul's policies, many pro-Seoul members of the Diet are so strongly committed to cordial relations with South Korea that they might find it difficult to support bold sanctions. But of course, as we have noted, relations with Korea are subject to wide emotional swings, and one cannot rule out Diet support for anti-Seoul measures. And it is uncertain, given "Koreagate"-stimulated pressures, whether the pro-Seoul lobby will remain as effective as it has been.

The inescapable conclusion is that it would be dangerous to fall back on the comforting assumption that Japan and the United States can easily employ economic leverage to discourage the South Koreans from developing a nuclear-weapons capability. To be sure, certain economic levers can be used to good effect, particularly if they are employed in a noncrisis atmosphere, as was the case when the United States acted to squelch the French sale of reprocessing facilities to Seoul in 1975. Finally, it is important to think of leverage, not merely in terms of sanctions but also as positive incentives to persuade the Koreans that they can satisfy their needs without going nuclear.

KAMIYA: The basic problem, however, is that if the South Koreans decide to go nuclear, it will, in all likelihood, be because they feel desperate. In such a situation, they are not likely to be influenced by economic levers. As noted by Rowen, economic leverage may be effective in noncrisis situations, but the real danger is that there will be a crisis that leads Seoul to conclude that the nuclear option is its only hope for survival. And even if some of our analyses show that nuclear weapons may not be so effective in defending Seoul, the South Koreans, as Whiting has pointed out, may believe that nuclear weapons would provide the necessary margin of security. Moreover, would the United States or Japan really be willing to exercise economic sanctions that would reduce South Korea to a shambles? If they did, then what would happen?

ROWEN: Assuming that all efforts to exert leverage on Seoul fail and that South Korea comes to possess a small number of nuclear explosives, what impact is this likely to have on the stability of the peninsula? There is little doubt that South Korean possession of nuclear weapons would put pressure on the D.P.R.K. to acquire them. One possible response by North Korea to signals of a South Korean nuclear-weapons program would be a preemptive attack. It is questionable whether the Soviet Union or China would allow the R.O.K. to use nuclear weapons against North Korea, especially in deep attacks, say against Pyongyang or near the Yalu River, without making a nuclear response. As already noted, if the Soviet Union made a nuclear response to an R.O.K. attack on the North, the results could easily be devastating to the South.

WHITING: There is, in fact, no prospect that North Korea could acquire a nuclear-weapons capability. China certainly will not equip North Korea with such weapons. In October 1975, Teng Hsiao-p'ing privately informed Cyrus Vance that China was in principle opposed to nuclear proliferation and would not practice it. (The author was present.) It is inconceivable that the Soviet Union would supply either weapons or the manufacturing capability to Pyongyang. Relations with the USSR have been poor since the early 1970s; the decline in military deliveries to the North gives evidence of this. Finally, the North lacks the material and human resources to emulate the South at least within the next decade.

A nuclear capability in the South, however, would compel the North to appeal for renewed deterrence from Peking and Moscow. Their responses might differ, depending on the degree of competition and confrontation in the Sino-Soviet relationship. The greater their rivalry, the more probable is a strong reaffirmation of the Sino-Korean military tie. A slightly weaker response would come from Moscow. China might amend its present no-first-use posture to include retaliation in the event that weapons are used against an ally, although an explicit statement of this policy is unlikely. Moscow would probably strike an even more ambiguous note. In this context, any such strengthening of alliances and commitments would tend to increase tension in the region and make the larger powers more vulnerable to manipulation by the smaller ones.

WEINSTEIN: There is a consensus among the members of this working group that a nuclear South Korea would be highly undesirable and that every effort should be made to exert leverage on Seoul to restrain it from seeking nuclear weapons. But even if it proves impossible to hold back the South Koreans, one can argue that this "worst case" scenario might not be so dire. As we have seen, the Japanese might well react calmly. Although there are real uncertainties, it seems likely that Tokyo would not take any drastic action, such as moving toward a nuclear capability of its own. Furthermore, Pyongyang would have a hard time acquiring nuclear weapons, though an aggressive South Korean posture, especially threatening the nuclear destruction of Pyongyang or of areas close to the Yalu, could provoke a response from Moscow or Peking. The most dangerous period would be the interval between the discovery that Seoul was moving toward nuclear weapons and Seoul's acquisition of such a capability. During that period, the temptation to stage a preemptive attack would be high. As Imai noted, the time immediately after the first test of a crude nuclear explosive could also be very dangerous, for the South Koreans might be quite vulnerable. At that point, they would lack enough weapons of proven reliability to deter effectively a conventional assault by desperate North Korean forces.

Some South Koreans have suggested, however, that if this dangerous period could be safely negotiated, the long-term result might be a more stable situation from Seoul's standpoint. While the arguments against Seoul's going nuclear are compelling, we should be aware of the possible arguments for such a course. In the first place, it seems inevitable that doubts about the reliability of the U.S. commitment will persist. With the passage of time, these doubts will probably grow. A modest nuclear-weapons capability might give the South Koreans the psychological boost needed to counter their fears about the asymmetry resulting from Seoul's geographic location, which stimulates concern about the capital's vulnerability to a blitzkrieg attack. Nuclear weapons could make Pyongyang as vulnerable as Seoul. Furthermore, a South Korean nuclear deterrent would have a kind of permanence that U.S. forces could never possess. It could be argued that if South Korea had the capability, through nuclear weapons, of devastating major North Korean centers in a short time, then whatever hopes Pyongyang may still have of staging a successful surprise attack on Seoul would vanish.

South Korean spokesmen, while asserting that they have no intention of seeking nuclear weapons, point out that nuclear weapons in Seoul's hands would be usable only for deterrence and for a last-ditch defense. They could not be used offensively, because a threat to unleash a nuclear holocaust on other Koreans would not be credible except as an act of desperation. The idea that Seoul could hope to reunify the country through a nuclear assault, and then to govern a populace on which it had rained nuclear destruction, is difficult to accept.

Even if the North Koreans were somehow to obtain nuclear weapons, which is by no means assured, South Koreans ask why they would be more likely to use these weapons against other Koreans than the United States would against Soviets or the Soviets would against the Chinese. To assume that mutual assured destruction would be a less-effective deterrent between the two Koreas than it is between the superpowers is to assume that the former nations are less rational. It is possible that the emotionalism of relations between the two Koreas would encourage more reckless behavior, but some would argue that the awesome threat of nuclear destruction would help to rein this emotionalism. They might even argue that by introducing the threat of rapid escalation to the nuclear level, possession of nuclear weapons could, in fact, reduce the likelihood of a conventional war on the peninsula. In short, nuclear weapons could be a force for stability in Korea.

The point of this exercise has been simply to show that even the "worst case" may conceivably have its positive elements and that it is important to avoid facile generalizations in dealing with a subject as complex as Korea's nuclearization. Even if a credible case could be made for nuclear deterrence in Korea, the risks of miscalculation, especially in the transitional stages, are just too high. And even if one could be confident that nuclear weapons would have a stabilizing effect on Korea, they would increase in some measure the pressures for nuclear proliferation elsewhere (though, as Whiting notes, these pressures are not likely to have much impact on the decisions of countries outside the East Asian area).

To sum up, it should be clear that it is an oversimplification to predict flatly, as some have, that the withdrawal of U.S. troops and tactical nuclear weapons from Korea would lead South Korea to go nuclear and that this in turn would lead Japan to follow suit. Tactical nuclear weapons, we have seen, are probably not needed for the defense of South Korea, though the Koreans seem to attach some importance to them. To the extent that nuclear deterrence is required in Korea, however, it should be possible to provide at least some measure of it from weapons stationed off-shore. While there is no consensus as to whether South Korea is likely to seek nuclear weapons, it is clear that the option has not been ruled out. But it would be erroneous to ignore the disincentives to go nuclear. The occasional South Korean intimations that they are considering the nuclear option may be a bluff aimed at persuading the United States to maintain its presence in Korea.

If the South Koreans decide to move toward a nuclear capability, there are a number of possible scenarios. The fastest route would be the seizure of U.S. weapons, a possibility that should not be ignored. According to Imai, an effort to build their own nuclear weapons might take the Koreans no more than a year, after they have acquired the necessary fissionable material. Experts cited in U.S. government reports estimate that it would take the South Koreans "a few years." [18] It would probably take three to five years for the Koreans to develop and deploy facilities for the production of fissionable material.

All of the working-group members recognize that the reactions of various countries to a South Korean nuclear capability would depend on the specific circumstances surrounding the event. Unless the circumstances are particularly threatening, this capability alone would probably not lead Japan to go nuclear. Nor is it likely that North Korea would be in a position to match the South's nuclear capability, since neither Moscow nor Peking is likely to be responsive to requests by Pyongyang for nuclear assistance, unless Seoul adopts an aggressive posture. It is even conceivable that Korea's nuclearization might have some positive effects. But the working-group members agree that the risks associated with nuclear weapons in Korea are such that the United States and Japan should exercise all the leverage at their disposal to dissuade Seoul from seeking such weapons. A Korean move toward nuclear weapons could well lead to the abrogation of the U.S. commitment to Seoul. It is not certain how effective economic levers would be, or, for that matter, how willing Washington and Tokyo would be to exercise them if that would ruin the South Korean economy. The best deterrent to a nuclear South Korea is a greater feeling of security on the part of Seoul. In the short run, at least, this must include a reliable U.S. commitment, backed by some military presence. Over the longer run, all members of the group share the hope that improved relations between the two Koreas will create an environment in which neither Seoul nor Pyongyang feels the need for nuclear weapons.

Notes

1. *Nihon Keizai,* June 6, 1977.
2. *Washington Star,* June 14, 1977.
3. *Boston Globe,* July 10, 1977.
4. Ibid.
5. Ibid.
6. See Robert Gillette, "How the U.S. Stopped Korea's A-Bomb Plans," *San Francisco Chronicle,* November 28, 1978.
7. *Hanguk Ilbo,* June 30, 1977.
8. *Haptong,* October 18, 1977.
9. See William Beecher in the *Boston Globe,* July 10, 1977.
10. *Tonga Ilbo,* March 29, 1978.
11. These and several of the following estimates are based on the work of Bryan Jack for Pan Heuristics.
12. According to simple "back-of-the-envelope type" calculations, reactor-grade plutonium with less than 70 percent Pu-239 will require a half micro-second (a two-millionth of a second) as implosion time for a sphere with a diameter of 13 centimeters or larger. Weapons-grade material, on the other hand, would require 4 to 5 microseconds with a somewhat smaller diameter.

13. The achievement of 200 meters per second peripheral speed is not too difficult. This would be only half the speed attained by URENCO (the Anglo-German-Dutch consortium) machines and, thus, theoretically only one-sixteenth as efficient. But the efficiency would be important only if the economic mass production of weapons were the goal.

14. *Haptong,* February 9, 1979. According to this report, "vast deposits of raw uranium" were discovered in Okchon, central Korea. Confirmed domestic uranium ore deposits were said to total 20.35 million tons. The latest strike involved a new stock of 7.1 million tons of raw uranium.

15. *Washington Star,* July 17, 1977.

16. See *Haptong,* July 4, July 5, and October 18, 1977.

17. *Asian Wall Street Journal,* April 19, 1979.

18. U.S., Congress, Senate, Committee on Foreign Relations, *U.S. Troop Withdrawal from the Republic of Korea,* report by Senators Hubert H. Humphrey and John Glenn, January 9, 1978, p. 33.

5
Arms Control and a Stable Military Balance

WEINSTEIN: There has been growing concern, stemming in part from the now-suspended plan to withdraw U.S. ground-combat forces from South Korea, that the arms race between the two Koreas will grow more intense. Can formal arms-control measures help maintain a stable military balance on the Korean peninsula and reduce the likelihood of conflict? Three kinds of arms-control measures have been suggested as applicable to Korea: (1) establishment of a nuclear-weapons-free zone (NWFZ); (2) restraints, formal or informal, on the transfer of arms to the two Koreas; and (3) mutual force reductions on the part of Seoul and Pyongyang. We shall consider each of these in turn.

Under What Circumstances, If Any, Would a Nuclear-Weapons-Free Zone Be Feasible on the Korean Peninsula?

WHITING: An NWFZ on the Korean peninsula is conceivably feasible provided that the South has not already acquired nuclear weapons. It is difficult to see what available leverage the United States would actually use to persuade the South to give up this capability if it were already in hand. A second condition for the NWFZ is the complete and credible withdrawal of all U.S. nuclear weapons from the South. But insofar as these weapons were justified as necessary to deter the North, their withdrawal cannot but unsettle Seoul. This means that, in order for Washington to withdraw its nuclear weapons, it must provide fresh evidence of its will and ability to defend Seoul, probably including provision of the R.O.K. forces with the most advanced defensive capabilities. This in turn increases the prospect of a conventional arms race, a subject to be considered later.

The NWFZ proposal most likely to win agreement among all relevant parties (the P.R.C., USSR, United States, D.P.R.K., and R.O.K.) would be the nontransfer of nuclear weapons from an outside state to either Korean regime. A prohibition on the domestic production of nuclear weapons would be accepted by all except the South, with Seoul's acquiescence dependent on the aforementioned conditions and circumstances. A pledge by the nuclear states not to use nuclear weapons on the peninsula (no-first-use, or NFU) would require a major change in U.S. policy. Were this forthcoming, China and the Soviet Union would follow suit. However, as previously indicated, the South would be more likely to accept the prohibition on domestic production if the use of nuclear weapons in Korea remains a credible U.S. option. The South would be less likely to agree if NFU became U.S. policy.

It should be stressed that all of the foregoing is wholly speculative and inferential. There is no direct evidence of Chinese or Soviet policy on these questions so far as the Korean peninsula is concerned. By contrast, there is some basis for predicting Communist postures on an NWFZ for all of Northeast Asia. In the late 1950s, Moscow proposed an NWFZ for "the Far East." In 1959, Peking concurred, but without any fanfare. No details or subsequent developments emerged at that time or thereafter. In 1963, Peking proposed an NWFZ for all Asia and the entire Pacific region, including the United States, the Soviet Union, China, and Japan. This obviously was entirely for propagandistic purposes because it had no chance of gaining serious consideration by either superpower. More recently, in 1976 China supported NWFZ schemes for South Asia, the Middle East, Latin America, Africa, and the Indian Ocean, with varying degrees of specificity and formal governmental commitment. But no such proposal has addressed Northeast Asia.

It is inconceivable that a Northeast Asian NWFZ—which would necessarily include the Soviet Far East and northeast China—would win acceptance by the Soviet Union and China so long as they remain in mutual military confrontation. Moreover, in the event of a Sino-Soviet détente that defuses this confrontation, it is unlikely that either side would sufficiently trust the other to agree to a Northeast Asian NWFZ. It is also conceivable that future inspection capabilities may prove so reliable under all climatic and topographic conditions that they would obviate those inspection procedures that are unacceptable to both sides. However, this is so far in the future that it is beyond the purview of this analysis. In sum, an NWFZ for Northeast Asia is not feasible now or in the foreseeable future.

ROWEN: Even concerning the Korean peninsula, there would probably have to be some major changes in the relationship between the two Koreas before an NWFZ could become a genuine possibility. But it is still a possibility worth exploring.

SAEKI: The basic problem has to do with the attitude of the Koreans themselves. While an NWFZ has a certain value, such as providing a cover for the withdrawal of U.S. tactical nuclear weapons, such a zone on the Korean peninsula will only be feasible when both South and North Korea decide that the NWFZ serves their respective interests. The concept cannot be imposed on the two Koreas by outside powers. And the reality is that neither of them is likely to consider it advantageous to accept an arrangement that would tie their hands. Each would prefer having the freedom to turn to nuclear weapons as a last resort. Nor would either the North or the South argue that the establishment of an NWFZ on the Korean peninsula will eliminate the possibility of nuclear attack on either of the two Koreas. Also, the fact is that the South Koreans are not prepared to accept an NWFZ.

WEINSTEIN: South Korea is particularly adamant regarding its opposition to an NWFZ because under current circumstances such a measure would operate mainly to the advantage of North Korea. Since there are U.S. nuclear weapons in South Korea but no nuclear weapons in the North, only the South would give up anything if an NWFZ were established. Indeed, a spokesman for Pyongyang whom I interviewed in Tokyo in July 1978 asserted that North Korea wanted the whole of Korea to be an NWFZ. In December 1978, when the chairman of the Japanese Socialist party proposed the withdrawal of nuclear weapons from the Korean peninsula, the Seoul press portrayed this as an initiative undertaken on behalf of Kim Il-sung. The proposal was denounced as nothing more than a call for unilateral action to remove U.S. nuclear weapons from South Korea, even though nuclear weapons just across the Chinese and Soviet borders are capable of reaching South Korea very rapidly.[1]

MOMOI: An NWFZ is conceivable only after the parties concerned have reached agreement on the following points:

1. a definition of nuclear weapons
2. the scope and nature of the zone
3. inspection-verification measures and procedures for implementing them
4. practical measures for enforcing the nuclear-free status of the high seas within the zone
5. assurances that the existing nuclear-weapons states would abide by restrictions imposed by the NWFZ concept

Since there is as yet no agreement, an NWFZ must be regarded as impractical. The proposal might, however, be politically useful as a means of developing the dialogue between the two Koreas and providing a way for the nuclear-weapons states to participate in arrangements aimed at preserving stability in Korea. As Saeki notes, an NWFZ could be the first step toward cross-recognition, since it might involve arrangements in which all of the concerned states would have to deal with one another. Conversely, cross-recognition could open the way for creation of an NWFZ. Kosaka has observed that if North Korea sought an NWFZ in connection with a nonaggression pact between the two Koreas, this would be reasonable.

It will be difficult, however, to open a dialogue on an NWFZ before there has been some improvement in the political climate between the two Koreas. Until improvement occurs, there is probably no point in pursuing an NWFZ. There is also going to be a major problem concerning nuclear weapons on the high seas. Will it be possible to impose restrictions on the nuclear-weapons states to limit their capacity to transport nuclear weapons on the high seas? Thus, an NWFZ is likely to be feasible only after several other preconditions are met.

IMAI: The prospects for an NWFZ, then, must be viewed within the context of the broader problems of military stability on the peninsula; they cannot be meaningfully considered in isolation. An NWFZ will become a realistic possibility only if there has been progress toward some kind of political settlement on the peninsula. Such a settlement could involve either a process of peaceful reunification or an acceptance of peaceful coexistence on the part of a permanently divided North and South. The former is highly desirable, but it must be regarded as unlikely in the near future. The chances for an NWFZ would thus seem to hinge on the willingness of the two Koreas to accept the stability of the thirty-eighth parallel as a long-term dividing line. There is, of course, a kind of circular logic at work here. If both Seoul and Pyongyang are prepared to accept the continued division of the peninsula, then there is less need to worry that either will feel pressed to seek nuclear weapons. In that case, an NWFZ will be a genuine possibility.

What Steps Might Be Taken by Outside Powers to Discourage the Two Koreas from Engaging in an Intensified Arms Race? Is It Possible for Outside Powers to Impose Restraints, Formal or Informal, on the Transfer of Arms to the Two Koreas?

KOSAKA: The most important need at present is for measures to avoid a spiraling of the arms race between the two Koreas as a result of concerns about a possible withdrawal of U.S. forces. It would be highly desirable to develop an understanding between the United States and the Soviet Union concerning the exercise of self-restraint. But it is clear, as Whiting has pointed out, that this will be difficult to make explicit because of the Sino-Soviet dispute. At the very least, the United States should be careful in transferring arms. Washington should explain fully to Moscow and Peking the goals of its policy. As Saeki has noted, the United States must make it clear to the Soviets and the Chinese that its military assistance to South Korea is aimed only at maintaining a military equilibrium on the peninsula, not at attaining superiority over the North. The Communist powers must be persuaded that in the short run the only feasible solution to the Korean problem is the maintenance of peaceful coexistence between the two Koreas, based on a military balance.

OKIMOTO: This is consistent with the Carter administration's overall posture on limiting the transfer of conventional arms. The administration's policy, stated by the president in May 1977, specified among other things that the United States would not be the first supplier to introduce a newly developed weapons system into a region where this would create a significantly higher combat capability. While this is ambiguous enough to permit the supply of most conventional weapons, including F-16s, it does indicate the government's concern about avoiding arms sales that might upset the regional equilibrium. It should also be noted that the United States and the Soviet Union have engaged in talks about limiting conventional arms transfer, although Northeast Asia has not been one of the areas on the agenda up to this point. In November 1978, U.S. officials believed that the Soviets might propose that bilateral negotiations set for December on the limitation of arms sales along regional lines include sales to South Korea (as well as to China and Iran). The United States, concerned about the political implications, was unwilling to enter such discussions.[2] Because of Soviet concern about China's arms sales to Pyongyang and the U.S. desire not to upset already sensitive relations between Washington and Seoul, it seems unlikely that Korea will be placed on the agenda for the U.S.–Soviet talks in the foreseeable future.

WHITING: The real question concerns the demands the North Koreans are likely to make on their allies in response to increased U.S. aid to Seoul. In recent years, Soviet military deliveries to the North have declined while Chinese deliveries to the North have increased. This is true both quantitatively and qualitatively. Specific information is fragmentary and sensitive. But it is clear that Pyongyang has capitalized on Sino-Soviet rivalry for the procurement of advanced electronic equipment, aircraft, and submarines. While this does not match the South's acquisitions, it confirms the likelihood of a long-term conventional arms race should Seoul and Washington continue their present interaction.

Furthermore, it is evident that the North Koreans can carry on sustained combat without immediate assistance from Moscow and Peking. According to one informed estimate, the North has sufficient weaponry and capability to undertake two months of full combat in the South without any resupply from China or the Soviet Union, provided that U.S. ground forces do not intervene. This stockpile includes spare parts, ammunition, and oil. A serious obstacle to monitoring the North is Pyongyang's proclivity for building important military facilities and factories underground.

WEINSTEIN: To what extent would compensatory aid of the kind that the Carter administration proposed giving to South Korea in connection with a U.S. troop withdrawal stimulate counterdemands from Pyongyang for additional support from its allies? The initial proposed compensatory aid package consisted of annual FMS (foreign military sales) credits of $275 million (cut to $225 million in 1979) for four years, plus the transfer of about

$800 million worth of equipment and weaponry from the departing Second Division. The transferred equipment would augment the R.O.K. army's mobility (with helicopters, armored personnel carriers, and self-propelled mortar carriers), firepower (with new tanks, TOW antitank missiles, and artillery), and antiaircraft capabilities (with surface-to-air missile batteries).[3] In the judgment of the late Senator Hubert Humphrey and that of Senator John Glenn, a package of this kind would allow the South Koreans to assume greater responsibility for their own defense without providing sufficient offensive capabilities for a successful attack on North Korea. Furthermore, the senators noted that even if the North Koreans acquired only enough new equipment to modernize their current inventory, in 1982 they would still retain a numerical advantage over the South in all key categories except armored personnel carriers (APCs) and surface-to-air missile (SAM) launchers. Although some of the equipment to be transferred may be regarded as moderately sophisticated, the senators felt that this would not create any imbalance favoring the South. In short, they did not believe that the North would use the compensatory aid package as a basis for escalating the arms race in Korea.[4]

Some observers have noted that the most escalatory aspect of the South Korean response to the troop withdrawal was their request to purchase 60 F-16 aircraft worth $1.2 billion. Senators Humphrey and Glenn pointed out that the introduction of these sophisticated aircraft might prompt the North Koreans to seek more advanced equipment from the Soviets and that it might be inconsistent with the president's policy on arms transfers. When asked why Washington was considering the sale of F-16s to Seoul, a U.S. official with expertise in military affairs asserted that "the basic reason is that this may enable us later to withdraw our air." Besides, he added, there is a natural desire to procure the next generation aircraft. He acknowledged that some officials had expressed their concern in government meetings that the sale of F-16s would lead to an escalation of the Korean arms race. But the concern "never gets anywhere because the Koreans want the F-16s and people are afraid of upsetting the Koreans." Some officials also doubted whether the Soviets would respond positively to any North Korean requests for more sophisticated aircraft to counter the F-16s.

As Okimoto has reported, President Carter vetoed the early

sale of F-16s to Seoul, following an intense debate within the government; but there have been indications of an "agreement in principle" to provide the aircraft at some point. The South Koreans have also urged Washington to permit the coproduction of F-16 engines in Korea, but, as of mid-1979, the United States remained opposed.[5] The sale of F-16s has not been the only source of controversy. Doubts have also arisen about the desirability of selling Seoul more F-4s. Congressman Clement Zablocki, chairman of the House International Relations Committee, suggested that it might be necessary to keep U.S. forces in Korea to avoid having to sell the South Koreans more sophisticated equipment. Indeed, the argument against withdrawal has sometimes been made on explicit arms-control grounds—namely, that keeping U.S. troops in Korea makes it unnecessary for the South Koreans to accelerate their own defense buildup and for the North Koreans to do the same in response.

There is evidence of a strong feeling in Congress that the United States should not feel obligated to make available to Seoul, as the price of withdrawal, whatever weaponry the South Koreans may request. These concerns have been expressed both by liberals, such as Senator George McGovern—who argued that the proposed aid package overcompensated for the planned reduction of forces—and by politicians like Congressman Zablocki. Former Congresswoman Helen Meyner put it well when she described the "trap" in which Washington finds itself on Korea: "If we withdraw our troops, we are told we must increase our aid. But if we increase our aid, we will strengthen an undemocratic regime." Another liberal legislator said he could envisage an increase in government repression as a result of the troop withdrawals. He worried that this could lead to an increase in domestic opposition and ultimately to the disintegration of the South Korean political situation.

Up to now there has been a kind of de facto arms control in Korea as a result of restraints observed by all of the major powers in not providing the most sophisticated weapons to their respective Korean allies. As Okimoto has noted, the Soviets have failed to provide Pyongyang with MIG-23s, even though they have made such aircraft available to Iraq, Libya, Syria, and other nations. Could the superpowers agree to make explicit those restraints in order to avoid an escalatory spiral? According to State Department officials, this is unlikely to happen until political changes occur in relations among the great powers. According to U.S. officials, the competition engendered by the Sino-Soviet dispute makes it virtually impossible for either Moscow or Peking to engage in such "collusion" with Washington. One would think, however, that the North Koreans, perceiving that Seoul is likely to gain more sophisticated equipment than Pyongyang, might press their allies to establish an arrangement that would restrain the South Koreans from gaining too pronounced a superiority. In any case, the hope remains that the United States, the Soviet Union, and China will continue to exercise self-imposed informal restraints in arming their respective Korean allies.

Administration officials assert that, even though the United States may still eventually decide to sell F-16s to Seoul, Washington is continuing to show restraint in the kinds of equipment it makes available to South Korea. These officials strongly deny that a compensatory aid package would be destabilizing. "We will never give the South Koreans as many tanks as they want," said a State Department official. "Instead, we will give them more TOW antitank missiles." Indeed, antitank missiles are clearly the easiest items to justify in the aid package, since they are purely defensive. At present, the U.S. Second Division possesses more TOW missiles than the entire R.O.K. army, although it was reported in early 1979 that the Pentagon was seeking to sell 1,800 TOW missiles and 10 TOW launchers to Seoul.[6] Furthermore, the equipment proposed for transfer from the Second Division to the R.O.K. army was less than that originally requested by the South Koreans. Rather than providing the South with the Second Division's M-60 tanks, which the Koreans had requested, Washington proposed to give them a larger number of M-48s. Seoul's requests for two Lance battalions and for Stinger SAMs were also rejected.

The Korean lobbying scandal delayed consideration of the administration's request for authority to transfer the $800 million worth of equipment from the Second Division. In April 1978, President Carter announced that the pace of the troop withdrawal would be slowed, with only 3,400 troops (one combat battalion of 800 men and 2,600 support personnel) being withdrawn in 1978, rather than the 6,000 (including two additional combat battalions) originally scheduled to be pulled out that year. The administration left no doubt that the reason for the delay was the difficulty of gaining approval for the transfer in the then scandal-ridden atmosphere. Congressman Zablocki was quoted as saying that the transfer could not have been authorized in light of "the present climate in Congress on Korea."[7] The $800 million transfer was subsequently approved by the Congress, though it is now presumably in abeyance in view of the suspension of the troop withdrawal. The annual allocation of FMS credits was also approved, but the amount was cut from $275 million to $225 million.

The question of U.S. military aid is gradually becoming less important, given the dynamic growth of the Korean economy. If Congress should refuse to provide continued credit to South Korea, Seoul may seek to purchase the needed equipment on commercial terms. The distinction between sales under FMS credits and conventional sales is not so great, since the former include only a minor concessional element. South Korea has amassed record foreign exchange holdings, estimated at $5 billion in early 1979.[8] If present trends continue, the Koreans may be increasingly able to meet their needs through commercial purchases. Moreover, if restrictions on arms sales should obstruct the transfer of certain kinds of equipment, Seoul has the option of seeking other suppliers (though there is a clear preference for U.S. equipment).

Finally, as noted in Chapter 1, South Korea's arms industry has made impressive strides in recent years. The South Koreans handle all of their own vehicle overhaul and repair, and manufacture many of their heavy trucks. They can rebuild M-47 and M-48 tanks and manufacture many spare parts. They have a fledgling helicopter industry and are developing a capability to construct fast patrol boats. The South Koreans reportedly produce their own smaller hardware, including mortars, M-16 rifles, grenade launchers, and submachine guns, as well as heavier armaments and some ammunition. According to a Congressional Budget Office study published in May 1978, South Korea was then producing locally 50 percent of all military equipment used in South Korea. Some observers have predicted that by the early 1980s South Korea will be able to manufacture enough equipment to meet all its military needs, except for highly specialized electronic equipment and aircraft. But in the above study this is regarded as an optimistic assessment.[9]

The members of the working group generally agree that it is desirable to continue the de facto policies of restraint in providing military aid to Seoul and Pyongyang and, where possible, to make those restraints explicit through U.S. discussions with Moscow and Peking. Rowen, however, questions the basic assumption that an intensified conventional arms race is necessarily undesirable. In the Korean situation, he argues, a first-strike capability is not the central issue. In any case, it is highly unlikely that North Korea can attain such a capability. Rowen believes, furthermore, that the Carter administration's reluctance to transfer sophisticated non-nuclear weapons to other nations is inconsistent with its goal of reducing incentives for acquiring nuclear weapons.

At the other end of the spectrum, Harrison is skeptical even about the planned compensatory aid package. But though the question of arms-transfer policies may be important at present, it is likely to become less central as the two Koreas increase their capability to produce their own weaponry and as Seoul develops a greater diversity of sources for sophisticated equipment. Any explicit and comprehensive agreement to limit the transfer of arms to the Korean peninsula would require the consent of Seoul and Pyongyang. Thus, it seems evident that if the arms race between the two Koreas is to be kept within bounds, it will ultimately depend on the willingness of Seoul and Pyongyang to impose restraints upon themselves.

Is There Any Possibility That the Two Koreas Might Negotiate Mutual Force Reductions? What Are the Incentives and Disincentives for Pyongyang and Seoul to Do So?

HARRISON: In order to assess the prospects for mutual force reductions, it is necessary to recognize the harsh demographic and economic realities that confront Pyongyang in its continuing conflict with Seoul. With a population less than half that of the South, the North has nonetheless attempted to maintain armed forces comparable in size and sophistication to those of its rival. Just as the South has treaty ties to Washington, the North has defense links with its allies, nominally assuring protection in time of war. But Pyongyang, in conspicuous contrast to Seoul, has not had foreign forces on its soil since 1958.[10] In the military aid sphere, Moscow and Peking have supplied much less and, by all accounts, have charged much more than Washington.[11] The North has necessarily geared its economic planning to defense needs, holding

down consumer-goods production to levels that have been notably
low even by the standards of most Communist economies. By
contrast, the South has given consumer goods a significant place
in its economic development pattern, primarily because it has
enjoyed the massive economic subsidy represented by U.S. forces,
U.S. bases, U.S. military aid, and such ancillary economic assistance
as Food for Peace.[12]

Despite the difficulties involved in obtaining hard economic
data from a closed society, there can be little doubt that the
North has allocated a much greater share of its limited resources
to defense than the South. As noted in Chapter 1, some estimates
indicate that the North devotes three to four times as much of
its gross national product to military expenditures as Seoul. There
are those who believe that North Korea spends as much as 30 percent of its GNP on defense.[13] This is based on the assumption
that Pyongyang hides significant defense-related expenditures
(e.g., for paramilitary, militia, and part-time national guard forces)
under nondefense budget headings. It is particularly difficult to
make meaningful budgetary comparisons of defense spending by
the two Korean regimes because the North, seeking to project a
peace-loving image, plays down its military spending, while the
South emphasizes its increases in military outlays to counter U.S.
congressional sentiment that it does not bear enough of its own
defense burden. Broadly speaking, however, there is widespread
acceptance of the view expressed by a South Korean scholar that
"the arms race will present extraordinary burdens for both Koreas,
but North Korea will suffer more because of its relatively small
GNP."[14]

The low population density of the North has created a favorable environment for the development of a capital-intensive,
mechanized industry and agriculture. But this has also meant a
built-in conflict between the maintenance of large standing armed
forces and civilian labor needs, especially in the mining sector.
For the Kim Il-sung regime, therefore, the economic pressures
resulting from a disproportionate defense burden have gradually
produced subtle subsurface political stresses. As we shall see, these
stresses have contributed to the desire for a new pattern of relations with the South that would permit economic interchange and
mutually agreed military force reductions. In the North, where the
military is only one element (albeit an influential one) in the

power structure of the governing Korean Workers party, Kim does not depend primarily on the support of the armed forces. This would make force reductions relatively manageable, from a political standpoint. In the South, on the other hand, political power is clearly centered in the army. The Seoul regime not only finds a large military establishment politically desirable, but is fearful that demobilization on a major scale would lead to widespread dislocations of the labor market.

WEINSTEIN: It is worth noting here that the CIA's 1978 study of Korea supports the view that the North Koreans have strong economic incentives to reduce their military burden. The study cites Pyongyang's overriding commitment to defense expenditures as "a key reason" why the South has moved ahead in economic development. The report also notes the "tremendous resource drain" of large military manpower requirements and its contribution to chronic labor shortages in the North. About 12 percent of North Korea's working-age males are in the regular armed services, compared to only 6 percent in the South. North Korea's emphasis on underground construction was cited as another heavy resource drain. Underground construction demands heavy manpower and is three to four times more expensive than similar above-ground construction.[15]

HARRISON: Pyongyang's repeated proposals for mutual force reductions have been made seriously, quite apart from their tactical utility as a means of putting the South on the defensive in the propaganda arena. When I interviewed Kim Il-sung during my visit to the North in 1972, I was struck by the intensity and animation with which he spoke of the importance of force reductions. On this subject, there was none of the canned, propagandistic flavor that is characteristic of some of his recitative discourse on the history of the revolution. After the formal interview, he made a point of taking me aside and urgently insisting—amid toasts with Korean champagne—that it was time for Seoul and Washington to take Pyongyang more seriously when it put forward proposals for North-South cooperation, especially with respect to force reductions.

In my interview with Kim, the North made a significant concession in the terms of its long-standing proposal for force reductions, a concession that, to the best of my knowledge, has yet to be explored diplomatically by Seoul or Washington. In its usual references to force reductions, Pyongyang argues for reductions *to* a level of 100,000 men on both sides. But in my interview, Kim suggested that the forces on both sides should initially be reduced *by* 150,000 to 200,000 men, which would leave the existing North-South balance at any given time undisturbed. Under this latter plan, the South would still maintain its numerical superiority. Subsequently, Kim suggested, once Seoul had demonstrated its good faith by embarking on force reductions, Pyongyang would enter into the no-war pact long sought by the South. The two sides could then work toward the long-term goal of reducing their forces to 100,000 men each, provided that U.S. forces were removed following conclusion of a no-war agreement. Significantly, Kim was ready for first-stage force reductions and a no-war pact, even if U.S. forces were not immediately removed.[16]

This change in the North's position came as the climax of several weeks of negotiations concerning the questions that Kim would discuss during the interview. I had pointed out that my editors and readers (of the *Washington Post*) would not be satisfied with a mere repetition of previously stated positions, as had been the pattern in many of Kim's interviews with foreign visitors. In the written list of proposed questions submitted at the request of my hosts, I asked for specific information on a number of issues. I sought, among other things, amplification on how any force-reduction plans would work, including details on how reductions would be verified and how they would be phased with regard to projected North-South contacts and U.S. force withdrawals. I was told that Kim had not been previously asked such detailed questions and that these were quite unreasonable. So I had to submit two more drafts before we arrived at a mutually agreed agenda as well as an understanding that I would be free to ask several impromptu questions. In our meeting, however, Kim began by saying that he wanted to give me "something new" and that he wanted to dispel my apparent suspicions that the North did not really have a serious plan for force reductions. He then suggested first-stage reductions of 150,000 to 200,000 men, together with another new proposal for demilitarization of the demilitarized zone. This modification in Pyongyang's standard position on force reductions was officially chronicled in the North in a 1975 review of important statements by Kim[17] and was also implicitly suggested in a 1972 interview with Kim by Harrison Salisbury.[18]

Since 1972, the idea of balanced force reductions has not been emphasized by Pyongyang, which might lead some to argue that this may have been put forward for propaganda purposes in the expectation that the South would not be likely to follow up on it. But my own view is that it revealed a malleability on the part of the North that has yet to be seriously explored in the North-South talks, in which Seoul has refused to discuss force reductions. My clear impression was that Kim and his aides had never before been asked substantive questions about their attitude toward force reductions, at least in a public context. I believe that there would be considerable potential for diplomatic give-and-take if a serious effort were made to pursue the North's initiative.

It should be recalled, in this connection, that the immediate occasion for the rupture of the North-South talks in 1973 was an impasse over the force-reductions issue. Initially, the South had agreed, following the North-South communiqué in July 1972, that subcommittees of the North-South Coordinating Committee (NSCC) would be established to deal with political, military, diplomatic, economic, social, and cultural problems. At the second NSCC meeting, in March 1973, however, the South reversed this position, declaring that the creation of the military, diplomatic, and political subcommittees would be "untimely." The North responded by stressing the importance of the military subcommittee, and by proposing a four-point agenda for such a body: (1) the discontinuation of the arms race, including a mutual ban on the introduction of weapons and equipment from foreign countries; (2) the mutual reduction of force levels and armaments; (3) the withdrawal of foreign forces from the South; and (4) the conclusion of a North-South peace agreement. Pyongyang argued that because armed confrontation was the "root cause of mistrust," the best way to establish trust would be to start by phasing down the arms race. Seoul's rejection of this proposal at the third and last NSCC meeting, in June 1973, and its plea for "small things first" marked the rupture of the talks.[19]

Looking back on the collapse of the talks, Rinn-sup Shinn has concluded that the force-reductions proposal was more important to the North Koreans than their other demands. Thus, while Pyongyang had insisted on the abrogation of the South's "anti-Communist laws" from the outset of the North-South dialogue, Shinn suggests that the North might "have dropped or modified this demand in exchange for some concession by the South on the issue of mutual force reduction."[20] He points to Pyongyang's desire for relief from its defense burden as the principal reason for this assessment. As I have suggested elsewhere in this study, however, the North may also have been using the force-reductions issue as a way of testing whether the South was prepared for an accommodation on a basis of coequality or was seeking a position of dominance reflecting its numerical superiority.

WEINSTEIN: Interviews I conducted in July 1978 with two leaders of the pro-North Korean community in Tokyo show the lengths to which the North Koreans are prepared to go in order to persuade others of their eagerness for arms-reduction talks with the South. The individuals were Choe U Gyun, editor-in-chief of the Choson Sinbosa Company and director of the Korean International Peace Institute, and Kim Myong-chol, editor of *The People's Korea*. While it is impossible to know how accurately they represent Pyongyang's thinking, both insisted they were authentic spokesmen for the North Korean government, and they have often been treated as such by the Western press.[21]

In the interviews, these leaders emphasized the readiness of the North Koreans to talk at any time with the South Korean government about force reductions. They asserted that force reductions applied not merely to troops, of which the South had larger numbers, but to weapons and equipment—including tanks and aircraft—in which the North holds a substantial numerical advantage. Despite obvious differences in the quality of armaments, they said, North Korea was prepared to support reductions that would leave the two sides with equal numbers of each item. Acceptance of equal numbers, said Kim, was "the only way to reach an agreement." They asserted that inspections should be conducted for verification. The two sides should exchange equal numbers of specialists—military, civilian, or joint military-civilian teams—who should be allowed to go anywhere without restrictions. They also noted that the United States had "spy satellites" capable of verifying compliance with any agreement. Verification, they suggested, was a relatively easy matter, since the territory involved was limited and the weapons were "simple conventional weapons." They added, finally, that North Korea would never allow either a Soviet or a Chinese base on its territory and that South Korea should similarly ban foreign bases.

The precise meaning of these statements is hard to judge. It is somewhat difficult to believe that the North Koreans would permit unrestricted inspections or that they would agree to equal numbers of aircraft, because the South holds a significant qualitative advantage. But even if the assertions of these North Korean spokesmen cannot be taken at face value, they do suggest Pyongyang's intense desire to convey the impression that North Korea is prepared to make significant concessions in order to achieve an agreement with the South on force reductions.

HARRISON: The North's seriousness of purpose with respect to force reductions could be determined quickly enough by efforts to reactivate the issue in the North-South talks. Would Pyongyang be prepared to discuss a meaningful approach to inspection procedures? Even if adequate verification procedures were agreed on, could Seoul be induced to cooperate? If the experience of earlier years is any indication, the South could well be more of a problem on this issue than the North.

In 1971, William J. Porter, former U.S. ambassador to South Korea, attempted to promote a unilateral force reduction by the South of 125,000 men, spread over the five-year period of the force modernization program that was then beginning.[22] In part, this was viewed as a way of facilitating the progressive reductions in grant military aid expected to accompany what was then seen as the "last" modernization program. To a lesser extent, it was also viewed as a prelude to a possible diplomatic initiative designed to obtain reciprocal reductions by Pyongyang. But the Park government, with the backing of U.S. military authorities in Seoul and Washington, quickly torpedoed the proposal. The case against the plan did not rest solely on military agreements as such, for it was conceded by many in Washington that reductions to a level of sixteen divisions would not upset the North-South balance.[23] Officially, Seoul addressed its strongest objections to the idea of linking any future reductions to reciprocal moves by Pyongyang. Unofficially, it was evident that the military hierarchy in the South saw the projected reductions as the harbinger of a potentially more serious threat to its power and prerogatives. More importantly, with South Korean troops then in Vietnam, Washington was in no mood for a confrontation with Seoul.

WEINSTEIN: Viewed from the perspective of 1979, a major obstacle to any discussion of force reductions was the South

Korean belief that the military balance would shift in their favor by the mid-1980s and that any arms-control discussions should be deferred until then. A highly placed South Korean leader with whom I spoke in August 1978 indicated that verification of an arms-control agreement was possible, at least with respect to aircraft, and that inspections could be useful. But he added that Seoul expected to be "well ahead" of North Korea militarily by the mid-1980s and thus did not want to talk about arms control until the existing asymmetries in Pyongyang's favor had been "rectified."[24] Nor did this official believe that Pyongyang really wanted force reductions at present. North Korea's proposals, he argued, had been advanced "only because they know we will reject them." He also said that although there was some sentiment among members of the South Korean government to the effect that the removal of all troops from the DMZ might be a useful arms-control measure, Seoul was reluctant to propose such action until there was a greater likelihood that North Korea would agree.

HARRISON: In order to work effectively toward a mutual reduction of force levels in Korea prior to the mid-1980s, the United States would have to make its future arms sales to the South conditional on cooperation in such an effort and would have to seek parallel Soviet and Chinese restraint in dealings with the North. This approach should not be difficult to defend in the U.S. Congress as an appropriate concomitant to continued support of the South during the transition period accompanying a withdrawal of U.S. ground forces. There is a reluctance in Congress to see the South "abandoned." This explains the widespread support for continued military equipment transfers and credits despite the "Koreagate" controversy. On the other hand, it is assumed that the United States would like to see a North-South thaw, and there could well be substantial congressional opposition to arms sales perceived as sustaining unnecessarily high force levels.

WHITING: The problem of mutual force reductions in the two Koreas is more a function of internal than external politics. It was very difficult to conceive of Park facilitating a diminution of tension and threat by such a step and thereby undermining his professed need for authoritarian, self-perpetuating rule. But Kim might well agree to such reductions in order to relieve his hard-pressed economy. If, indeed, Park's personal power was the prime obstacle, prospects for the negotiation of mutual force reductions may be improved now that Park has been removed.

Kim has proposed such a move wholly in terms of manpower, with both sides being cut to 100,000 troops. The South's higher population, which provides a larger reserve potential, could make this attractive. But the North's attempts at total mobilization, whether troops are formally in uniform or in civilian dress, makes Kim's proposition of doubtful validity. Moreover, to be meaningful, Kim's suggestion of force reductions would have to be coupled with limitations on arms sales. While something symbolic might emerge from prolonged negotiations, it is doubtful that anything short of serious economic need would reduce force levels substantially on either side.

MOMOI: Nevertheless, arms-control talks between the two Koreas would be useful in themselves, even if they do not lead to an agreement. At least, one can assume that the two Koreas are unlikely to go to war with one another while they are negotiating. Other arms-control agreements may be easier to achieve than force reductions—for example, exchange of observers (one or two on each side) and notification of exercises. A basic problem with any force-reduction agreement, however, is that the South Korean reserves are likely to be poorly motivated compared to those of North Korea.

KOSAKA: Still, it must be acknowledged that the chances are not great for an agreement between the two Koreas on mutual force reductions. Unsuccessful arms-control talks could worsen the situation by raising the level of frustration and animosity. So I would oppose initiating such talks unless there are greater assurances than at present that they would be successful in achieving agreement.

HARRISON: It is important to recognize that the issue of force reductions is important in political terms, whether or not such reductions can actually be achieved as an arms-control measure. Because force reductions matter to the North, this issue can be used to initiate and sustain a larger process of negotiation and interchange between North and South. In Northern eyes, the South's willingness to discuss such reductions seriously would be a significant sign of good faith; and in Southern eyes, the North's willingness to do so would signify a more solid de facto recognition of Seoul than in the past. There are, of course, many uncertainties as to what the North Korean position would actually be on various specific issues. The North Koreans have wavered on the matter of timing—specifically, whether or not an agreement is possible while U.S. forces remain in the South. It might be possible to reach a force-reduction agreement with U.S. forces remaining in Korea, so long as there is a commitment in principle to withdrawing them later.

WEINSTEIN: Whether the blame is placed on Seoul or Pyongyang, there seems to be general agreement that a force-reduction agreement, or any other arms-control measure, is unlikely unless there are basic changes in the attitudes of the two Koreas toward one another. As Harrison noted, the principal reason for raising the force-reduction issue at this stage is political. It may be the best way to encourage North Korea to undertake serious efforts to work out a modus vivendi with the South. The issue, then, is broader than arms control. What can be done to reduce tensions between the two Koreas, with the aim of bringing them to negotiate long-term arrangements that might be feasible and effective in maintaining peace? That question is the subject of the next two chapters.

Notes

1. *Dong-A Ilbo,* December 16, 1978.

2. *New York Times,* December 20, 1978, and information supplied by a U.S. government official.

3. For a complete list of the items proposed for transfer, see U.S., Congress, Senate, Committee on Foreign Relations, *U.S. Troop Withdrawal from the Republic of Korea,* by Senators Hubert H. Humphrey and John Glenn, January 9, 1978, p. 46.

4. Ibid., p. 47.

5. *Asian Wall Street Journal,* May 17, 1979.

6. *Asian Wall Street Journal,* April 11, 1979.

7. *New York Times,* April 22, 1978.

8. *Korean Newsletter,* December 4, 1978, p. 8.

9. U.S., Congressional Budget Office, *Force Planning and Budgetary Implications of U.S. Withdrawal from Korea,* May 1978, p. 15.

10. Seoul argues that while the North does not need the regular stationing of foreign forces, given the proximity of Soviet and Chinese territory, U.S. forces should be maintained in the South in order to compensate for an

"asymmetrical" strategic environment. This argument is challenged in Selig S. Harrison, *The Widening Gulf: Asian Nationalism and American Policy* (New York: Free Press, 1978), which examines U.S. strategic mobility capabilities with respect to Korea. See especially pp. 377–379.

11. According to the U.S. Arms Control and Disarmament Agency, the North received only $1.1 billion in military aid from its allies from 1967 to 1976, compared to $2.6 billion received by the South (*World Military Expenditures and Arms Transfers, 1967–1976,* ACDA Publication 98 [Washington, D.C.: Government Printing Office, 1978], p. 137).

12. This view is elaborated in Selig S. Harrison, "One Korea?" *Foreign Policy,* winter 1974–1975, pp. 35–62; and in a related exchange with Chongsik Lee, *Foreign Policy,* spring 1975, pp. 71–72. See also Harrison, "The United States, Japan, and the Future of Korea," in *United States–Japan Relations and the Security of East Asia: The Next Decade,* ed. Franklin B. Weinstein (Boulder, Colo.: Westview Press, 1978), pp. 189–227.

13. Sang-woo Rhee, "The Future of North-South Korean Relations" (Paper delivered at the Symposium on Northeast Asian Security, Washington, D.C., June 20–22, 1977), p. 14. See also "Pyongyang's Armed Forces Huge Economy Burden," *Korea Herald* (Seoul), June 25, 1977, p. 1, and *Far Eastern Economic Review,* May 18, 1979, p. 43.

14. Rhee, "The Future of North-South Korean Relations," p. 14.

15. U.S., Central Intelligence Agency, National Foreign Assessment Center, *Korea: The Economic Race between the North and the South,* January 1978, pp. 6–7.

16. *Washington Post,* June 26, 1972, p. 1.

17. *Kim Il-sung, Choguk t'ongil e kwanhan widaehan suryong Kim Il-song tongji ui munhon* [Documents of the great leader comrade Kim Il-sung on the unification of the fatherland], Samhaksa (Pyongyang), 1975, p. 144.

18. In his interview with Harrison Salisbury of the *New York Times* on May 26, 1972, Kim proposed "the reduction of the numerical strength of the armed forces of the two sides," avoiding his usual reference to achieving equal levels of 100,000 men. This interview was published by the official Korean Central News Agency in Pyongyang ("Talk of the Respected and Beloved Leader, Comrade Kim Il-sung, with Reporters of the *New York Times* of the United States," p. 15).

19. Rinn-sup Shinn, "The North-South Korean Dialogue in Perspective" (Paper prepared for the Conference of Japanese and U.S. Parliamentarians on Korean Problems, Washington, D.C., September 19–20, 1977), p. 26.

20. Ibid. (revised version), p. 30.

21. See *Far Eastern Economic Review,* March 2, 1979, which reported on a letter from Kim Myong-chol; and *Asian Wall Street Journal,* March 24, 1979, which carried an interview with another leader of the pro-Pyongyang community in Tokyo.

22. See Selig S. Harrison, "U.S. Asks Korea to Cut Force," *Washington Post,* July 4, 1971, p. A15.

23. The reduction to sixteen divisions was not considered in relation to the Porter proposal itself. It was one of the options considered during an earlier debate on Korea in September 1969. In that inconclusive debate, the Joint Chiefs of Staff argued that the possibility of Chinese intervention should be considered in any assessment of the force levels needed by the South. This view was questioned by the Nixon White House during the prelude to its China initiative. The issue was still unresolved when former Secretary of Defense Melvin Laird negotiated the 1971 modernization agreement.

24. An editorial in *Dong-A Ilbo*, December 16, 1978, indicated that "the day will come" when the South would have to engage in arms-control talks "to reduce tensions in this part of the world." The editorial added that "we may have to have an international meeting on arms control in East Asia in the mid-80s."

6
The Search for a Modus Vivendi:
Long-Term Perspectives

WEINSTEIN: Whatever one may think about the wisdom of withdrawing U.S. forces from Korea, it is regrettable that there have not been more substantial efforts aimed directly at easing tensions between the two Koreas. The members of the working group agree on this point. Because of the Carter administration's 1977 troop-withdrawal decision, discussions of the Korean situation in recent years have been dominated by questions relating to the military balance. Too little energy has gone into the search for ways to transform the political environment on the peninsula to help ensure that any withdrawal of U.S. forces will enhance, rather than diminish, the prospects for peace and stability.

There should be no illusions that the United States and Japan can establish a modus vivendi between the two Koreas. The future of the peninsula ultimately resides in the hands of Seoul and Pyongyang; the influence of even the most powerful ally is limited. But there are certain diplomatic and economic measures that can be taken by the United States and Japan to lessen the possibility of conflict and, indirectly, to promote a dialogue between the two Koreas.

There is sharp disagreement among the members of the working group as to the most effective course of action in promoting détente and in establishing a modus vivendi between the two Koreas. In this chapter we shall examine various perspectives on how the interests of the two Koreas might, in the long run, be reconciled with the desire for reunification. We shall consider the implications of alternative approaches, including cross-recognition. In the next chapter, we shall take up the more limited objective of détente, exploring the factors affecting the prospects for productive

North-South talks and the potential contribution of U.S. and Japanese relations with Pyongyang. Particular attention will be given to the merits of Japan's taking further initiatives with Pyongyang.

How Do the Koreans, Both North and South, Define Their Basic Objectives?   What Kinds of Long-Term Solutions Do They Envisage?   What Kinds of Arrangements Seem Feasible?

KOSAKA: Any realistic discussion of the Korean formulas for reunification must begin with the realization that both Seoul and Pyongyang want, above all, to strengthen their respective positions vis-à-vis one another. Although they both speak of reunification as an ultimate goal, neither side will accept an arrangement that promises to place it at a disadvantage compared to its rival. Whatever positions may be adopted for propaganda purposes and whatever statements may be issued by factions or dissident groups, it is essential to keep in mind the central role of that competitive dynamic.

WHITING: Viewed in that light, the respective proposals of North and South Korea must be regarded with some skepticism. When examined critically, the proposals of both seem unlikely to be accepted and neither offers a convincing solution to the question of unification. The specific proposals of Seoul and Pyongyang will be described in greater detail by Harrison. Basically, Kim asks for "top-down" confederation beginning with large-scale consultations, while the South has sought step-by-step measures that start with the reunion of families. But there is no credible, systematic proposal from either side that details how the two fundamentally dissimilar, if not explicitly antagonistic, socioeconomic systems can be jointly ruled.

It is, of course, impossible to determine the private perspectives and policies of Koreans, either North or South. This is as true for individual leaders as it is for subgroups inside and outside of government. There is simply no adequate basis for such analysis other than the public rhetoric. If taken at face value, the rhetoric indicates that neither Kim nor Park had any intention of conceding any personal control or risking it for the sake of compromise. As Kosaka has suggested, any proposals for reconciliation and reunification are almost invariably devised to place the opposite side at a disadvantage, either by forcing immediate rejection or by exposing a vulnerability that can be exploited.

On the other hand, we cannot ignore the desire among Koreans, both North and South, to reunify their country. All evidence suggests that formal acceptance of the status quo is politically unlikely in both North and South, at least for the next several years. Korean unity is a powerful emotional goal for a people whose history provides no precedent for the present division. Korea was not a defeated enemy in World War II, but was liberated from Japanese colonial rule. Division was imposed by external forces manipulating internal factors. Moreover, the Asian significance of symbol compared with substance inhibits the formal abandonment of one-nation identity and the acceptance of two-nation reality. These circumstances, however, appear to be less constraining on Seoul than on Pyongyang, as evidenced by the former's willingness to accept dual representation in the United Nations and to invite dual recognition by other countries.

HARRISON: While it is indeed difficult to envisage a credible scenario leading to joint rule of the two Korean entities, the confederation idea does not necessarily imply joint rule, and it deserves serious study. It would be a grave mistake to dismiss this idea as nothing more than North Korean propaganda. Let us examine the respective proposals of North and South Korea.

NORTH KOREA

HARRISON: Although the North continues to espouse the cause of reunification, Pyongyang has increasingly distinguished between the long-term goal of an integrated national state, embracing the entire peninsula, and the interim objective of confederal institutions that would permit separate regimes to coexist in the North and South for an unspecified transition period.

In my interview with Kim Il-sung on June 23, 1972, he stated that the North envisages "creating a supreme national council with representatives of the governments of North and South Korea, primarily for the purpose of jointly consulting about questions concerning the national interest of Korea and coordinating them in a uniform way, while maintaining the present different political systems of North and South Korea as they are for the time being." This formulation has been echoed in numerous statements by Kim and others. In an October 1977 interview in New York, Vice-

Premier and Foreign Minister Ho Dam stated that the confederal body or bodies would be composed of an equal number of representatives of the governments of the two sides. This point, it should be noted, could well become a major focus of contention, given the population imbalance between the two Koreas; Seoul's election proposal (described on page 180), by contrast, would give the South dominant representation commensurate with its population superiority. According to Ho Dam, a "Supreme National Committee" could deal with "such questions as cultural and economic exchange and the reduction of our military forces. On international issues, also, we could discuss our differences and arrive at a common line."

In seeking to elicit Ho Dam's views concerning the possible duration of any confederal arrangements, I pointed out that two very different systems had developed since 1948 and asked whether it would be unreasonable to conclude that a confederation would have to last for a comparable period of 25 to 30 years before full unification could take place. "This would be a political process," Ho replied, "so it is very difficult to say how many years it would require. Foreigners tend to think of a confederation as formed of two separate states but we see it as something that would be created by one nation in the process of moving toward unification. Our common objective would be unification, and the sooner the better." Then he added, "We are a homogeneous nation, with a history of many centuries as one people. In this light, 30 years is a short period. But the main point is this: if the American troops go out of Korea, the period of solution will be greatly shortened."

In the near term, confederation is viewed by the North as a way of rationalizing the de facto existence of two Korean regimes without acceding to a de jure two-Korea settlement that would prolong the division of the country any longer than necessary. In the longer run, North Koreans assume that the process of North-South political interaction within a confederal framework would work to the advantage of Pyongyang. It is an article of faith in the North that the South requires anticommunism to compensate for the lack of a positive political ethos. They feel the South will gradually fall apart psychologically if there is a meaningful relaxation in North-South tension.[1]

In evaluating the North's motives in advancing the confederation concept, two key factors should be emphasized. One is

Pyongyang's desire for a reduction in a defense burden that consumes at least twice the percentage of its GNP as it does in the South. The other is the North's need for a credible demonstration of progress toward unification to satisfy the domestic political imperatives of the Kim Il-sung regime.

KOSAKA: It is important, however, to remember that North Korea does not necessarily require a confederation to reduce its defense burden. North Korea has not been forced to spend large sums on armaments and to take an aggressive posture. Rather, it has chosen this course. If the North Koreans genuinely wish to relieve themselves of their heavy defense burden, they can begin the process through their own actions.

HARRISON: It is true that economic considerations, as such, do not adequately explain why the North is so wedded to the confederation idea. Pyongyang and Seoul could, if they so desired, negotiate force reductions and economic interchange even in the absence of confederal institutions. But unilateral action on the part of North Korea is another matter. It is one thing to reduce military expenditures when apparent progress is being made toward the long-term goal of reunification and quite another to do so in the absence of such progress. Moreover, there is evidence of a division within North Korea on the urgency of reducing military expenditures. In a climate of North-South détente in which there is an appearance of progress toward national unity, those in the North who favor a reduction in the defense burden through accommodation with Seoul would be strengthened in arguing for a conciliatory approach toward the South and for a postponement of efforts to achieve an integrated Pan-Korean regime.

In any case, the underlying reason for the North's interest in a confederation—and its corresponding refusal to accept a two-Korea framework on the German model—lies in the political symbolism that a confederation would have for North Koreans, as a step toward eventual unification. Elsewhere I have elaborated on the significance of the unification ideal to Koreans in both North and South.[2] In the case of the North, Kim has based the legitimacy of his regime in large part on his carefully cultivated mystique as the nationalist leader who helped to deliver Korea from Japanese colonialism and U.S. imperialism and who alone personifies the hopes of all Koreans for national unification. To be sure, the ultimate sanctions on which his regime rests are those of an unusually rigid and monolithic totalitarianism; but Kim has skill-fully used nationalism as a psychological reinforcement to sustain these sanctions over the years. One of the strongest impressions I gained in the North was that Kim and his colleagues could not abandon, or appear to abandon, the unification goal without seri-ously tarnishing their leadership image.

At the same time, Kim confronts the reality of a South in which Communist-oriented forces are extremely weak and the prospects for early political changes favorable to the North appear remote. Shifts in the strategic environment make a militarily enforced unification more difficult to achieve than in 1950, and economic compulsions make a peaceful relationship with the South desirable. Thus, a confederal setup might be a satisfactory compromise for Kim, providing a hopeful symbol of progress toward national unity sufficient to satisfy his domestic political needs. For example, Pyongyang envisages that a confederal setup would make it possible for Korea to have joint representation in the United Nations and other international bodies. To foreign observers, this might seem like an insubstantial, cosmetic change in the context of a de facto two-Korea situation where separate economic systems and military command structures continue to exist. But in North Korean eyes, this would have considerable psychological importance, as the first assertion of Korean national identity on the contemporary world stage and as a vindication of Kim Il-sung's policies.

In addition to the economic pressures and the domestic politi-cal importance of the unification issue, there is still another critical reason why the confederation proposal should not be dis-missed as a mere propaganda ploy. As previously indicated, Pyongyang believes that the process of political interaction within a confederal framework would work to its advantage. The North is confident that it could make good use of such a forum for stimulating desired political change in the South, without the need of direct interference or subversion. Thus, one can easily project what Kim might have had in mind when he alluded to "jointly consulting about questions concerning the national interest of Korea and coordinating them in a uniform way." To take an obvious example, Pyongyang could argue in a confederal forum that Korea as a whole faces the threat of neocolonial exploitation by Japan. The North would thus win sympathy among those in the South who feel that Seoul has permitted excessive Japanese economic influence on overly generous terms. The South, for its part, could stress the dangers of excessive dependence on Communist countries. But Pyongyang expects to get the better of such exchanges, given the sensitivity of relations with Japan in the aftermath of the colonial period. Pyongyang believes there is a basic difference between its purchases from Japan, for nationally controlled state enterprises, and the economic and political inroads gained by Tokyo through private investment in the South. From the North's perspective, the South's economic growth has been achieved at the cost of multiplying foreign dependence, constituting a betrayal of long-term Korean interests. The North believes that it is no trick to "grow" by deliberately inviting such a heavy dependence. Nationalists in both the South and the North could find common ground on this issue, as well as on other issues involving Korean interests vis-à-vis external powers.

While the South appears to feel that time is on its side economically, the North believes that it would have an advantage politically if the economic and psychological props provided by U.S. and Japanese support could be dislodged. This conviction on the part of the North appears to explain why Pyongyang has placed so much emphasis on the withdrawal of U.S. forces. The intent goes beyond the immediate utility of this issue as a nationalist propaganda symbol and beyond its direct relationship to the military power balance. To the extent that the United States reduces its support of the South, Pyongyang calculates, Seoul will face the same conflict between economic and military priorities long faced by the North. According to this thinking, the South will eventually be forced to adopt a more conciliatory posture. The North appears persuaded that even if Seoul does not soften its approach, the political impact of a complete U.S. withdrawal from the South would erode the government's support. They feel that it would gradually bring to the surface political leaders in the South, such as Kim Dae-jung, who favor a more flexible approach to North-South contacts.

SOUTH KOREA

HARRISON: There are two broadly differing approaches in the South to the unification issue. As defined by the Park regime, the South's long-term objective has been a unified Korea with a government chosen "by means of free general elections held according to the proportions of the indigenous populations in the South and North."[3] This electoral approach, advanced as "more reasonable and realistic" than the North's proposal for coequal representation in a confederal Supreme National Council, would clearly leave areas now constituting South Korea in control.[4] By contrast, Kim Dae-jung has left the door open for negotiations on a variation of the confederation proposal. Publicly, Kim has called for a "loose federal system" linking the North and the South. According to Kim's plan, each would be free to "conduct in its own way its own foreign policy, military affairs and domestic politics" but would seek to "adopt a joint diplomacy toward all countries of the world." Kim sees this as the first stage in a gradual movement toward unification.[5] In my private conversations with Kim Dae-jung in Seoul and Tokyo prior to his arrest in 1973, he frequently expressed the view that the possibilities for a limited confederation should be actively explored in talks with the North. He stated that any confederal bodies would have to be based on the coequal representation of North and South.

Let us first review the government approach under Park. Park argued in his "Three Major Principles for Peaceful Unification" that the first step toward unification must be "the consolidation of peace on the Korean peninsula through the conclusion of a non-aggression agreement."[6] He stated that this must be followed by a "small steps first" approach to the North-South dialogue. Resolution of difficult issues, such as mutual force reductions, should be deferred until greater trust developed through multifaceted exchanges and cooperation. This approach is in sharp contrast to that of the North, in which simultaneous efforts are made to resolve both big and small issues. Only through a gradual, step-by-step approach, Seoul has maintained, can the ground be properly prepared for U.N.-supervised elections throughout Korea leading to unification.[7]

Examining other official pronouncements, one finds that the "small steps first" approach has been designed not only to develop mutual trust but also to buy time during which the South can build up its relative power position and thus dominate any future unified Korea. In his 1971 New Year's press conference, Park said that "the easiest road to unification is to strengthen our national power. When the national power is expanded to such a degree as to surpass North Korea, and when the urge to freedom moves from the republic to the north of Korea, Kim Il-sung's dictatorial system will surely collapse."[8] In his third-term inaugural address six months later, Park added that "by the mid 1970's, we should have become strong enough to achieve unification."[9] By 1977, the president told a group of his senior military officers that "we are about to enter a stage of surpassing North Korea."[10] That same year, Park's defense minister informed the National Assembly that the South will be "completely superior" to the North militarily when it completes its current program of military modernization in "several" years.[11] This confident military assessment was reflected in the comments of a government-oriented scholar, who stated that the South can "foresee a time when its economic power will dwarf North Korea's to such a point that it can easily dictate the conditions for national unification."[12]

To some extent, the posture of the South Korean government reflects the emotional and ideological legacy of the Korean War years, especially in the case of many military officers. But it would clearly be naive to take government statements about unification at face value. The status quo in the peninsula is eminently satisfactory for those who have a vested interest in the present power structure in the South, including certain military officers, civil servants, and big businessmen (especially those with foreign ties). The many changes likely to accompany a reduction in North-South tensions clearly threaten the positions of these groups.

Conversely, it is among the out-groups, which do not have so great a stake in the present order in the South, that one finds a greater ambivalence with respect to North-South relations.[13] These include low-paid and underemployed industrial laborers, small businessmen, members of the lower middle class, underemployed tenant farmers, and many students and intellectuals. Among those who do have full-time jobs, there is some fear of rocking the boat and a reluctance to see a sudden volte-face in dealings with the North that might add to the immediate problems of everyday life. Even among the fully employed, however, one finds fluctuating undercurrents of discontent and gnawing feelings that the in-groups are exploiting the North-South impasse to their own advantage. Feelings of uneasiness have increased among all groups in the South as Korea's external environment has changed—as the Sino-Soviet split has sharpened, as Washington's relations with Communist nations have improved, and, above all, as all Koreans have confronted the shadow of growing Japanese economic power. Park's opponents accused him not only of perpetuating tensions with the North for selfish political purposes,[14] but of mortgaging the country to Japan, an allegation that was particularly damaging to him in view of his record as an officer in the Japanese colonial army.[15] Many politically conscious South Koreans believe that the extent of their external dependence prolongs the division of the peninsula by continually increasing the vested interest of those with a stake in the status quo. For the most part, public debate about these issues has been suppressed by the Anti-Communist Law. There have, however, been periodic outbursts of sentiment in favor of more serious efforts to arrive at a modus vivendi with the North that would enable Seoul and Pyongyang to reduce their external dependencies and to adopt a stronger, more concerted posture toward other powers.

One such outburst occurred during National Assembly hearings held in 1966. These hearings, designed as a token gesture to unification-minded groups, released a flood of pent-up nationalist feeling. Another indication of the subsurface nationalism in the South was the strong support for Kim Dae-jung when he stressed the issue of liberalized contacts with the North in his 1971 presidential campaign. Park indirectly acknowledged Kim's success in using the North-South issue by entering into North-South talks in 1972. In a revealing comment, Lee Hu-rak, who represented Seoul in the initial exchanges in 1972, also inadvertently conceded that there is widespread subsurface hunger in the South for a more flexible posture toward Pyongyang and that the Park regime favored a policy of "small things first" because it feared the domestic political consequences of a more direct approach to unification. Defending the "small things first" policy in a press briefing following his return from Pyongyang, Lee said that

> even though unification is urgent, if South-North Korean discussion is limited to political talks for unification only, there is every danger that there might be an explosion of hidden sentiments among the people. Thus I think it vitally necessary for various exchanges in many fields to precede political talks, so that we could all understand what the capitalist society is like and what the Communist society is like, through mutual visits.[16]

More recently, Kim Young-sam, shortly after his May 1979 election as leader of the New Democratic party (the principal opposition group), challenged Park's stand on talks with North Korea and criticized the president for making little progress toward reunification in his eighteen years in office. Kim declared his willingness to meet with Kim Il-sung.[17]

KOSAKA: There is, however, need for caution lest excessive significance be attributed to the views of opposition elements in the South. In the first place, though sentiments of the kind just described undoubtedly exist, it is not clear how widespread they are, beyond the small group of vocal dissidents. It is hard to ascertain whether Kim Dae-jung's strong showing in the 1971 election indicates support for his views on approaches to the North. In any case Kim has, by his excessive reliance on foreigners as his political constituency, lost a good deal of the domestic support he once enjoyed. Moreover, we should not ignore South Korea's outstanding record, compared with other developing countries, in combining rapid economic growth with a high degree of equity. It is well known that incomes in the rural areas have been increasing faster than urban incomes, and there is little evidence of dissidence among the majority of the populace residing in the countryside. Park's critics may feel that he exploited North-South tensions for his own political advantage. But there is no reason to question the sincerity of the critics' belief, and the belief of most others in the South, that reunification, however desirable as a long-term goal, is not acceptable at the price of Communist rule. One can even ask whether the opposition leaders, if they were in power, might not be subject to the same pressures that led Park to reject compromise with the North. Taking into account all of these considerations, it is highly questionable whether the views of dissident groups in South Korea should be considered an important element bearing on the question of reunification.

In short, North Korea has put forth a confederation proposal that it views as a step toward unification under its control. The South has advanced proposals that are equally self-serving. Neither approach seems at all promising.

KAMIYA: To reinforce the points made by Kosaka, it is worth recalling that Kim Il-sung initially advanced his confederation proposal in the last days of Syngman Rhee's rule. At that time, Pyongyang saw the unstable situation in the South and advanced the confederation proposal as a means of exploiting the perceived weakness of the South. The idea did not, therefore, originate as a plan for stimulating a North-South dialogue, and there is no evidence that Kim ever really regarded it as such. Since the days of Rhee, moreover, nearly every important aspect of the Korean situation has changed dramatically. Thus, it is extremely difficult to see how the confederation proposal can serve as a realistic basis for a North-South dialogue.

WEINSTEIN: There is, however, another way of looking at the question of whether the confederation idea is realistic. There is no disputing the observation that neither side has presented, nor seems likely to present, a credible scenario leading to "joint rule" of the two Korean entities as a single confederal state. Any proposal suggesting that the two Koreas can in any sense be ruled by a single government is obviously out of the question at present, and there is, as yet, nothing to indicate that this situation will change. Indeed, in many respects the two Koreas are growing more dissimilar. Although no one can predict what possibilities may eventually emerge, the prospects for unification are likely to grow dimmer, not brighter, in the near term.

It is essential, however, to distinguish between confederation as a step toward a unified state and confederation as the end point of the process—in effect, a substitute for joint rule. To be sure, the North Koreans, as Harrison has reported, emphasize that they view confederation as a step toward unification. Ho Dam stated that Pyongyang sees confederation as part of a process leading to unification, not as an end in itself; and he indicated an expectation that a "common line" would emerge on international issues. As Harrison noted, Pyongyang's confidence that confederation will lead to unification seems to be based on the belief that cooperative relations between North and South will hasten the political collapse of the southern state. That belief would appear to be wishful thinking on the part of Pyongyang. Although the "threat from the North" played a certain role in helping Park extend and consolidate his control, the proposition that détente would lead to the disintegration of the Seoul government seems dubious. Fear of a North Korean attack is not the only thing holding South Korea together; nor, for that matter, would fear of such an attack be entirely dissipated by the formation of a confederal entity, though such concerns would certainly diminish.

Although the North Koreans are likely to continue to speak of confederation as a step toward unification, this does not mean that the confederation idea has to be considered in those terms. The idea of confederation may be a good deal more realistic if it is not tied in detail either to Kim Il-sung's proposal or to other existing models but is devised to reflect the particular requirements of the Korean situation.

In the coming decade, the economic and military realities are likely to be such that North Korea will be under increasing pressure to make the one real concession sought by the South—namely, an accommodation with the Seoul government based on the acknowledgment that unification on Kim's terms is becoming an increasingly remote possibility. Moreover, the economic and political costs of Pyongyang's holding to a hard-line position, though not unbearable, are likely to become more burdensome. The South Koreans are correct in their assessment that the indispensable factor, if Pyongyang is ever to seek a modus vivendi with the South, is a strong South Korea. Many observers have noted, however, that it will be difficult for Kim Il-sung to abandon the goal of unification without jeopardizing the legitimacy of his rule. The appeal of confederation as an approach is that, if properly defined, it could enable Kim to claim a "victory" in his struggle for progress toward unification even as he makes the key concession of agreeing to the establishment of a framework within which both Korean states, with equal legitimacy, can begin to search for possible areas where they might share an interest in cooperation.

Kim would, of course, seek to make the most of his "victory" in Pyongyang's propaganda. But the reality is that South Korea would be trading an essentially symbolic concession for a more substantive concession on the part of the North. Such an exchange is dictated by the weakness of North Korea's position. This is a face-saving way for the North to accept a status quo it has vowed to change. From Seoul's standpoint, it could be advantageous to provide Pyongyang with a fig leaf in the form of a confederation that gives symbolic recognition to the long-term ideal of unification. This would make it easier for North Korea to make the key concession of accepting the South as an independent entity. Such a concession will only come when Pyongyang concludes that the costs of holding to the goal of unification under its own auspices, measured against the remoteness of the prospects for achieving that goal, have grown too high. But insistence on Kim's capitulation to a formal recognition of two Koreas will make it hard for him to do anything but hold to his hard-line position, whatever the cost. The principle suggested here—offering North Korea symbolic concessions in exchange for the North's real concessions—appears to be a sound one from the standpoint of South Korea.

Confederation would place a de jure one-Korea umbrella over the de facto reality of two separate regimes. A very loose confederation, as once proposed by Kim Dae-jung, would in fact leave the two governments intact with full authority over the territory they now govern. The two states would retain complete authority over their own foreign and defense policies. A confederation that implies the adoption of common external policies is unrealistic. The confederal entity's functions would be essentially coordinative—in some respects, similar to the functions exercised by regional organizations like the Association of Southeast Asian Nations (ASEAN), though, in this case, the framework would be national rather than regional. A loose confederation could make possible the creation of instrumentalities to facilitate economic and cultural exchanges of the kind proposed by Park Chung-hee, but within a framework similar to that advocated by the North. Any commitment concerning the long term would have to be very cautiously formulated. Both sides might agree that the confederation should move toward unification of the two Koreas only when there is agreement that conditions permit such a move; such a statement would not depart from what Seoul and Pyongyang have already said. By failing to specify either the time when the next step is to be taken or what the next step will be, the two sides might lessen the possibility that one would try to force the other into premature moves toward integration. There would, in short, be no obligation to move further along the road to unification unless both sides were convinced of the desirability of doing so.

For a very long time, if not indefinitely, the principal external manifestation of the confederal "one Korea" might be at the United Nations. As Harrison has noted, Kei Wakaizumi has suggested "a special arrangement for joint representation," but without specifying the details.[18] Glenn Paige has proposed a more specific formula for "co-representation with a single national voice," i.e., two delegates with one vote. When the two sides agree, Korea's vote would be so recorded; when they disagree, the Korean vote would be recorded as an abstention.[19] Thus, Korea would be treated as a single state at the United Nations, even though Seoul and Pyongyang would continue to carry on independent relations with other states. As Whiting has noted, there is a precedent for such an arrangement in the United Arab Republic (U.A.R.), which consisted of Egypt and Syria. The U.A.R. had a single vote in the United Nations, but in all other forums Egypt and Syria maintained their own sovereignty.

Whatever merit this approach may have, it is clear that the initiative must come from the two Koreas themselves. The United States and Japan can offer their analyses of alternative scenarios, as we have done here. But one point on which both North and South Koreans agree is that the modalities of any relationship between them must be determined by the Koreans themselves. Are the two Korean states likely to accept a confederal arrangement that includes joint U.N. representation through some formula similar to that suggested by Paige?

HARRISON: Paige points out that Ho Dam, in a 1974 speech, implicitly indicated a readiness to accept such an arrangement. After enumerating the possibilities for North-South cooperation on internal issues that would result from a broadened North-South dialogue, Ho added that "as to external questions, we might also discuss and decide on measures for proceeding together to the international arena and defending the interests of the whole nation, entering the United Nations under a single national title and jointly countering the aggressive threat of foreign countries, if there is any."[20] When I asked Ho about this point in October 1977, he expressed confidence that the North and South would be able to agree on common policies and would need only one U.N. delegate. He did not, however, explicitly rule out the two-delegate, one-vote idea.

WEINSTEIN: Interviews I conducted in July 1978 with Korean spokesmen for the pro-Pyongyang community in Japan also indicate some potential receptivity to this approach, although the extent to which the pro-Pyongyang group in Japan accurately represents North Korean thinking may be questioned. Choe U Gyun, editor-in-chief of the Choson Sinbosa Company and director of the Korean International Peace Institute, and Kim Myong-chol, editor of *The People's Korea,* described the Paige proposal as "quite possible" and insisted they were speaking for Pyongyang.

Korea, they said, should speak with one voice in the United Nations, even though the two governments would have to continue functioning in their present manner in any confederation scheme. They asserted that confederation was, in fact, a way of preserving the status quo. But they felt that it was different from recognizing two Koreas because it assumed "eventual" unification, rather than perpetual division. They did, however, repeat the standard formulation that the confederation should have a single foreign policy, though they excluded foreign economic policy.

The South Korean leaders have, of course, opposed any confederal arrangement, while advocating the admission of both Koreas to the United Nations. There is no real evidence that this position is likely to change. Still, it is noteworthy that in an August 1978 discussion of the confederation plan and the Paige proposal, a well-placed official of the Seoul government did not categorically rule out this approach. He asserted that two elements are central from South Korea's standpoint. First, Seoul must retain the right to manage its own foreign and defense policies. Second, it is necessary for the South Koreans to retain the legal basis for asking U.S. forces to come to their defense.

It is conceivable that the South might at some point decide that something along the lines of the Paige proposal for joint U.N. representation has some real advantages. It is an improvement over Korea's present lack of any representation in the United Nations, and it would imply at least a degree of recognition of Seoul by the North. To be sure, the South Koreans want to represent themselves in international gatherings and they feel that they have every right to do so. But one might ask how much is really sacrificed by South Korea's loss of an independent voice in the United Nations. The United Nations is, in many respects, largely a symbolic body. As such, it would be a most appropriate place for the symbolic expression of the one-Korea ideal. Besides, if a disagreement between Seoul and Pyongyang is recorded as an abstention, is that really different, in effect, from casting votes that would otherwise cancel each other out? Of course, as Paige has suggested, this arrangement might lead the two Koreas to discover that they have more in common than they suspected. As for the North Koreans, the Paige proposal would at least provide recognition of Korea as a single entity in a confederal form. Though it would represent far less than a genuinely unified Korean state, this formulation could provide a face-saving way for Pyongyang to reach an accommodation with Seoul, while claiming to have stood by its commitment to the long-run goal of reunification.

On the other hand, it would be a mistake to ignore the potential dangers of this approach. Increased contact between North and South need not lead to cooperative relations. It could provoke intensified conflict on a variety of issues that are now largely dormant, or that are at least addressed only infrequently. If a confederation were attempted and later broke up in acrimony, the situation might be more tense than if confederation had never been attempted. Furthermore, Pyongyang might well feel that confederation gives it a more legitimate basis for criticizing political and economic conditions in the South. From South Korea's standpoint, the status quo may not be so unsatisfactory that serious risks should be taken in an attempt to produce a more desirable situation.

These risks do not loom very large in comparison to the prospects of creating an arrangement that might help to defuse a tense and dangerous border situation by providing a face-saving way for Pyongyang to accept the reality of a viable South Korean entity. Although almost any effort to change the status quo entails some risks, the fact is that the failure of the 1971–1972 dialogue produced no catastrophic results. Increased conflict, if it occurs at the conference table within a framework in which each side accepts the other's right to exist, may not be so worrisome. And the status quo, though it may favor the South, is far from satisfactory. Besides the ever-present danger of war, the costs of an intensifying arms race—though perhaps more easily borne by the South—are significant. Confederation would not solve this problem, but it might create a more conducive climate for the negotiation of arms-control arrangements. And it is in South Korea's long-term interests to create a basis for its own security that is independent of a perpetual U.S. military presence, with all of the problems and uncertainties this dependency relationship creates.

To be sure, it is unlikely that the two Korean governments will move toward a confederal arrangement in the near term, though it is hard to predict the impact on Korean attitudes of Peking's developing ties with the United States and Japan. The eventual establishment of a modus vivendi between Peking and Taipei could also influence Korean thinking. Assuming that South Korea continues its impressive development and the North Koreans come to see the hopelessness of their ambition to reunify the country on their terms, the confederation approach, as a long-term scenario, may prove to have merit.

TRADE AS A BASIS FOR A NORTH-SOUTH RELATIONSHIP

WHITING: The most practical basis for a de facto relationship between Seoul and Pyongyang is trade. The two economies had a natural complementarity before division and might still prove mutually supportive, though to a much lesser degree than 30 years ago.

HARRISON: In the short run, the potential for North-South trade does not appear to be very great, given the "structural similarities of the two economies, attained through a costly duplication of industrial structures."[21] There are, however, certain complementarities in resource endowments, and the two Koreas could profit from diverting to one another some of the trade presently conducted with other nations.

In the long run, both South and North Korea could gain considerably if each specialized in accordance with relative cost-price factors. In addition to resource complementarities, each possesses a comparative advantage in certain manufacturing sectors. Moreover, as one study has noted, South Korean exports to the North would require less labor and capital than corresponding exports to the rest of the world. Indeed, some exports to the North would require less labor and capital than comparable goods produced for domestic consumption.[22]

As for the specific commodities that might be traded, several studies indicate that the general pattern would be one of exchanging North Korean raw materials or semiprocessed products for more sophisticated manufactures from the South. The most promising North Korean exports to the South are iron ore, pig iron, steel, semiprocessed iron and steel products, zinc and copper alloys, coal, magnesite, and barite. To demonstrate the advantages to South Korea of importing these items from the North, one study notes that in 1970 the South was paying $125 per ton for pig-iron imports, while North Korea was selling pig iron to Japan at $70 per ton; similarly, the South Koreans were paying $326 per ton for zinc and $1,721 for copper, whereas North

Korea was exporting those commodities at $294 and $1,526 per ton, respectively. Potential South Korean exports to the North include petroleum products (from plastics to synthetic textiles), chemical products, telecommunication equipment, electrical appliances, rubber products, tools, sewing machines, leather goods, clothing and footwear, chromium concentrates, elemental sulfur, edible fats, and food.[23]

In a 1977 study, Chung Wun-hwak, a South Korean scholar close to the Park government, proposed that there be North-South discussions on five basic principles for economic cooperation before any trade is initiated between the two Koreas:

1. The exchange of advanced industrial know-how which the south and north have introduced into their respective economies.
2. Mutually beneficial participation in economic development through a regional division of labor between north and south.
3. The positive promotion of development projects all over the Korean peninsula, *using the abundant manpower resources of South Korea.* [Emphasis added.]
4. A triangular trade system toward the respective markets which the south and north have already secured.
5. Increased interlocking transportation along the roads and sea-lines which would be reopened between the south and north in the course of such exchanges, resulting in closer though limited linkage of the divided halves of the peninsula as well as bolstered maritime transportation along the east, south and west coasts.[24]

Chung blamed the North for an overall approach toward the North-South talks that, in his view, dims the possibility of economic exchanges. But he pointed out that the North has proposed economic exchanges, including the possibility of direct passenger service between Seoul and Wonsan and between Shinuiju and Pusan. The North has also proposed the opening of the North Korean ports of Nampo, Chongjin, and Hungnam to the South, and the South's ports of Inchon, Mokpo, and Kunsan to the North.[25]

Of course, any significant development of North-South trade depends on a willingness of both states to circumscribe their independent approaches to industrialization and to undertake specialization in production based on economic considerations.[26]

At present, there is little evidence that either side is prepared to consider any significant sacrifice of independence in order to achieve economic gains.

WHITING: There are other problems standing in the way of North-South trade. Economic relations between the two Koreas will encounter some of the same obstacles that would impede expanded trade between North Korea and Japan or the United States. At least in the short run, Pyongyang's bad credit rating and limited prospect of future export earnings would pose problems. Moreover, North Korea's economy is basically geared to Soviet-bloc products, as far as the compatibility and specifications of industrial equipment are concerned. Of course, these obstacles can be overcome in time.

There are some areas, however, in which even short-run North-South economic cooperation, possibly within a multilateral regional framework, would be very desirable. For example, there is a pressing need to settle the exploitation of offshore resources, particularly oil. Joint activity between Seoul and Tokyo has already progressed to the point where both Peking and Pyongyang have a legitimate basis for protesting. Peking has already officially warned against this development and insisted that the matter is for "consultation among the countries concerned." The studied ambiguity of this phrase opens the possibility of compromise, tacit or explicit, that would evade the question of sovereign, legal rights.

Less dramatic steps might be explored in handling the 200-mile economic zone where fishing, an age-old problem in the region, takes on new importance. It is well worth studying whether the North and South could be assisted by third-party mediation or drawn into a multilateral approach that focuses on the entire region. Even if the Sino-Soviet dispute does not lessen in intensity, Moscow and Peking might be inveigled into indirect cooperation in reaching an accommodation on fishing rights.

Conceivably, the North's energy needs could make Pyongyang dependent on multilateral arrangements in Northeast Asia that would collectively serve a useful purpose. But these agreements are years away and would require major changes in U.S. policy, as well as in Sino-Soviet relations. Reference has already been made to the possible multilateral exploitation of ocean resources such as fish and oil. More ambitious and far-reaching in its implications is Moscow's scheme for the development of Siberia. There appears to be immense potential for development of natural gas reserves in Soviet territory east of Lake Baikal. But the vast amount of capital and technology required makes this development inconceivable within the next decade unless Japan joins the project. Tokyo is unwilling to move unless Washington does, not only to protect itself against Peking's displeasure but also to share the risks and to improve the performance of later Soviet shipments in payment for earlier investment.

Conventional wisdom, particularly in the United States, holds that any Siberian growth threatens the security of the area. This zero-sum game attitude prejudges the situation, perhaps wrongly. One preliminary analysis suggests that a developed Soviet Far East would be an even greater security liability to the Soviets than the undeveloped area is at present and would not be an asset for attacking other countries. On the one hand, development will produce high-cost, high-technology complexes that are vulnerable to damage by aircraft or missiles. On the other hand, the area will remain deficient in both population and the resources for supporting large defensive forces.

On the positive side, should this area's energy resources become available for Japan, Korea, and the United States, the potential benefits would be felt for decades to come. Although Moscow's plans for the westernmost portions of Siberia are likely to serve primarily the western portion of the USSR and Eastern Europe, the Far Eastern program looks more promising for Northeast Asia. In this larger context multilateral interests, including those of North Korea, would tacitly inhibit aggression on the part of Pyongyang. If indicators of aggressive intent did emerge, control over the flow of energy resources to North Korea would offer some leverage to dissuade Pyongyang.

KOSAKA: We have to accept as a given, however, that China will not look favorably on any triangular U.S.–Japanese–Soviet cooperation. Peking may well seek to lessen Sino-Soviet tension on its own, but U.S.–Soviet cooperation to develop Siberia would concern the Chinese.

HARRISON: It is also doubtful that any economic relations between the two Koreas, whether in a bilateral or multilateral framework, can precede a breakthrough on other issues. The political issues cannot be circumvented.

WHITING: One should, however, avoid thinking about the prospects for regional economic development in a static, monolithic mold. We should not exclude the possibility that Chinese attitudes may change in time; they could well be ameliorated. We need to study various possibilities—not merely the alternatives of Sino-Soviet alliance or dispute, but some intermediate position, perhaps involving limited cooperation. Projecting ahead ten years, one can imagine the development of cooperative relationships between Moscow and Peking in certain areas of trade and technology. The Chinese may feel that they need to minimize the possibility that Japan will play off China and the Soviet Union against each other. The central point here is the need for a basic reassessment of the possible relationships among the nations of the region. The Sino-Japanese Peace Treaty, the development of U.S.–China relations, and the economic ties that those developments help facilitate may create new opportunities that could involve the two Koreas. We may come to see that it is not a zero-sum game.

How Do Japan and the United States View the Long-Term Future of Korea?

OKIMOTO: Some Japanese believe that their national interests will be best served if the Korean peninsula remains divided. Many conservative leaders feel that a partitioned Korea would permit Japan the greatest flexibility, while posing the fewest problems. This view, presumably, is based on the following assumptions.

1. Peace and stability can be maintained on a permanently divided peninsula, perhaps on the pattern of the "German solution."
2. Reunification does not appear to be a realistic possibility for the foreseeable future.
3. A unified Korea, combining the economic and military power of North and South, could pose a formidable threat to Japan if it were to adopt a strongly nationalistic, explicitly anti-Japanese, attitude.

Each of these assumptions, of course, is open to question.

As Kamiya noted in Chapter 1, Japan's overriding objective is the maintenance of peace and stability on the peninsula. Whether

this can be achieved more easily by reinforcing the status quo or
by unifying the peninsula would depend, inter alia, on (1) the likelihood of conflict if Korea remains permanently partitioned,
(2) the attitude of whatever government is established through
unification, and (3) the relationship among the four major foreign
powers (the United States, the Soviet Union, China, and Japan)
and their policies toward Korea. A volatile, tense, divided Korea,
always on the brink of conflict and war, would probably be less
desirable from Japan's point of view than a stable and unified
Korea, even under Communist rule, assuming that it is genuinely
independent of outside powers and pragmatic in its dealings with
Japan. On the other hand, a Communist regime closely aligned to
either Moscow or Peking and openly hostile to Japan would
probably be viewed as a real menace. Speculating in vacuo whether
two divided states or one consolidated regime would best serve
Japan's national interests is not only difficult but pointless. A
great deal would depend on the specific circumstances and attitudes of those governing Korea.

SAEKI: Even though it is clear that the unification of Korea
under Communist auspices would have serious negative political
and economic consequences for Japan, it might conceivably have
a positive military impact on the security of the Korean peninsula
and its periphery. The unification of Korea would reduce the likelihood of hostilities on the peninsula. And a unified Korea would
not have any strong reason to attack Japan. It is even possible that
there might develop on the peninsula an independent buffer zone,
free of Soviet and Chinese influence.

This does not, of course, alter the fact that the system and
ideology of a unified Communist Korea would force Japan to seek
new bilateral relations dramatically different from the current
political and economic cooperation between South Korea and
Japan. Such a change could cause confusion and instability in
Japan, especially with respect to the way the Japanese people
view their national security.

OKIMOTO: Regardless of whether or not Korea is reunified,
Japan will undoubtedly seek to maintain cordial relations with
whatever government or governments hold power on the peninsula. Korea is, after all, Japan's closest neighbor. Given the history
of Japan's involvement in the peninsula, hostile relations would be
deeply unsettling. The desire to maintain cordial relations with

Korea also flows naturally out of the wellspring of Japan's broader framework of "omnidirectional" diplomacy. Nevertheless, even a unified Korea, open to cooperation with Japan, may cause some anxiety among the Japanese simply because a strong, united Korea would represent a major new force in the Asian power balance. Although Japan's relations with South Korea are likely to grow increasingly competitive, even in the absence of reunification, the problem would be magnified if reunification occurred.

KAMIYA: Whatever one may feel about the reunification of Korea, Japan's principal interest clearly lies in détente between North and South. In order to ensure peace on the peninsula, some kind of modus vivendi between the two Korean governments is necessary. The desirability of unification, as against maintenance of the present division, as a means of ensuring peace and stability does not lie within the scope of Japan's national interest. This question must be resolved by the Koreans themselves. Under certain circumstances, either course could serve Japan's interests. But there is a strong predisposition to emphasize the importance of stability, which can mean either the maintenance of the present situation or moderate change.

WEINSTEIN: As for the United States, most of the officials whom I interviewed in Washington assumed that some version of the "German solution"—the indefinite division of Korea—is the only viable alternative. To be sure, one State Department official who follows Korean affairs closely argued that it is unrealistic to expect that North Korea will ever accept the concept of two Koreas. The central question, he stated, is whether the United States can bring itself to recognize that Pyongyang will never give up its goal of reunification. But his position, he acknowledged, is not accepted by most of his colleagues in the government.

Most U.S. officials reject Kim Il-sung's confederation scheme on the grounds that Kim would insist on democratic reforms that grant the Communists freedom to operate in the South. Nor do these officials believe that a North-South congress, as proposed by Pyongyang, could accomplish much. All the United States really seeks from Pyongyang, it was asserted, is a credible renunciation of the use of force. But a North Korean declaration to that effect could be made credible only by some gesture that signifies recognition of the South Korean government's legitimacy.

Although the mention of confederation evoked a largely

negative response from the U.S. officials I interviewed in late 1977, there was a good deal of interest in the novel proposal concerning U.N. representation. Of course, some officials dismissed it as mere "gimmickry" or a "grandiose attempt at a quick fix." One added, "We should not always be worrying about trying to find ways of helping Kim save face. The important thing is to provide an arrangement that will secure the interests of South Korea." This view ignores the fact that such an arrangement is impossible without concessions from Pyongyang. The reason for trying to help Kim save face is that this will increase the likelihood of his making the necessary concessions. In any case, most of those interviewed considered the "two-delegate, one-vote" idea worth pursuing.

What Are the Prospects for Cross-Recognition? What Do the Soviets and Chinese See as Desirable Long-Term Solutions to the Korean Problem? What Is the Extent of Soviet and Chinese Economic Interests in Korea? Under What Circumstances Might the Soviet Union and China Be Disposed to Establish Informal or Formal Diplomatic Relations with South Korea?

KAMIYA: The idea of cross-recognition—that is, the simultaneous extension of diplomatic recognition by the United States and Japan to North Korea and by the Soviet Union and China to South Korea—was first broached in 1969. In fact, I must accept responsibility for having originated the idea, which I discussed in an article entitled "Divided Countries and Japan's Foreign Policy," published in the June 1970 issue of the monthly *Chuo Koron.* In that article, I also proposed a multilateral conference on Korea in which all of the countries concerned—the two Koreas, the United States, Japan, the Soviet Union, and China—would have an opportunity to participate in working out a solution. For several years these ideas gained little support in either Japan, Korea, or the United States because neither Seoul nor Pyongyang was prepared to recognize the other's legitimacy. In 1975, however, Secretary of State Henry Kissinger officially adopted the ideas of cross-recognition and a multilateral conference as U.S. policy. Had the United States backed these proposals several years earlier when an atmosphere of détente prevailed on the peninsula, some progress might have been achieved; but by 1975 it was too late. The two Koreas are not likely to give serious consideration to cross-recognition until more time has passed and the international situation has undergone certain changes.

WHITING: There is no doubt of Seoul's eagerness for relations with the Soviets and the Chinese. Seoul has repeatedly made overtures toward Moscow and Peking, with mixed results. The only confirmed contact with Peking involved a single meeting in Hong Kong, ostensibly to discuss the sale of kim chee. A "leak," probably by a disgruntled R.O.K. official, evoked a denial by both sides and nothing followed. Moscow, however, has been more open in its issuance of visas to South Korean athletes, scholars, and journalists and even to one government official, the minister of health. This policy has evoked oblique protests from Pyongyang and public criticism from Peking.

It seems evident that both Communist powers are more concerned with each other's activity in competition for Pyongyang than with Pyongyang's reaction per se. Thus, an easing of the Sino-Soviet dispute might reduce the reluctance of both China and the USSR to proceed further with Seoul, although it is unlikely that these steps will ever add up to formal recognition and acceptance of the status quo. Under these circumstances, a less visible effort by the United States to bring about dual recognition would be more productive, since it might subtly enhance Seoul's chance of eroding Pyongyang's confidence in Moscow and Peking.

How will the development of U.S.–China relations affect the prospects for cross-recognition? Those relations have come a long way from the détente of 1972 to the rapprochement of 1979. Technology transfer, joint declarations against "hegemony" (read the Soviet Union), and personal summitry will characterize relations between Peking and Washington at least through the early 1980s. While a formal Peking–Tokyo–Washington entente is unlikely, the tripartite linkage will dominate the politics of each toward other states in Asia.

The two Koreas' view of this development is uncertain and confused. On the one hand, South Korean hopes for improved relations with China are offset by the fear that Chinese exports to the United States will reduce Seoul's market, particularly in textiles and light industrial products. On the other hand, North Korean expectations of credits and technology, from Japan if not from the United States, may be countered by concern that Peking will lose all interest in its welfare. This could jeopardize the flow of oil, coal, and military supplies from Moscow, which are less available now than in the past.

These considerations highlight the mixed nonzero-sum game aspects of closer China–U.S. relations as seen from North and South Korea. In one sense, the die was cast in 1972. Nothing fundamentally new occurred in the final negotiations on normalization between Peking and Washington that could not have been anticipated, although the particular timing was presumably a surprise. Nevertheless, the rapidity and extent of change in Chinese domestic policy, predicated on major changes in foreign economic relations, added a wholly new dimension to normalization that could not have been foreseen so long as Mao Tse-tung and the radical ideologues were present.

Teng Hsiao-p'ing's open call for an anti-Soviet entente linking Western Europe, Japan, and the United States goes far beyond the indirect hints and significant silences of Chinese statements prior to 1976. At the very least, this implies tacit acceptance of the status quo in Korea by removing the issue from the agenda of problems to be discussed between Peking and Washington.

Still, it seems highly unlikely that Peking will accept any proposal for formal cross-recognition. Kamiya is correct in warning us not to be too helpful about the prospects that the new international climate may induce Peking to develop a relationship with Seoul. There is no visible gain for Peking in risking Pyongyang's wrath. With no other pro-Peking Communist government in Asia, a North Korean–Chinese split would please Moscow. At home, Teng, as the presumed advocate of pragmatism and moderation, would add still another brickbat to the pile with which his various opponents hope one day to strike back.

Moscow's move into Indochina, especially the Soviet-Vietnamese political-military agreement of November 1978, poses a sober warning to Peking and a suggestive alternative for Pyongyang. During the rising tension between Phnom Penh and Hanoi in the late fall of 1978, Pyongyang publicly sided with the Pol Pot regime. Pol Pot's ouster by Hanoi's forces, however, redounded to Moscow's credit and Peking's loss.

These developments would not in themselves prompt Kim Il-sung to reject China in favor of the Soviet Union. His need to avoid total dependency on either country is rooted in 30 years of dealing with the two Communist nations, as well as in the entire history of Korean nationalism. But the new situation does require Chinese policymakers to take greater care than before, lest they provoke Kim to the point of no return and thereby create an opportunity for Moscow to cultivate still another position of influence on China's borders.

HARRISON: It is clear that both the Soviets and the Chinese view the Korean problem primarily in relation to one other. Since each wants to be certain that the other does not gain the upper hand in Pyongyang, each is prepared to support the North in its opposition to a two-Korea approach. In Soviet eyes, a two-Korea solution might well seem desirable, because Moscow fears that racial affinities could ultimately lead to a unified Korea oriented toward China. Moscow is also concerned lest Korean unification serve to open up the German question and the Kuriles issue. Nevertheless, both Moscow and Peking are likely to give nominal support to the goal of unification and are most unlikely to be responsive to overtures for formal relations with the South in the foreseeable future.

My assessment on this issue differs from that of some Americans who have met the same Soviet Far Eastern specialists I have met and who have come away with the impression that Moscow can be induced to accept a cross-recognition formula. In my view, Moscow seeks to give this impression for tactical reasons, while carefully avoiding explicit undertakings. By encouraging Washington to expect a Soviet change of heart, Moscow seeks to delay U.S. contacts with Pyongyang, which it greatly fears in the context of Sino–U.S. and Japanese–U.S. ties. More importantly, Moscow hopes to keep Pyongyang from going too far in its relations with Peking by holding out the implicit threat of dealing with Seoul.

Neither Moscow nor Peking has critical economic interests in North Korea. China gets some magnesia clinker, machine tools, pig iron, cement, and iron ore from Pyongyang, and Moscow gets some important metals. (North Korea formerly sent 71 percent of its zinc exports, 48 percent of its lead exports, and 32 percent of its copper exports to the Soviet Union; but these levels have dropped.) Imports from the North are convenient for the Soviet Far East, and this is the destination of most Soviet imports from the North.[27] The North is not vital economically to either the Soviet Union or China, however, and may even be regarded by them as a burden in some respects. Moscow and Peking supply Pyongyang with all of its oil (about one million tons from China, primarily in the form of crude, and a similar amount from the Soviet Union, divided equally between crude and petroleum products). Although North Korea's dependence on imports from China and the Soviet Union dropped from 83 percent in 1970 to 48 percent by 1974, reflecting the North's conscious attempt to diversify, Pyongyang continues to be critically dependent on both China and the Soviet Union, not only with respect to petroleum, but also in certain spheres of military aid—especially air-to-air missiles, aircraft, and submarines.

According to a recent South Korean analysis, because the North's debts to the Soviet Union exceed $700 million, Moscow holds the key to peace on the peninsula. Kim Youn-soo suggests that the Soviets could defer repayments, relax other terms, and that they could

> mediate the arrangement of "European dollar credits" for North Korea via the "North European Industrial Bank" in Paris as they had consistently done in the past until 1974. There is no other way for Kim Il-sung to free North Korea from its foreign debts unless it cooperates with Soviet policy. Therefore, it is possible to argue that the north may be forced to "cooperate" with the R.O.K. for a political and military détente should Brezhnev really press for this, realizing that to be one of the preconditions for realizing the success of his plan for a collective security system in Asia.[28]

This analysis assumes that Moscow wants peace in Korea on the South's terms, but my discussions with specialists on the Soviet Far East do not support such an interpretation. Moscow, like Peking, would be likely to use its leverage to prevent an adventurist northern military policy that might provoke U.S. intervention. But at the same time, Moscow is not prepared to challenge the North's opposition to the "small things first" approach in the North-South dialogue and appears to see some practical possibilities in the confederation approach.

I see little hope for cross-recognition, except in the context of significant movement toward a North-South détente. If there is a significant movement toward détente and the eventual creation of some form of one-Korea superstructure as an outgrowth of the North-South dialogue, the North might not view cross-recognition as a juridical impediment to unification. Similarly, only in conjunction with a North-South nonaggression agreement and negotiations on mutual force reductions can one envisage meaningful moves to limit arms sales and, eventually, discussion of mutual decoupling of treaty commitments to the two Korean regimes. External powers can only orchestrate a Korean settlement if it is directly related to an intra-Korean settlement. This, in turn, is likely to take place only if a timetable can be established projecting steps toward some form of confederal arrangement or some other substantial gesture toward the goal of unification.

South Korean economic links with Moscow and Peking would be useful, but not determinative, for realizing cross-recognition. The South, in time, may find some areas of significant economic interchange with the Soviet Far East. But as Stephen Uhalley, Jr., points out, Seoul may also compete with the Soviet Far East in seeking to attract foreign economic collaboration.[29] With respect to China, there may be some possibilities for indirect crude oil sales through third parties. As I have suggested elsewhere, however, the most significant opportunities for oil collaboration between China and the two Korean regimes are likely to be part of a larger pattern of North-South economic cooperation.[30]

WHITING: One suspects, albeit without good evidence, that in their most private moments Chinese and Soviet policymakers see a Korean peninsula united under Communist rule as the most desirable solution. But this view is not advanced openly, so that Pyongyang will not be encouraged to take risky action or to disturb Japan and the United States from their respective, relatively relaxed, postures in Northeast Asia. Such a solution would end the problem of contingency planning for another Korean war and would also fit the ideological imperative. Although this might lead to a less manageable Korea, it would also reduce the likelihood of a dependent, demanding Korea.

But this optimal solution has no visible, viable means of attainment short of war, which both Moscow and Peking hope to avoid. Therefore, their pragmatic adaptation to the status quo over the past 25 years is likely to continue for the next 25. Their economic interests are minimal or marginal. Their competitive political interests outweigh their direct political interests, so long as the North remains a protective buffer against any "worst case" contingencies from the South. While Korea has a higher priority for

China than for the Soviet Union, compared with relations and objectives elsewhere it ranks well below most other concerns in Northeast Asia and elsewhere in the world. It also ranks below the domestic development goals of both Moscow and Peking, which in turn depend intimately on stability in the region and good relations with Japan. In short, whatever dangers exist on the peninsula are far more likely to result from the behavior of North and South Korea than from that of external powers. On the other hand, relations among the external powers may well play an important role in creating an environment conducive to an improvement of relations between the two Koreas.

Notes

1. For a more complete discussion of this point, see the two articles summarizing my trip to North Korea, *Washington Post,* July 2–3, 1972. See also Selig S. Harrison, *The Widening Gulf: Asian Nationalism and American Policy* (New York: Free Press, 1978), pp. 231–237.

2. Harrison, *The Widening Gulf,* pp. 209–231.

3. Park Chung-hee, "Three Major Principles for Peaceful Unification," Liberation Day Message, August 15, 1974.

4. Ku Pom-mo, "Comparison of Unification Policies of South and North Korea," in *Theses on South-North Dialogue,* Seoul Side of South-North Coordinating Committee, July 4, 1977, p. 28.

5. Kim did not take this position publicly in Seoul, where he would have been vulnerable to prosecution under the Anti-Communist Law, but rather in an address to the Foreign Correspondents Club of Japan, March 1973. Cited in Tokuma Utsonomiya, "The Relaxation of Tensions and Korean Unification" (Paper presented at the Conference of U.S. and Japanese Parliamentarians on Korean Problems, Washington, D.C., September 19–20, 1977), p. 12.

6. Ku Pom-mo, "Unification Policies of North and South Korea," p. 32.

7. For an elaboration of the "Three Major Principles," see Kim Young-jun, "Analysis and Prospects of Three Principles for Peace," *Sedae* (Seoul), no. 135 (October 1974): 160–169; Kim Hak-jun, "The Holding of Free General Elections and the South-North Issue," *Sedae,* no. 135 (October 1974):170–179; and Lee Ki-taek, "Principles for Peaceful Unification and the U.N. General Assembly," *Sedae,* no. 135 (October 1974):180–187. See also Min Pyong-chon, "A Study of the Logic of a South-North Non-Aggression Agreement," *Unification Policy* (Seoul) 3, no. 1 (spring 1977):61–62.

8. Park Chung-hee, *Decade of Confidence and Achievement,* The Presi-

dent's Annual New Year Press Conference for 1971 (Seoul: Ministry of Culture and Information, Republic of Korea), p. 13.

9. "Inaugural Speech by President Park Chung Hee," July 1, 1971, pp. 4–5.

10. *Korea Herald,* January 28, 1977, p. 1.

11. *Korea Herald,* April 29, 1977, p. 1.

12. Sang-woo Rhee, "The Future of North-South Korean Relations" (Paper presented at the Symposium on Northeast Asian Security, Washington, D.C., June 20–22, 1977), p. 10.

13. Mikio Sumiya provides a careful economic analysis of the plight of labor, indigenous business, and underemployed tenant farmers in "Growth Economy and Unstable Society: The Mechanism of the South Korean Economy" (Paper presented at the Conference of U.S. and Japanese Parliamentarians on Korean Problems, Washington, D.C., September 19–20, 1977).

14. In the controversial manifesto that led to their arrest in March 1976, Kim Dae-jung, former President Yun Po-sun, and ten other opposition leaders attacked Park for his political repression and for economic policies that "foster corruption, foreign indebtedness and ever widening disparities of wealth." They also strongly implied that he was partly to blame for the continued division of the country. In their "Declaration for Democratic National Salvation," signed in Seoul on March 1, 1976, they stated,

> The tragic rupture of our land for the thirty years since liberation has given an excuse for dictatorships in both north and south. . . . For the north and south to have a combined standing army strength of over a million men, and to maintain these forces with modern weapons, imposes an impossible burden on the economies of the Korean peninsula without foreign military aid. . . . Accordingly, "National Unification" is today the supreme task which must be borne by all the 50 million Korean people. If any individual or group uses or obstructs "National Unification" for its own strategic purpose, it will be impossible to escape the strict judgement of history. Depending on the attitudes of politicians, north or south, the opportunity for "National Unification" can either be brought closer or delayed. Those who truly believe in the nation and our common brotherhood, clearly perceiving the changing international situation, and seizing the chance when it comes, ought to have the wisdom and courage to deal with it resolutely. This is precisely what we must pursue as the goal of an independent foreign policy inspired by our own Korean interests.

15. An example of a significant underground document stressing the anti-Japanese theme is *Declaration on the Contemporary Situation of Korea,* issued by the Student Government of Korea University with the approval of the Contemporary Conference on the New Order of Korea and Asia, Seoul, September 29, 1970. See also the veiled anti-Japanese allusions in South Korean poet Kim Chi-ha's "The Five Thieves," a satirical poem confiscated by the Park regime but available in Japanese translation in Sentaro Shibuya, *Nagai Kyrayamai no Kanata ni* (Tokyo: Chuo Koron-sha, 1971). Park's

official biography (April 1969, p. 5) notes that he graduated at the head of his class in the two-year elementary course at the Manchukuo Military Academy in 1942, winning entry to the advanced course at the Japanese Imperial Military Academy and serving as a first lieutenant until the end of World War II.

16. See the text of Lee's briefing, circulated by the Korean Press Service, Seoul, July 4, 1972, especially part 9.

The 1966 episode is discussed in detail in "After Korea: The Stresses of Division," in Harrison, *The Widening Gulf,* Chapter 7. The hearings of the Special Committee on National Unification were held from September to December 1966, and the 190-page proceedings were reprinted in full in Korean in the committee report. See "T'ongil Paekso" [White paper on unification], Taehan Minguk Kuk-hoe [National assembly], mimeographed (Seoul, 1967). The committee report and numerous other Korean-language materials relating to the unification issue were translated for the author with the support of the Brookings Institution. See a series of thirteen articles by the committee's chairman, Sun In-sok, in *Choson Ilbo,* August 1966; an article by Professor Kim Hong-ch'ol of the South Korean National Defense College, "Concept of a Friendly Nation," *Chong Maek,* March 1966; and *Han'guk ui minjokchuui* [Report of a conference on Korean nationalism] (Seoul: Korean Association of International Relations 1967), especially the address by the association's former president, Yi Yong-hui, "Han'guk minjokchuui ui chemunje" [The problems facing Korean nationalism], p. 13. See also Ch'a Ki-byok, "Han'guk minjokchuui ui tojon kwa siryon" [Trials and challenges of Korean nationalism], pp. 33–34, 183–215—especially comments by Ha Kyong-gun, Yi Ki-yong, and Ko Yong-bok. For a partial English summary of this symposium, see *Korea Journal,* Korean National Commission for UNESCO, December 1966. This was one of the last open discussions of the unification issue among Korean intellectuals permitted by the Park regime prior to the consolidation of authoritarian rule in 1969. The unification issue also figures prominently throughout *Han'guk kundaehwa e issosoe kaldungggwa chohwa* [Conflict and harmony: report of conference on modernization], April 20, 1968, publication no. 8 (Seoul: Korean Association of International Relations, 1969).

17. *Asian Wall Street Journal,* June 13, 1979.

18. Kei Wakaizumi, "Japan's 'Great Experiment' and the Japanese-American Alliance," Woodrow Wilson International Center for Scholars, October 9, 1975, p. 37.

19. Glenn D. Paige, "The United States and Alternative Approaches to Korean Peace: Recommendations, 1973" (Report to the Assistant Secretary of Defense for International Security Affairs, grant no. DAHC-15-73-G-5), pp. 4–5.

20. Ho Dam made this statement in his address to the sixty-third meeting of the Central Committee of the United Front for the Liberation of the

Fatherland in Pyongyang on November 8, 1974. See the press release issued by the office of the Permanent Observer of the D.P.R.K. to the United Nations, November 19, 1974, p. 4.

21. Lee Joong-koon, "North Korean Foreign Trade in Recent Years and the Prospects for North-South Trade in Korea" (Paper presented at the twenty-sixth annual meeting of the Association for Asian Studies, Boston, April 1–3, 1974), p. 27.

22. Lim Young-il, "South Korea's Foreign Trade: Possible Impacts of Trade with North Korea" (Paper presented at the twenty-sixth annual meeting of the Association for Asian Studies, Boston, April 1–3, 1974), especially pp. 9–14, 24–25.

23. Lee Joong-koon, "North Korean Foreign Trade," p. 28.

24. Chung Wun-hwak, "The Possibility of Economic Exchanges between South and North Korea," in *Theses on South-North Dialogue,* Theme Papers at Seminar Held on the Occasion of the Fifth Anniversary of Issuance of South-North Joint Communiqué (Seoul: South-North Coordinating Committee, July 4, 1977), p. 93.

25. Ibid., p. 77.

26. Lee Joong-koon, "North Korean Foreign Trade, " p. 28.

27. Boris N. Slavinsky, "Siberia and the Soviet Far East within the Framework of International Trade and Economic Relations," *Asian Survey* 17, no. 4 (April 1977), p. 322.

28. Kim Youn-soo, "Russia Can Exercise Pressures on N.K. for Detente With R.O.K.," *Korea Herald,* November 4, 1977, p. 2.

29. Stephen Uhalley, Jr., *The Soviet Far East: Growing Participation in the Pacific,* American Universities Field Staff, East Asia Series, vol. 24, no. 1, September 1977, p. 12.

30. Selig S. Harrison, *China, Oil, and Asia: Conflict Ahead?* (New York: Columbia University Press, 1977), pp. 144–145.

7

Steps Toward Détente

WEINSTEIN: Progress toward détente between the two Koreas may be indicated in many ways. These include a diminution of hostile rhetoric, the avoidance of border incidents, and the easing of the arms race between the two Koreas. But because the dispute between Seoul and Pyongyang is one in which each challenges the legitimacy of the other, the clearest indication of the prospects for détente may be the willingness of the two sides to talk with one another. In this chapter, we shall continue our analysis of the search for a modus vivendi between the two Koreas, considering first the prospects for North-South negotiations, and then initiatives that might be taken by the United States and Japan to help create an environment conducive to détente and the establishment of a modus vivendi on the peninsula.

What Can Be Done in the Short Run to Produce a Détente Between the Two Koreas? What Are the Prospects for North-South Negotiations?

HARRISON: Before discussing the future of the North-South talks, it is necessary to understand why the 1972–1973 negotiations broke down. The rupture of the talks in 1973 was not the result of minor disagreements or mere tactical errors by either party. Rather, it reflected a basic conflict over an acceptable basis for peaceful unification. As already noted, the North, with a population less than half that of the South, has sought agreement on ground rules for a process of movement toward unification in which the principle of coequal representation is established at the outset. The South has envisaged a unified government based on

U.N.–supervised elections, in which the areas now constituting South Korea would rightfully dominate by virtue of their numerical superiority. The confusion and bitterness resulting from the failure of the 1972–1973 exchanges can be fully comprehended only in the light of these differing perspectives.

In Pyongyang's eyes, the critical significance of the 1972 North-South communiqué was the South's agreement to seek unification "without external interference" through the newly established North-South Coordinating Committee.[1] By implication, Seoul had relaxed its insistence on U.N.–supervised elections. But Pyongyang remained suspicious. Was Seoul really prepared to accept the principle of coequality as the basis for a transition to unification, or was it merely seeking to convey the illusion of progress toward that goal, while working to crystallize a de jure two-Koreas settlement in which the status quo would be prolonged for as long as possible?

With this question in mind, Pyongyang sought to test Seoul's sincerity by pressing for the establishment of a military subcommittee empowered to consider mutual force reductions and restrictions on arms flows into the peninsula. By agreeing to discuss "small things first," the North feared, it would only be tricked into protracted negotiations that would, by the South's design, never go beyond "small things."

It quickly became apparent that the two sides had entered the dialogue with sharply conflicting approaches to the question of unification. South Korean leaders began to tone down references to unification in the communiqué of July 4, 1972, even before the ink was dry. In briefing reporters following the release of the communiqué, Lee Hu-rak, then director of the Korean CIA and Seoul's representative in drafting the North-South statement, stressed that the dialogue was "primarily aimed at forestalling war by all means possible."[2] He added that Seoul would adhere to its long-standing position that unification could only be achieved through U.N.–supervised elections. He specifically rejected the idea that the United Nations was an "external power" and therefore disqualified from playing any role.

While Park and other South Korean officials gave lip-service to unification, most of them had no intention of permitting the North-South dialogue to proceed very far.[3] What Park appears to have had in mind in entering into the North-South exchanges was a limited deal between dictators in which each would have let the other rule unimpeded in his own domain under the protective cover of a nonaggression agreement and related security arrangements designed to keep the DMZ quiet. Whereas an expanded dialogue and confederation could serve Kim's political purposes by providing a credible means of making progress toward the goal of unification, which was the basic legitimizing raison d'être of his regime, Park's political requirements were different. Park saw certain dangers in a structured process of North-South interchange, because Pyongyang could consciously tailor egalitarian and nationalist appeals to the predilections of Park's opponents. Above all, he was chary of the North's emphasis on mutual force reductions, because the armed forces provided his principal political base and a North-South thaw would jeopardize the privileged position of the military leaders. Although both sides would eventually benefit economically from reduced force levels, Kim had much more to gain because he was confronted with a severe labor shortage. In any event, many of those in the Park camp argued that the North, in stressing force reductions, was merely seeking to induce an artificial relaxation of tensions that would soften the South psychologically, paving the way for political subversion and a subsequent reversion to military pressure.

The South's retreat from the July 4 communiqué was formalized in the proclamation of its "Special Foreign Policy" on June 23, 1973, advocating a two-Koreas approach through the admission of both states to the United Nations and the recognition of Seoul by the Communist powers.[4] North Korea responded with an attack on the southern leaders for "openly revealing their ulterior intention to perpetuate the division."[5] Pyongyang gradually shifted to a new policy, emphasizing bilateral negotiations with the United States to conclude a peace treaty, rather than a resumption of the North-South talks. Seoul, eyeing world opinion, adopted a posture of injured innocence and stressed its readiness for a resumption of negotiations without conditions. Spokesmen for the South indicated their belief that the North would return to the negotiating table when the South had established an overwhelming lead in economic and military capabilities.[6]

By contrast, the North stipulated stiff conditions that appeared to rule out resumption of the dialogue for the foreseeable future. Pyongyang called on Seoul to renounce the "Special Foreign

Policy" and to free all those imprisoned under the Anti-Communist Law.[7] Later, the North added the condition that the Park government must be replaced by a "government committed to human rights and democracy."[8] These conditions undoubtedly reflected, at least in part, Pyongyang's bitterness over what it regarded as Seoul's betrayal of the 1972 agreement. Any future formula for a fruitful North-South dialogue will have to take into account the circumstances surrounding the 1973 rupture.

KOSAKA: It should be noted, however, that there is another way of interpreting the events leading to the suspension of the dialogue in 1973. The foregoing analysis seems to accept Pyongyang's view that the basic cause of the ruptured dialogue was the South's "betrayal" of the July 4 communiqué. This analysis fails to take into account the fact that the actions of both North and South Korea have been dictated less by any deep conviction about how unification can be achieved than by a desire to strengthen their positions vis-à-vis one another. North Korea's proposals for force reductions should be viewed not as a test of Seoul's sincerity about working toward a confederation but as a move that would have worked to the advantage of the North. And it is inaccurate to imply that the South has been unwilling to engage in force reductions mainly because this would threaten the privileges of certain generals. The southerners, with good reason, feel that they cannot show any weakness that might invite a northern attack. In addition, both sides have, over the years, reversed their positions on some of the key issues—such as dual U.N. membership and the desirability of a nonaggression pact. These changes have occurred in response to various international and domestic developments that affect calculations of relative advantage. The central point is that neither side can conceive of unification in terms other than ultimate domination by one side or the other.

While it is indeed clear that Seoul and Pyongyang had dramatically different interpretations of the July 4 communiqué, the fact remains that North Korea broke off the dialogue. Nor can the South's approach of "small things first" be dismissed as intrinsically meaningless or duplicitous. Such an approach, if pursued, might help to ease tensions in modest ways without requiring that essentially irreconcilable issues be confronted directly. And although this approach might well help to preserve two separate Korean states, this would seem to be in accord with reality, because neither side is willing to submit to the other.

Finally, Harrison has mentioned the South's "posture of injured innocence" and the need to take account of the North's feelings of "betrayal." In my opinion, the North's feelings of betrayal probably should be viewed in the same light as the South's injured innocence. One may, in fact, question whether Pyongyang was so naive as to expect the South to participate in a process that would lead to unification on North Korea's terms and to demonstrate its seriousness by agreeing to arms-control moves that would give disproportionate advantage to the North. In the case of both Koreas, the posture of injured innocence should not be taken at face value but should be viewed as a part of the overall competition between the two sides.

WEINSTEIN: It is reasonable to hope that progress on small issues will ease tensions, but two points should be kept in mind. First, the small issues may in some ways be even more difficult and complex than questions related to certain larger issues, such as the confederation proposal. Reunion of families, for example, is more than a simple humanitarian measure. From Pyongyang's standpoint, it may not be entirely unreasonable to question the South's Anti-Communist Law. How would it apply to Communists who go South to visit their families? It seems obvious that such exchanges would increase possibilities for subversion on both sides. Thus, it is not hard to imagine that some of the small steps proposed by the South would actually increase, not ease, tensions. Some social and economic exchanges, even though narrowly defined and "small" in scale, may require more trust than the establishment of a confederation with functions that are largely symbolic.

Second, if we remember that unification and confederation are not the same thing, then one can argue for confederation as an interim step to ease tensions without assuming resolution of the basic issue of whether the North or the South will ultimately prevail. A largely symbolic confederation based on coequality would not resolve the major, seemingly irreconcilable issues that divide North and South. But it could create a framework within which the North, having achieved a de jure one-Korea umbrella, will find it easier to put aside the irreconcilable issues and accept for an indefinite period the de facto division of the peninsula.

HARRISON: In any case, although Pyongyang's feelings of

betrayal should be taken into account, this does not mean that every North Korean pronouncement must be taken at its face value or that a meaningful dialogue must await the replacement of the current South Korean leadership. Given a larger process of diplomatic interchange involving Washington, Pyongyang, Seoul, and possibly others, one can envisage a pattern of trade-offs in which productive North-South talks would take place as a central element of the overall search for accommodation.

WEINSTEIN: In January 1979, Seoul and Pyongyang agreed to resume talks, and on February 18, the first North-South meeting in nearly six years took place at Panmunjom. At that meeting, which was held in a cordial atmosphere, the two sides tentatively agreed to reopen the hot line and to meet again. Subsequent meetings made little progress, and the talks soon faltered, primarily over differences concerning the status of the two delegations. Seoul insisted that all negotiations had to take place between "responsible authorities" of the two sides, and it initially demanded that the South-North Coordinating Committee (SNCC) established during the early 1970s be used. It was clear that the South wanted government-to-government contacts, which would convey implicit North Korean recognition of Seoul's legitimacy. North Korea, however, identified its representatives as a liaison delegation from the Democratic Front for the Unification of the Fatherland (DFUF), which was said to speak for all political and social organizations in the North. In response to the South's objections, the North agreed that its representatives would come as a "liaison delegation of parties, social organizations and authorities" in North Korea; subsequently, the North Koreans referred to their representatives merely as "liaison working-level representatives." The South, for its part, dropped its insistence on the revival of the SNCC, which Pyongyang dismissed as defunct and, in any case, too narrow in scope. At the same time, another set of talks was held in an unsuccessful attempt to create a joint team to participate in the world table-tennis championships held in Pyongyang in late April and early May.

While South Korean leaders saw their exclusion from the table-tennis tournament as further evidence of North Korea's "cold bloodedness" and "madness," the North Koreans made effective use of the opportunity to open their capital to Westerners and to display a conciliatory attitude. Members of the U.S. table-tennis team were told of Pyongyang's desire for cordial relations with the United States. U.N. Secretary-General Kurt Waldheim also visited Korea in early May, stopping in both Pyongyang and Seoul. Although his discussions with Kim and Park were cordial and Waldheim indicated his intention to keep in touch with both sides through their observer delegations at the United Nations, there seemed to be little prospect of any concrete result. Following his departure, the North Koreans continued their efforts to project an image of reasonablesness. Kim Yong-nam, a leading member of the Communist party politburo, gave details of the North's current thinking about reunification, and he emphasized that Western interests in the South would not be affected if, after a period of confederation, North and South Korea were to reunite.[9]

Southern officials were reportedly skeptical about the North's intentions in launching its "offensive of reasonableness." They took the position that North Korea's decision to open a new round of dialogue was a disingenuous move that represented no basic change in Pyongyang's attitudes or strategies. Seoul suspected that the talks were aimed at creating an image of flexibility and moderation in order to lure the United States into bilateral talks and to encourage implementation of the U.S. troop-withdrawal plan. Still, some reports indicated that the South Korean government had come to the conclusion that Pyongyang, for whatever reasons, was genuinely interested in talking with the South. Although there was agreement that the initial round of meetings had proved sterile, some observers in Seoul felt that the North Koreans might be working toward new proposals aimed at easing tensions.[10]

In May and June 1979, both Kim Yong-nam and Foreign Minister Ho Dam indicated a possible shift in Pyongyang's attitude toward the idea of three-sided talks involving the United States and the two Korean governments. The North Koreans were apparently prepared to accept South Korean participation in talks *after* North Korea had entered into negotiations with the United States "to settle differences."[11] Pyongyang contended that it had to talk first to the United States because Seoul had not been a signatory to the 1953 armistice. In Ho Dam's words: "If South Korean authorities radically change their stand on reunification, not division, it may be taken into consideration to accept the form of tripartite talks by letting them attend our talks with the United

States when these reach a definite stage."[12] The foreign minister's statement makes it clear that Pyongyang's acceptance of three-sided talks was heavily qualified.

In early July, during President Carter's visit to Seoul, he and President Park jointly proposed three-way talks among U.S., North Korean, and South Korean officials to discuss ways of reducing tensions on the peninsula. They also proposed the admission of both Koreas to the United Nations pending the start of negotiations that could lead to reunification. While there were unofficial reports that Pyongyang had encouraged the proposal, the North Koreans rejected it as nothing new. In fact, the South Koreans had been known to be unenthusiastic about three-sided talks, and it reportedly took some persuasion to convince Park to join in making the proposal.[13] On the other hand, as Kamiya has noted, the 1979 proposal for three-sided talks did not seem to differ significantly from a proposal advanced by Secretary of State Kissinger in 1976. Furthermore, the linking of the new proposal in the same communiqué with a call for the admission of both Koreas to the United Nations suggested that the move might have been calculated to elicit a negative response from Pyongyang, aimed at reinforcing the latter's image as recalcitrant.

WHITING: It is no mere coincidence that the second round of North-South talks began shortly after the normalization of U.S.-China relations was announced, just as the first round had come in 1971 in the wake of Henry Kissinger's secret trip to Peking, which foreshadowed President Nixon's 1972 visit. Both Seoul and Pyongyang are sensitive to changes in U.S.-China relations. They must hedge against the possibility of being compromised by their powerful patrons in tacit or explicit agreements on a wide range of matters, extending from limitations on military aid to a virtual settlement of Korean affairs.

At the very least, they feel pressed, directly or indirectly, to adopt postures that parallel those of their patrons. For instance, Pyongyang initially greeted the announcement of President Nixon's 1972 trip to Peking with derision, claiming he would bear "the white flag of surrender." After a visit from Premier Chou En-lai, however, North Korean propaganda was muted. Meanwhile, Pyongyang began a dialogue with Seoul. The public announcement of new Chinese aid was probably accompanied by private Chinese remonstrations, a combination that persuaded

Kim Il-sung to change his posture.

The linkage between Peking-Washington relations and Seoul-Pyongyang relations provided a propitious setting for the resumption of the North-South dialogue in early 1979. Its role was even more evident in 1979 than in 1971–1972 because Peking had gone much further in softening its line on Taiwan, thereby inviting—although not compelling—a parallel move by Pyongyang.

The future impact of this linkage on developments in Korea is impossible to predict. The two situations are far from analogous. But it is worth noting that Peking has stressed travel, trade, and family contacts between the mainland and Taiwan. This could make it easier for Kim to accept Seoul's proposals for initiating negotiations on smaller, less sensitive matters, rather than beginning with more far-reaching and difficult problems like the establishment of a unified governmental structure.

In fact, one can envisage an informal modus vivendi between the North and South similar to that which has long existed in the Taiwan Strait. According to this scenario, hostile contact and confrontation would be replaced by a genuine cease-fire and cooperation. Rather than seizing ships and firing on border violations, the Koreans would render assistance to fishermen in distress and vessels that inadvertently stray across specific boundaries. This pattern has prevailed around the offshore islands of Quemoy and Matsu, and it might serve as a model for the Korean peninsula.

But such developments are likely to stop far short of the demands of Pyongyang and Seoul, which will remain fundamental obstacles to any overall settlement of the Korean problem. Each side insists that it is the one de jure sovereign state on the peninsula. Each insists that unification must be the ultimate goal of the Korean people. Each defines the other as an enemy lacking legitimacy and popular support. And each seeks to justify authoritarian rule as necessary to guard against attack from across the DMZ. In the past, these uncompromising positions reflected not only the mutually incompatible socioeconomic systems and political ideologies of the two Koreas but also the personal interests of Kim and Park in perpetuating confrontation and preventing final accommodation. Whether South Korea's new leaders will have a greater interest in accommodation remains to be seen.

KAMIYA: Whiting is quite correct in pointing out that the sources of conflict between the two Koreas are complex and deep-rooted. At the same time, the continued tension on the Korean peninsula seems increasingly anomalous in the spreading atmosphere of East-West détente in Asia. Korea is now the only place in Asia where tensions between East and West remain high. The question is how the Koreans can break out of the confrontational postures into which they seem to have become frozen.

Some people, including Richard Holbrook, assistant secretary of state for East Asia and the Pacific, advocate a gradual resolution of the problem through step-by-step communication between the two Koreas. I frankly doubt that such a firmly established confrontational relationship can be altered through an incremental approach. It is easier to bring about such a dramatic change in a single stroke, through a summit meeting. For example, Kissinger's secret meeting with Chou En-lai, leading to the 1972 U.S.–China summit meeting, and President Sadat's lightning visit to Israel in 1977 were spectacular moves that played an essential role in making possible the rapid transformation of relationships from hostility to cooperation. I believe that the top leaders of South and North Korea should meet to discuss the future of Korea and East Asia with as broad and open-minded a view as possible. When Carter and Park proposed three-sided talks with Pyongyang in July 1979, it was predictable that the North Koreans would reject this overture, but I was hopeful that it might help prepare the way for a Kim-Park summit meeting. Of course, it will be difficult to find workable solutions, but a step as dramatic as a summit meeting may be necessary if there is to be any chance of progress. Once this process starts, the United States may be able to contribute to it by playing a mediating role between the two Koreas, as it did between Egypt and Israel.

WEINSTEIN: In mid-1979 North Korea did indicate a willingness to meet with Park, but, as in the case of the abortive contacts earlier in the year, there were certain ambiguities about status. In late June 1979, a statement on the subject issued by the official Korean Central News Agency (KCNA) was broadcast over Pyongyang radio. It declared that the KCNA had been authorized to state that "we are always ready to meet not only the president of the New Democratic party [presumably a reference to Kim Young-sam's offer to meet personally with Kim Il-sung] but also the president of the Democratic Republic party [Park's party], if he wants it, and meet representatives of any political party or organization, persons in authority or individual personages in South Korea for the reunification of the country." The statement did not make clear whether the North Korean representative would be Kim Il-sung. Nor was it known whether the North Koreans would meet with Park as a "person in authority" rather than as a mere party leader.

Pyongyang took its most unambiguous step toward a revived dialogue in January 1980 when it agreed to deal with Seoul on a government-to-government basis. Up to that time, North Korea's reaction to the Park assassination had consisted mainly of exhortations to South Korean intellectuals and political leaders to demand a rapid dismantling of Park's Yushin constitution. In his New Year's address, Kim Il-sung had urged North Koreans to heighten their readiness for war. Then, on January 12, North Korean Prime Minister Li Chong-ok proposed a face-to-face meeting with his South Korean counterpart for an "unreserved exchange of views" on Korean reunification. Li's letter, addressed to Prime Minister Shin Hyon-hwak, referred to South Korea as the Republic of Korea for the first time. Roughly two weeks later, Seoul accepted this proposal, addressing North Korea for the first time as the Democratic People's Republic of Korea. Seoul suggested that officials of the two sides begin meeting in February to prepare procedural matters. A second North Korean proposal, calling for "a comprehensive political consultative conference" involving representatives of general and political organizations, was rejected by Seoul on the grounds that it seemed designed merely to bring out political differences within the South.[14]

North Korea's motivation in putting forth a conciliatory proposal was, of course, difficult to fathom. Some South Koreans suspected that the underlying purpose was to sow confusion in the South at a time when the elements of the post-Park political system were still being worked out. They feared that Pyongyang, known to be seeking new contacts in the West, might also be seeking to isolate South Korea from the United States. But they also noted that the North Korean move could be a sign that Pyongyang was moving toward recognition of the South's political legitimacy. There was added reason to be hopeful when, in February 1980, the vice-chairman of a North Korean citizens association in Tokyo, who usually reflects Pyongyang's thinking, indicated that North Korea might agree to a series of economic and cultural exchanges with the South before attempting to achieve political unification. He added that the North was willing to pursue official talks for some time even in the absence of the broader-based discussions it was demanding. According to the vice-chairman, Pyongyang's attitude had changed because of Park's removal.[15] But most South Korean observers remained skeptical about the prospects for real progress in the North-South dialogue.

What Initiatives Might the United States Take to Improve the Prospects for Détente in Korea?

HARRISON: How might the larger process of diplomatic interchange concerning Korea be initiated? Washington has consistently reaffirmed its blanket support for the South Korean approach to the normalization of Seoul-Pyongyang relations. The United States has called on Pyongyang to resume the North-South dialogue without conditions and has pledged that the United States "would not enter into any negotiations on the future of Korea with North Korea without the participation of the Republic of Korea."[16] In recent years, however, scattered voices in the United States have begun to question this blanket opposition to bilateral Washington-Pyongyang contacts. Senator George McGovern and former Representative Helen Meyner, among others, have made general references to the desirability of U.S. contacts with the North.[17] Specific proposals have been suggested by a number of writers, including Robert Shaplen and Gareth Porter.[18]

WEINSTEIN: The suspension of the troop-withdrawal program, a move that has been enthusiastically received in Seoul, may have strengthened the case for Washington's taking a more active role in negotiations to ease tensions on the Korean peninsula. With Seoul now "reassured" by the suspension of the withdrawal, the United States may not need to be so concerned that a diplomatic initiative would unsettle the South Koreans. Congressman Les Aspin, in a June 1979 statement endorsing a suspension of the troop withdrawals, urged that the United States "recognize the political value of its military presence and encourage serious military and political negotiations" between the two Koreas. "Until now," Aspin noted,

the United States has allowed the ROK to dominate all consideration of negotiations and to establish the terms under which they
would proceed. The ROK refuses even to consider military talks,
although the North Koreans (whether sincerely or for propaganda
purposes) have offered several proposals in recent years. This situation should be changed. The United States should not allow its
foreign policy options to be determined by a country it is sup-
posedly protecting. It should take the initiative instead.

Aspin concluded by asserting that "Japan's much-noted objections to the troop withdrawal plan focused not so much on the
withdrawal itself as on the absence of any attempt to couple
the plan with negotiations toward a settlement on the Korean
peninsula." U.S. troops should be withdrawn eventually, he
argued, but the United States should first move to create a political context in which they could be withdrawn purposefully.[19]

HARRISON: There are a number of ways in which the
United States might contribute to the easing of tensions between the two Koreas. One might be to begin by recognizing
that a nonaggression treaty between the two sides, an important step toward a relaxation of tensions, will probably be
possible only if the South makes a serious response to Pyongyang's proposals for balanced force reductions. If the United
States links its arms sales to arms-control policies in Korea, then
it is possible that the conclusion of a U.S.–D.P.R.K. peace treaty,
as demanded by the North, could be used to facilitate a North-
South nonaggression treaty, long sought by the South. One can
envisage such a result through the following scenario.

As a first step, the United States could agree without
conditions to enter into bilateral talks with the North on a
peace or nonaggression treaty, in response to proposals that
Pyongyang has been making since 1974. The *conclusion* of
such a treaty, however, would be contingent on the North's
willingness to (1) join in reactivating the North-South Coordinating Committee and the Red Cross talks *without conditions* and (2) conclude a nonaggression or peace treaty with
the South (proposed by Park in January 1974) as an adjunct
to the North-South dialogue, provided that the South agrees
to link such negotiations with parallel negotiations on mutual
force reductions.

Should Seoul so desire, the United States could arrange for the South to have observer status at its negotiations with the North. Pyongyang has indicated informally that this would be acceptable. Before announcing its intention to accept the North's proposal for bilateral talks, Washington could give Seoul several months' advance notice. Thus, Seoul would have an opportunity to make suggestions but not to exercise a veto over the U.S. negotiating posture. The principal purpose of consulting with the South would be to make clear that the United States sees mutual force reductions not only as desirable in themselves but as an appropriate quid pro quo for northern agreement to negotiate the nonaggression agreement long advocated by the South. Washington might urge Seoul to develop a positive bargaining posture on the force-reduction issue, including specific proposals for inspection. In addition, Washington could make clear that future U.S. arms-sales policies would be governed by Seoul's response. Should Seoul refuse to enter into negotiations on mutual force reductions, the United States could suspend new arms-sales agreements. Such a line would be a natural concomitant to the continuance of U.S. obligations to the South under the security treaty. The rationale for arms sales is that they reduce the risk of a war in which the United States might become involved, and this rationale would be directly undercut if these sales were perceived as supporting unnecessarily high force levels that increase the danger of conflict.

Under this scenario, both the North and South would be pressed to modify the positions taken at the time of the 1973 rupture. Thus, while calling on Seoul to negotiate with the North on force reductions, the United States, by proposing an *unconditional* resumption of the dialogue, would also be implicitly prodding Pyongyang to couple negotiations on military matters with parallel talks on smaller issues. Among the issues that would lend themselves to early consideration might be postal, athletic, and cultural exchanges. In pressing for "small things first," the South has also urged family exchanges. As Rinn-sup Shinn has pointed out, however, such exchanges would not be a small matter for the North, given the large number of South Koreans of northern origin. For the South to push this issue would only arouse suspicions in the North that Seoul has subversive intentions.[20] Similarly, the South is suspicious of the North's intentions in pressing for contacts between nongovernmental groups, such as the "political parties and social organizations" envisaged in the North's recurring proposals for a "political consultative conference." Seoul alleges that the North has already attempted to get recognition of "fictitious" or "dummy" groups, contending that the groups in question operate underground in the South.[21]

It would be undesirable for the United States to link the timing of future force withdrawals directly to its agreement on a peace treaty with the North. It should be sufficient for Washington to indicate to Pyongyang that it intends to withdraw Korea-earmarked air force units to Pacific-based carriers at a time of its own choosing, following the withdrawal of ground forces. In other words, the United States would be asking Pyongyang to sign a nonaggression agreement with the South, based on a U.S. agreement in principle to withdraw its forces thereafter, but without any formal assurance as to when those forces would be removed. In this connection, an essential element of the proposed U.S.–D.P.R.K. peace treaty would be a mutual nonaggression pledge.

Kim Il-sung has told Tokuma Utsonomiya, "If we do sign a peace treaty with the United States, I will guarantee that we will not advance southward. But the United States would also have to guarantee it will not advance northward."[22] Here it should be recalled that Kim has shown flexibility regarding the timing of U.S. force withdrawals in relation to force reductions and a nonaggression pact. In my 1972 interview with Kim, and in other statements by him at that time, he proposed that as a first step the North and South meet to demilitarize the buffer zone along the Panmunjom armistice line and reduce the armed forces of both sides *by* 150,000 to 200,000 men. This was to be followed by a "no war" agreement and, finally, by the completion of U.S. force withdrawals, which would then set the stage for full-scale force reductions *to* parallel levels of 100,000 men on both sides.[23] In his 1974 meetings with Tokuma Utsonomiya, however, Kim gave priority to bilateral talks with the United States and said that a peace treaty should be followed first by the withdrawal of U.S. troops from the peninsula and then by a North-South nonaggression agreement.

In talks with the North, the United States could appropriately seek to hold Kim to his 1972 formulation. Washington could argue that a bilateral Washington-Pyongyang peace treaty, containing an explicit U.S. nonaggression pledge, would give the North a measure of security not contemplated in Kim's 1972 proposal. It could be argued that, coupled with a volte-face by Seoul on the issue of force reductions, this would merit a reciprocal move by Pyongyang to reassure Seoul in the form of a nonaggression or peace treaty.

Besides initiating talks with the North, the United States could take other steps to improve relations with Pyongyang and improve the negotiating climate. The United States could liberalize visa regulations to permit expanded journalistic, cultural, and commercial contacts and freer movement of North Korean officials within the United States. A logical next step would be the establishment of liaison and trade offices. Full diplomatic relations, however, might have to be deferred for some time, since an asymmetrical situation in which only Pyongyang is recognized by both Communist and non-Communist powers would lead to a destructive mood of insecurity in the South. Although informal contacts may be developed, the establishment of full diplomatic relations is likely to be possible only in the context of a confederation or some other arrangement that would facilitate cross-recognition beneath a de jure one-Korea umbrella.

Although the terms of such an arrangement would have to be worked out by the two Korean entities themselves, the United States—and Japan—could facilitate the process by defining an overall Korea policy that recognizes the long-term goal of unification as an integral part of efforts to stabilize North-South relations. Washington and Tokyo thus might encourage Seoul to propose a timetable for steps toward confederation over a period of, say, ten to fifteen years. This could include, in the interim, North-South agreements dealing with force reductions, family exchanges, trade, and, above all, coordination of foreign economic and diplomatic policies, as proposed by Kim Dae-jung. The United States and Japan could also lend their support to some form of U.N. representation— perhaps along the lines suggested by Glenn Paige—that would symbolize the Korean commitment to unification.

WEINSTEIN: The above speculations about possible U.S. actions to foster détente on the peninsula raise some fundamental questions concerning linkages between the role of external powers and that of the two Koreas. Even though Harrison acknowledges that ultimate responsibility rests with the Koreans, the scenario just sketched involves the United States in the process in a most direct way—using its leverage to press South Korea to adopt a particular position in negotiations with the North. A central issue here is whether such a role is appropriate.

KOSAKA: Indeed, there seems to be an underlying assumption in the preceding discussion that it is essential for the United States to do something to stabilize the Korean situation. It almost seems as if we are searching for diplomatic moves acceptable to North Korea merely for the sake of doing something. But it is not imperative for us to make a diplomatic move in Korea, if there is no good move to make. A realistic assessment of the situation suggests that there is really little the United States or Japan can contribute at this point.

We must begin by recognizing the existence of a set of impasses. Seoul and Pyongyang are basically at odds on questions of cross-recognition, confederation, force reductions, and other issues. So long as the two Koreas take such dramatically different approaches on the key issues, there is no way for the United States and Japan to change this. The situation of "two Koreas de facto but not de jure" is likely to persist for some time. The USSR is much wiser in saying that the question of Korean unification is one of the two problems in Northeast Asia that will not be settled during this century. Only the long process of history will decide the fate of the peninsula—either in the direction of one Korea, of de jure two Koreas, or of a legally unstable but politically stable situation in which tensions are reduced and the danger of conflict recedes even though the status of the two Korean entities remains unresolved.

The problem lies not so much in the particular nature of Harrison's scenario, although it is very unbalanced in its treatment of the two Koreas, as will be discussed later. A more fundamental problem is that it is simply inappropriate for the United States to determine and then to press for a particular solution to the Korean problem. Why should outsiders make efforts to force North and South Korea to pursue talks if the Koreans themselves are not eager to do so? My opinion, therefore, is that we should not make proposals as to how the two Koreas should get together.

This does not mean that there is no role for outsiders. The real problem for us is to reconsider the policy of insisting on cross-recognition or nothing at all. My premise is that only the Koreans, not the United States or Japan, can stabilize the situation legally, but the United States and Japan are restraining factors. In particular, the United States plays an important role in preventing the military unification of the country. This leaves little room for maneuvering. Perhaps the only feasible approach is to aim at the third possibility mentioned above—to seek a stable political situation even though the legal situation remains ambiguous.

Because of the U.S. role in preventing a military solution to the Korean problem, great caution must be exercised with respect to any U.S. initiatives. A U.S. overture to Pyongyang will have a much larger impact than a Japanese move. To put it simply, since the "American card" is much more powerful than the "Japanese card" vis-à-vis North Korea, it should be played very carefully. Any initiative must be thought through fully. Negotiations are not, in themselves, necessarily a good thing. It is essential to have a clear idea about matters of substance before negotiations are begun. For example, a peace treaty or nonaggression agreement between the United States and North Korea is not necessarily a bad idea. But what would be the substance of such a treaty? No one presumes that North Korea will ever attack the United States; the only country North Korea threatens is South Korea. Therefore, a simple bilateral nonaggression treaty is meaningless. Can North Korea pledge not to use force against South Korea? This would amount to a nonaggression treaty between North and South Korea. Harrison's scenario does aim at producing such a result, but is it wise to attempt this by pressing the South to accept force reductions that Seoul feels would jeopardize its security?

HARRISON: With respect to the role of outsiders, the position of the United States is quite different from that of Japan, since the United States continues to incur the risks arising from security obligations on the peninsula, while Japan eschews such obligations and risks. Since the United States is already playing a role in Korea in the security sphere, why is it barred from playing a role in the diplomatic and arms-control spheres? In order to minimize its risks, the United States could appropriately integrate its diplomatic and arms-control policies with its security policies to assure that its military presence and arms sales do not freeze, or even increase, North-South tensions.

The scenario I have described would not condition arms sales to Seoul on the adoption of any particular formula for mutual force reductions, but rather on a willingness to explore whether Pyongyang is, in fact, prepared for balanced force reductions accompanied by meaningful verification and inspection procedures.

Even if such a process of exploration should fail to produce results in the years immediately ahead, as seems likely, a readiness on the part of the South to enter into serious negotiations on this issue would test the North's intentions and could do much to improve the overall North-South climate.

OKIMOTO: Let us consider, however, the asymmetrical impact of the proposed scenario. North Korea would reap considerable advantages, including:

1. a peace treaty with the United States, which would be tantamount to de facto diplomatic recognition, without similar recognition of South Korea by the Communist powers
2. a U.S. commitment in principle to withdraw all of its armed forces
3. a guarantee that South Korea would either yield to Pyongyang's demand for force-reduction negotiations or face a suspension of U.S. arms sales
4. the introduction of new strains into the Washington-Seoul relationship as a result of U.S. abandonment of its previous pledge not to deal unilaterally with Pyongyang.

In contrast, South Korea would have relatively little to gain. Given the basic differences between the two sides, it is open to question whether the proposed North-South negotiations would make any progress. A nonaggression pledge by the North could represent a major breakthrough if undertaken in good faith. But, if the agreement fails to include sanctions for noncompliance, such a pledge could also prove worthless. It is not clear that the advantages of such an agreement would sufficiently offset the dangers created by forcing Seoul into force-reduction negotiations with the North. Pyongyang's proposals are excessively ambiguous. A reduction in the number of troops by 150,000 to 200,000 may seem desirable on the surface, since both sides maintain force levels far in excess of desirable thresholds. But the proposal is almost impossible to evaluate seriously without knowing such specifics as the types of forces to be cut, how reductions would be verified, and the impact of these reductions on the overall balance of power. From an economic standpoint, both sides would benefit from force reductions, but the North would gain a disproportionate advantage because it bears a heavier burden and has a weaker economy.

WHITING: What about the possibility that the United States might go beyond a peace treaty and extend recognition to North Korea in exchange for the latter's pledge not to use force as a means of reunifying Korea? If the United States makes such an offer, Kim might accept, conditioning his response on the withdrawal of U.S. military forces from the South. He has already made "peaceful" reunification litany in all statements from Pyongyang, thereby permitting Peking to echo its support. A further step in this direction would be relatively costless, especially since it has no additional sanctions in the event of noncompliance, beyond those already in effect with the U.S. treaty commitment. This would be a major step toward formalizing the status quo but would probably be viewed differently in Seoul and Pyongyang, depending on what other countries, as well as the United States, did at the time.

Assuming that Washington's recognition of Pyongyang is not accompanied by any reciprocal move by Moscow and Peking toward Seoul, Pyongyang will likely seek to exploit the U.S. move to Seoul's disadvantage. Seoul would initially see it this way. The extent to which the South Korean reaction would be destabilizing would depend on how Tokyo and Washington compensated Seoul via economic and political means. An initial wave of demonstrations against both the United States and Japan, officially sponsored but not so acknowledged, might be followed by shrewd exploitation of the situation for greater concessions and assurances. Beyond this, however, it is difficult to envisage any serious break in relations.

WEINSTEIN: There is an important distinction between the two scenarios discussed here. The Harrison scenario seeks to draw North Korea into serious talks with the South by pressing Seoul into concessions on the force-reduction issue. The second scenario—trading a diplomatic approach to Pyongyang for the latter's pledge of nonaggression against the South—does not seek to force any policy change on Seoul. The second scenario promises to yield a pledge of nonaggression by Pyongyang without any concession on the part of Seoul. But the North's pledge is to the United States, not to South Korea, meaning that North Korea would not have to go as far toward recognizing the legitimacy of the South. Nevertheless, as Kosaka suggested, such a pledge of nonaggression against the South, even if made to the United States, would, in fact, amount to a nonaggression treaty between North and South. The essential difference, then, is that the former approach involves a direct intervention by the United States into North-South relations, with Washington pressing Seoul to undertake arms-control negotiations with Pyongyang, while the latter involves only the U.S.–D.P.R.K. relationship, which is clearly a proper matter for U.S. initiative.

It may well be, as Kosaka suggested, that a North Korean pledge of nonaggression against the South, even if made to the United States rather than to Seoul, would be useful if it could be obtained without forcing the South Koreans into any unwanted policy changes. It would by no means solve the Korean problem, but it could help to ease tensions and add to the stability of the situation. It may not be necessary to establish diplomatic relations with North Korea to gain such a pledge. There is evidence that the North Koreans might be willing to make a nonaggression pledge in exchange for a peace agreement with the United States, though they might seek to impose some unacceptable conditions. The latter, however, could be resisted.

The North Korean position was sketched out in my July 1978 interview with Choe U Gyun and Kim Myong-chol, who insisted they were speaking for Pyongyang. They indicated North Korea's intense interest in talks with the United States that would focus on two issues: (1) a peace agreement to replace the present armistice agreement and (2) a North Korean pledge of nonaggression against the South, as a basis for discussing the withdrawal of U.S. forces from Korea and a future prohibition against the introduction of any new foreign weapons into the peninsula. They asserted North Korea's readiness to provide written assurance to the United States that it would never attack South Korea—not before the completion of the U.S. withdrawal and not after. They indicated an awareness that a U.S. withdrawal, for which no time period was specified, would require assurances of nonaggression from the North. They also said that they expected the United States to insist on the reinforcement of local forces to fill the vacuum created by the departing U.S. forces.

It is clear that the United States is in no position to make any concrete pledges concerning the time when U.S. forces will be withdrawn and the time when it might be feasible to prohibit further arms transfers to the peninsula. But the United States might consider making a pledge that expresses agreement in principle to the eventual withdrawal of all U.S. forces. This could be accompanied by a unilateral U.S. statement that the pace of withdrawals will be determined by the United States, in consultation with Seoul, based on Washington's assessment of the military balance between North and South.

This approach, in effect, would involve two sets of exchanges. A North Korean pledge of nonaggression against the South would be traded for U.S. acquiescence to a peace agreement with Pyongyang. Secondly, in exchange for a U.S. pledge to eventually withdraw its military forces, North Korea would implicitly accept the U.S. right to keep those forces there until the military balance permits their withdrawal. This scenario seems to provide a reasonably balanced exchange. But it remains to be seen whether the two Korean governments would see it that way.

MOMOI: My only concern with this approach relates to the ability of the United States to reintroduce its forces into South Korea. It is important that a U.S. agreement in principle to withdraw its forces not be construed as prohibiting the return of U.S. troops, if conditions on the peninsula require it. To be sure, there is nothing in the proposed scenario to prevent the United States from reintroducing its forces, should Washington decide that this is necessary to maintain the military balance or to deter an imminent North Korean threat. It may be awkward for the United States to assert that right explicitly as part of the agreement with North Korea, but it is essential that Washington and Seoul understand clearly that the pledge of eventual withdrawal does not preclude an increase in the number of U.S. forces if the circumstances so require.

KOSAKA: Some would argue that a major liability of this scenario is the legitimacy it might give to the North Koreans. But even if the United States, in negotiating directly with Pyongyang, does convey a certain measure of legitimacy to the North Korean government, this need not be viewed as undesirable. It is better that the North Koreans attach value to that kind of legitimacy than to other things. Of course, it would be preferable to have a nonaggression pact concluded between Seoul and Pyongyang, but a pledge made to the United States is better than nothing.

SAEKI: It is very important, however, that the South Korean government be consulted prior to the undertaking of any such initiative vis-à-vis Pyongyang. A serious attempt should be made to persuade the South Koreans that their interests are being safeguarded. It is not necessary that such an effort be successful, but it is essential to try.

ROWEN: I would go further. The United States should not make any approach to North Korea unless the Seoul government agrees. It is inappropriate for the United States to undertake negotiations with Pyongyang if Seoul objects. The United States has a mutual security treaty with the South, and it is inconsistent with that relationship for Washington to negotiate with Pyongyang over the objections of South Korea. If both Seoul and Tokyo approve of the proposed U.S. initiative, then it is all right to proceed.

WEINSTEIN: We must recognize, of course, that on the part of the U.S. government, there has been a notable lack of enthusiasm for any sort of diplomatic initiative vis-à-vis North Korea. This may change, for the Sino-Japanese peace treaty and the normalization of U.S.–China relations have set in motion changes that may, in time, affect the way the United States perceives the Korean question. But, as of late 1979, there was impressive resistance in Washington to any sort of approach to Pyongyang. U.S. officials have tended to regard diplomatic approaches to Pyongyang that are tied to the latter's pledge of nonaggression against the South as not particularly promising. This is due to the fact that the North Koreans have reiterated on numerous occasions their lack of any intention to use force in resolving their differences with the South. Therefore, a pledge of nonaggression against the South might be regarded by Seoul as nothing new and thus of little value as "compensation" for a U.S. move toward contacts with Pyongyang.

There is currently a general mood that the last several years have been an inauspicious time for any U.S. initiatives vis-à-vis North Korea, given the South's uneasiness about the Carter administration's troop-withdrawal plan. As a result, the added benefits of a formal, written North Korean pledge of nonaggression have not been seriously considered. As one Senate staff member stated: "We are already doing enough to the South Koreans." Some State Department officials have predicted that any Washington-Pyongyang contacts would have a "disastrous" effect on Seoul and Tokyo; the Japanese government was said to have made this clear. Most of those interviewed in Washington held to the position that contacts with North Korea would have little utility unless South Korea were allowed to participate. It is possible, however, that the suspension of the U.S. troop withdrawals may make it easier to build support for a diplomatic approach to North Korea.

Even when the implementation of President Carter's original troop-withdrawal plan was considered likely, a minority on Capitol Hill was prepared to contemplate seriously an overture toward Pyongyang. They pointed out that North Korea seemed quite receptive and, indeed, had been actively seeking such contacts for some time. It is generally known that President Carter communicated with Kim Il-sung via President Tito of Yugoslavia, who presented a diplomatic feeler from Pyongyang during his March 1978 meeting with Carter in Washington. Rumanian Communist party chief Nicolae Ceausescu was said to have carried a similar message to Washington in April 1978. According to Western officials, North Korea has sought direct contact with the United States on at least three occasions since Mr. Carter's election, twice through the Pakistani government and once in a letter sent directly to Plains, Georgia, shortly before the inauguration.[24] Senator McGovern has publicly proposed a diplomatic approach to Pyongyang, arguing that this could in no way jeopardize either South Korean or Japanese security interests. A Republican source in the House asserted that the acceptability of any U.S. approach to the North would depend on who made it. If the administration undertook such a move, Congress would "scream." But an exploratory mission composed of a centrist, bipartisan congressional delegation might be able to play a useful role. Even some individuals who strongly support South Korea might be willing to go on such a mission, which would be undertaken with the understanding that Seoul would be kept fully informed of the discussions. A Senate source, on the other hand, questioned the wisdom of sending an "underinformed" delegation of legislators, and proposed that some outsider—a man of the stature of Clark Clifford (but not Clifford himself, who was viewed as too close to the administration)—might be sent to Pyongyang.

But the overwhelming feeling in Washington has been that nothing should be done for the time being. There is strong evidence of an extraordinary residue of bitterness toward North Korea among the U.S. populace as a result of the war—a bitterness that has been reinforced by such incidents as the seizure of the Pueblo and the murder in 1976 of U.S. officers supervising the trimming of a poplar tree in the DMZ. Former Congresswoman Meyner noted that any initiative toward North Korea would be highly controversial because so many Americans still regard the North Koreans with enormous suspicion and hostility. And State Department officials were dubious about the suggestion that Pyongyang's economic distress might move the North to make concessions.

My own view is that the United States ought to think beyond a peace agreement to the gradual establishment of diplomatic relations with Pyongyang. Clearly, this will take time. A peace agreement and a North Korean nonaggression pledge would be an appropriate first step; diplomatic relations could be considered afterward. There is also a strong case, to be discussed later, for Japan's taking the lead in developing ties with Pyongyang. But it is important, in my judgment, that Washington consider a progression of steps leading toward a diplomatic relationship with the North.

Although cross-recognition, in which the Communist powers would establish relations with Seoul at the same time as the United States establishes relations with Pyongyang, would be the preferred course, it is not necessarily wise for Washington to wait for Moscow and Peking to act before taking this step. It is quite possible that Moscow and Peking will accord recognition to Seoul after Tokyo and Washington have taken the lead by establishing ties with Pyongyang, and after the latter has had a chance to savor its propaganda "victory." The Soviets already have fragmentary unofficial relations with South Korea. And as Peking's relations with Washington and Tokyo develop further, it may find its relations with Pyongyang cooling to the point that some move toward Seoul might not be out of the question. In any case, one can question whether Pyongyang's propaganda victory would have any real effect on the Korean balance.

The central point here is that, even in the absence of reciprocity, steps toward the establishment of relations with North Korea need not be narrowly viewed as a concession to the Communists that must be balanced by some concession on their part. As will be discussed later, economic and diplomatic ties with Pyongyang are useful in themselves for both sides. The promised

benefits are not significantly diminished by the absence of reciprocal relationships between the Communist powers and Seoul. While
the South Koreans would probably react with alarm to any U.S.
move to deal with Pyongyang in the absence of Seoul's representatives, there is little justification for such concern. Even South
Korean leaders privately admit that they would derive some benefit from U.S. or Japanese ties with Pyongyang. Most important,
it is likely that these relations, if developed to any significant extent, would serve in some measure as a restraining influence on
Pyongyang. In any case, there is no reason to assume that U.S.
or Japanese ties with Pyongyang would lead to any diminution in
relations that they or other countries maintain with the South. No
country is going to break relations with Seoul because it has established them with Pyongyang; Seoul's position is in no way analogous to that of Taipei. There is no danger that South Korea will
find itself isolated.

How Would U.S. Troop Withdrawals Affect the Prospects for North-South Negotiations?

In considering possible U.S. moves to ease tensions on the
peninsula, the withdrawal of U.S. military forces deserves some
attention. As already noted, some officials have contended that
because they make the South Koreans uneasy, U.S. troop withdrawals would make it harder for Washington to undertake any
overtures toward Pyongyang aimed at easing tensions. The assumption is that troop withdrawals represent a concession to the North
and that any moves toward Pyongyang would only compound the
asymmetry. This perception of northern advantage, it is alleged,
would raise tensions by stimulating new fears that the North
would be emboldened to attack. There are two dimensions to the
question: (1) what effect would U.S. troop withdrawals have on
North Korea's willingness to negotiate with the South? (2) how
would such withdrawals affect the self-confidence of the South
Koreans?

HARRISON: The North has often cited the presence of U.S.
forces as justification for refusing to deal with the South and, in
particular, for deferring the conclusion of a nonaggression agreement with Seoul.[25] Pyongyang has pointed to the U.S. forces
as proof that Seoul is a U.S. puppet, arguing that serious North-

South discussions cannot take place until the departure of U.S. forces and the concomitant removal of the U.N. Command's control over South Korean forces. In the North's view, the South Korean government is artificially emboldened by its U.S. military links. It is propped up by a structure of direct and indirect subsidies that ultimately rest on the economic and psychological foundations provided by the U.S. presence. Once these props are removed, Pyongyang believes, gradual political and economic changes will occur in the South, leading to a more conciliatory posture toward the North. Against this background, the withdrawal of U.S. military forces would probably increase the North's willingness to negotiate by removing one of its principal past excuses for refusing to enter into negotiations. But the North's attitude would not depend on the removal of the U.S. presence as such. It might not be affected much at all if the United States continued to maintain direct or indirect military aid at past levels and continued to refuse the North's overtures for bilateral contacts.

WHITING: It should be noted, of course, that the ending of the U.S. military presence on the peninsula lies beyond the terms of President Carter's original withdrawal plan and in time lies well beyond 1982. It cannot be systematically discussed without considering the attitudes of the political leadership in Seoul and Pyongyang that will be prevailing at that time. Assuming that the U.S. treaty commitment remains, the self-confidence of the South would not be irreparably damaged by the ending of the U.S. presence, especially if South Korea's economy continues to provide reasonably full employment and the expectation of a continued rise in living standards. While the North's willingness to negotiate would be superficially affected by the U.S. departure, the determining factor would be Pyongyang's assessment of gain and loss through negotiations, as opposed to confrontation. Key variables in this regard would be the economic benefit, the perceived state of the South in terms of prospective tensions, the military balance and the trend of military expenditures on the peninsula, and the domestic politics of negotiation versus confrontation. The state of these variables cannot be forecast for situations eight to ten years hence. And, in addition, the susceptibility of the North and South to pressure and persuasion by patron regimes cannot be predicted that far in advance. Much will depend on the relative economic interdependency or self-reliance of each side.

A mutual decoupling of treaty commitments to the two Koreas is a very long-term development the prospects of which depend on many prior changes in the situation, most of which have been alluded to above. It would also probably require multilateral understandings, if not formal guarantees, concerning the transfer of arms into the peninsula. Although this may be attainable as a distant goal, it is wholly infeasible in the next several years. For such a decoupling to occur further in the future, each side would need to have the will and ability to react in the event of a violation by the other. Given the proximity of Communist forces for rapid intervention in Korea, U.S. forces in Northeast Asia would have to be in a similar position. This in turn would require a full and formal Japanese agreement for the use of bases in the event of a Korean war. The trend of Japanese policy favors this prospect, but until it is securely in hand, no mutual decoupling of treaty commitments can be risked because of the superior ability of Communist forces to intervene in a conflict.

WEINSTEIN: In considering the relationship of U.S. troop withdrawals to the negotiating process, it is important to draw a clear distinction between the principle of troop withdrawals and the pace at which forces are removed. It has been observed that the ending of the U.S. military presence would remove an excuse for Pyongyang's refusal to negotiate with Seoul. A commitment to the principle of troop withdrawal might also have an effect on Pyongyang's thinking. But that effect, as Whiting suggested, is in some respects superficial. The key question is how troop withdrawals are likely to affect Pyongyang's calculations about the prospects for achieving its goal of unifying the peninsula under its control.

The real importance of troop withdrawals for the negotiating process is that they reflect South Korea's growing capability to defend itself and, in general terms, its increasing independence. That is why it is a mistake, in my view, to regard troop withdrawals as a concession that needs to be balanced by some reciprocal move on Pyongyang's part. Actually, insistence on a quid pro quo tends to undermine the rationale that the forces are being withdrawn mainly because they have become superfluous. While commitment to the principle of troop withdrawals can be appropriately considered part of the negotiating process, the actual pace of the withdrawals should not be conditional on that process. The pace of withdrawals should be governed only by the extent to which the South Koreans have acquired the capability to defend themselves and to deter a North Korean attack without the presence of U.S. forces.

If the North sees the withdrawals as a demonstration of South Korea's ability to stand on its own without a U.S. military presence, troop withdrawals will affect Pyongyang's calculations concerning the prospects for achieving its goals. As Pyongyang views the generally adverse trends, it seems to be clinging to the hope that a withdrawal of U.S. forces will rescue the situation for them by undermining the morale, and hence the stability, of the South. There is no reason to doubt that the North Koreans sincerely believe that the U.S. forces are decisive in sustaining the southern political system. Once U.S. forces have been removed and the South continues to thrive, the North Koreans will no longer be able to delude themselves that U.S. forces are the vital glue holding the South Korean regime together. Only after the U.S. presence has gone and South Korea's independence has been demonstrated are the North Koreans likely to feel that they must come to terms with the reality of a viable South Korea. If this evaluation is correct, then the achievement of any genuine modus vivendi between the two Koreas is likely to be impossible before the latter half of the 1980s at the earliest. This argues for withdrawing U.S. forces as soon as the military balance permits this to be done safely.

As for the impact of troop withdrawals on South Korea, it is important to avoid being too heavily influenced by the reactions of the moment. Many observers have noted that the South Koreans seem more self-confident and assertive than they were before the Carter administration's troop-withdrawal plan was announced. Having survived the shock of the announcement of the plan, they are the stronger for it. Whiting predicted that the ending of the U.S. military presence would not do irreparable damage to the self-confidence of the South. One might go even further. Although the initial cries of alarm may suggest the contrary, troop withdrawals, if tied to South Korean capabilities, may well help to build South Korea's self-confidence, a vital ingredient in any successful negotiations with North Korea. Thus, even moves that appear disquieting to the South Koreans may in the end prove beneficial. Troop withdrawals should not be viewed as undercutting the South Korean negotiating position. Over time, they will help create a more independent, more self-confident, and, hence, stronger South Korea, better able to negotiate with Pyongyang.

What Initiatives Might Japan Take to Promote a Korean Détente?

KAMIYA: Although, as I have indicated, the United States may eventually be able to play a mediating role between the two Koreas, there is a basic problem with any approach that accords the major role in the initial stage to the United States. If the United States takes the lead in initiating talks with North Korea in Seoul's absence, this will in itself create a one-sided situation, rather than one characterized by reciprocity. Japan should take the lead with North Korea. I think of the process as one in which the United States initially assumes the major responsibility for dealing with Peking and Moscow on the Korea issue, while Japan is primarily responsible for Pyongyang. There should be, in effect, a division of labor. Talks between Tokyo and Pyongyang should focus on economic matters, as well as some political topics—such as the need for productive North-South talks. It would be best if the agenda were not set in detail at the start. At the same time, Japan should make a serious effort to expand its economic relations with North Korea, while continuing to place the highest priority on its relations with South Korea. In developing this relationship, Japan should take advantage of every opportunity to urge Pyongyang to adopt a softer foreign policy line, especially vis-à-vis South Korea. Needless to say, there should be full consultation, in advance, with Seoul.

Why should Japan be the first to negotiate with North Korea? North Korea has much larger expectations of Japan in the economic sphere, and economic relationships represent an important way of establishing meaningful ties with Pyongyang. The talks might aim at the establishment of a Japanese trade liaison office in Pyongyang. This could be either semiofficial or official, but it should be regarded as a step short of a full diplomatic relationship. Since Japan already has more extensive economic relations with North Korea than any other non-Communist country, it would be a natural next step for Tokyo to establish a liaison office in Pyongyang, primarily for the purpose of overseeing and facilitating trade.

Of course, a major purpose of this initiative would be to use

Japanese economic power as a means of inducing Pyongyang to soften its confrontational foreign policy line. It is important to realize that North Korea may be more responsive to such efforts now than it has ever been before. While any analysis of North Korea's situation is inevitably based on inadequate data, it can nevertheless be safely concluded that Pyongyang presently faces an economic and political impasse.

PRESSURES FOR CHANGE IN PYONGYANG

KAMIYA: There is no doubt that this is a period of economic distress in North Korea. The most dramatic manifestation of Pyongyang's economic difficulties has been the North Koreans' inability to meet their fast-rising external debts. The country's economic stagnation is indicated by the fact that since the 1960s Pyongyang has been obliged to stretch out its economic plans. The North Korean economy has, in fact, been stagnant for most of the last decade. In 1976, North Korea failed to launch its new economic plan as expected, announcing instead an "adjustment period" to prepare for the next economic plan. The fact that North Korea needed a two-year "adjustment period" (1976–1978) suggests that the country's economic stagnation may be structural in character. If so, only basic changes in approach are likely to rectify the situation. Although Pyongyang would prefer to confine any changes to economic and foreign policies, without having to alter its domestic political structure, this is difficult to do. It will be hard for Pyongyang to deal effectively with its economic problems unless it significantly reduces the percentage of its resources devoted to military preparedness. But the political implications of such a shift would be considerable. Since it is a formidable task for a totalitarian regime to undertake such a major shift in policy, it is hardly surprising that Pyongyang has been slow in taking any definitive action to alter its policies. A recent report that North Korea has cut its defense expenditures, if true, may be an indication that Pyongyang has begun to act.

The situation must appear especially distressing to the North Koreans in light of the spectacular success of the South Korean economy during the same period. A decade ago the South Koreans lacked confidence in their ability to compete economically with the North. This is no longer the case. In economic terms, South Korea is now clearly ahead of the North, and this has increased

South Korea's self-confidence as a nation. It also had an impact on the willingness of the populace to support Park. Even if his government was not the best one imaginable, the majority of the people supported him for a very long time. Indeed, nationalism, which seemed to be monopolized by North Korea during the 1960s, is now manifested by both North and South Korea in a competitive fashion.

North Korea has experienced similar setbacks in the area of diplomacy. To be sure, the country's position in international politics has been improving over most of the last decade. In 1967, South Korea had diplomatic relations with 76 countries, North Korea with only 24. In 1976, however, the score was 95 for South Korea and 90 for North Korea (with 47 countries recognizing both states). Today, the score is almost even. North Korea's inflexibility has, however, caused a loss of popularity in the Third World over the last several years. A good example is Pyongyang's embarrassing experience at the conference of nonaligned countries held in Colombo, Sri Lanka, in August 1976. North Korea sent a 120-person delegation headed by Premier Park Sung-chul. The delegation had planned to present a proposal on the Korean problem, and Chairman Kim Il-sung was scheduled to attend the conference when Pyongyang's proposal was voted on. His presence was meant to dramatize another North Korean diplomatic triumph. As it turned out, however, it became clear that more than 20 of the 86 countries attending, including the major ones, would reserve their attitude on the North Korean motion, and no vote was taken on the issue. This was viewed as a defeat for North Korea, and, needless to say, Kim did not attend. While the Colombo conference was taking place, North Korean guards at Panmunjom beat to death two U.S. officers who were supervising the trimming of a poplar tree in the DMZ. While the United States swiftly mobilized its forces as China and the Soviet Union watched calmly, Kim expressed his regrets to the U.N. forces. Even though his apology was voiced in a roundabout way, the incident amounted to a considerable setback for North Korea's international prestige. Immediately after the Colombo conference, North Korea decided to withdraw the draft resolution already presented by countries supporting Pyongyang's admission to the United Nations. The withdrawal was humiliating, and since then Pyongyang has not felt confident enough to raise again the issue of North Korea's admission to the United Nations.

What do these events signify? First, the North Koreans are beginning to understand that a hard ideological line can be costly. Having already come to understand that they could not rely totally on either Peking or Moscow, the North Koreans now realize that they cannot necessarily expect full support from the Third World countries. North Korea is thus under pressure to reconsider its hard-line ideological foreign policy. Second, these developments may lead Pyongyang to shed its illusions that the present R.O.K. regime is on the brink of collapse. In this connection, it is regrettable that the domestic policies of the Park government and the illegal activities of the KCIA in the United States and Japan have damaged South Korea's international image and may have encouraged hope in the North that the South will come apart. But Pyongyang should not miscalculate either the situation in the South, which, as already indicated, is strong, or the viability of U.S. and Japanese ties with Seoul, which will survive whatever strains may exist at present. If Pyongyang continues to hold to its dogmatic policy line, the country's prized "independence" may degenerate into a self-righteous egocentrism that only serves to alienate the country from the rest of the world.

Furthermore, pressure for change also seems to be coming from Moscow. The Soviet Union clearly would prefer that Pyongyang soften its foreign policy line. Although North Korea—for ethnic, cultural, and historical reasons—feels closer to China, the Soviet Union is a more reliable source of economic assistance. Nevertheless, Soviet aid has not been easy to procure. Soviet–North Korean relations have undergone some serious strains in recent years. When Kim visited China and Eastern Europe in the spring of 1975, he did not set foot on Soviet soil. The official reason was the illness of General Secretary Leonid Brezhnev, but this is hard to accept as a reason for the North Korean leader not visiting Moscow on such a rare outing so near the Soviet capital. It may be reasonably assumed that Moscow turned down Kim's visit because prior negotiations for Soviet economic cooperation, including the matter of North Korea's outstanding debts to the Soviet Union, did not produce results. But since North Korea was economically hard pressed, it could not afford to let the talks die out. Thus, Premier Park Sung-chul visited Moscow in January 1977. No joint statement was issued, and not much was reported about the visit by either the Soviet Union or North Korea. Judging from the circumstances, the Soviet Union may have responded to the North Korean request for economic cooperation by stating a certain political price, and Premier Park may have taken this home for study.

The political price demanded by the Soviet Union must include a switch in North Korea's basic foreign policy, including that vis-à-vis South Korea, from confrontation toward a certain type of détente. Such a policy shift would serve to blunt the growth of Chinese influence in North Korea and would help to reinstate Soviet influence there. With the relations between Eastern and Western Europe increasing in stability in the past few years, the Soviet Union has achieved a remarkable expansion of its Asia-Pacific role. In this, they have benefited from the U.S. return to its traditional Asian policy principles, China's increasing preoccupation with its own development following the deaths of Mao Tse-tung and Chou En-lai, and Japan's continued reluctance to play an active role in international politics. If the Soviet Union successfully takes advantage of North Korea's economic needs to impose on it a policy of détente tailored to Soviet needs, the Soviet Union will be able to increase significantly its influence on the Asian diplomatic scene.

The Soviet Union backs North Korea's "independence and peaceful unification" policy. The Soviets know, however, that this policy will not bring about any significant change in the situation on the Korean peninsula. At a meeting of Japanese and Soviet experts in 1976, the Soviets, when asked whether they recognized the thirty-eighth parallel as an international border, refused to answer—a deviation from the North Korean position that there is no such border. During a coffee break at that meeting, a noted Soviet political commentator added, "There are two problems in Northeast Asia that will not be settled during this century. One is Korean unification and the other is the 'northern territories' dispute [between Japan and the Soviet Union]."

The Soviet Union is clearly in favor of maintaining the status quo on the Korean peninsula. Moscow cannot, however, abandon its official position in support of North Korea's "independence and peaceful unification" policy, for this would drive North Korea into the Chinese fold. Of course, Pyongyang's fierce obsession with "independence" also inhibits the Soviets from taking overt action to bring North Korea into line. But it is still fairly certain that Moscow is now pressing the North Koreans to soften their hard-line foreign policy and accept détente. Even the Chinese, though they are closer than the Soviets to Pyongyang, have their own reasons for preferring to maintain the present division of the Korean peninsula. But until North Korean policies change, neither Moscow nor Peking is likely to alter its public position for fear of losing Pyongyang to the other. The North Koreans, however, may well find it expeditious to yield to the diverse pressures, both internal and external, to modify their confrontational stance toward the South.

Indeed, Pyongyang may be on the verge of a major shift in policy. The situation is now ripe for the North Koreans to switch from the present line of ideological confrontation to a more practical one based on détente. The North Koreans will have to face the fact that it is too risky for them to attempt once again to unify Korea by force. It must be increasingly obvious to Pyongyang that, unless it modifies its basic policy of giving top priority to military needs, it cannot hope to catch up with the South economically. With its growing need for Soviet economic cooperation, there is a good chance that North Korea will capitulate to Soviet demands for a policy shift. Moreover, economic relations with the West are now more important to North Korea than ever before, if the North is to compete at all with the South. There is evidence that the North Koreans are beginning to see that they cannot have significant economic intercourse with the West if they hold to a confrontational policy. The low political posture taken by the North Korean economic mission that visited Japan in July 1977 is one example. The North Koreans should realize that, over the long run, cooperation with the Western countries can be more beneficial to them than greater reliance on the Soviets.

Nevertheless, North Korea, which is very self-conscious about being a revolutionary socialist country, will not give its relations with the West priority over those with socialist nations. It is necessary to separate rhetoric from action in dealing with North Korea. One must avoid trespassing on its national principles, especially those related to independence and peaceful unification, for these are very important from the standpoint of North Korea's domestic politics. At the very least, we should pay formal respect to such principles, while striving to lead the North Koreans toward greater realism. Furthermore, North Korea still insists that it is the only legitimate government on the peninsula. During the May 1978 visit to Pyongyang of Chairman Asukata of the Japan Socialist party, the North Koreans denied the possibility of normalizing relations with Japan under the present scheme of two Koreas. Although détente is impossible without a change in this stubborn attitude, the present difficulties faced by the North Korean government raise a real possibility of such change.

We should not rule out a softening of North Korea's foreign policy and attitude toward South Korea in the near future on the grounds that Pyongyang continues to make confrontative official policy statements. It would also be wrong to assume that there will be no détente during the chairmanship of Kim Il-sung, who, for the last 30 years, has followed a line of confrontation with the United States and South Korea. As in Mao's decision to pursue a more conciliatory policy toward the United States, the presence of a leader with absolute authority can facilitate a drastic change in policy. For all its outward appearance of adhering to a rigid, narrow policy, the Kim government, like Mao's, has demonstrated considerable rationality in practical matters.

JAPAN'S "TRIGGER ROLE"

KAMIYA: Japan has the capacity to encourage the desired changes in Pyongyang's policy by taking the kind of initiative I have outlined. There may be little Japan can do to affect the outcome of relations among such powers as the United States, China, and the Soviet Union; but Japan can play a "trigger role" with respect to Korea. In settling the Korean problem, Japan cannot afford to take the wait-and-see attitude that it took when normalizing relations with China, which it effectively left to the United States. Any Korean settlement is likely to develop into a diplomatic issue in which Japan will be required to act as an equal partner with the United States.

WHITING: Another reason why the first step toward Pyongyang should come from Japan, not the United States, is that the Japanese are in a position to develop such a relationship without prejudicing the future of the U.S. commitment to Seoul. A U.S. move toward Pyongyang at this moment might aggravate the uncertainties raised by the now-suspended troop-withdrawal plan and the recently concluded lobbying scandal. Nor should the Japanese rush to bring Washington and Pyongyang together for talks as a follow-up to the initial contacts. If Tokyo is to urge any further talks at all, the focus should be on North-South discussions. It would be a mistake to bring in the issue of U.S.–North Korean talks. Keeping the United States out of the process is the one thing that Japan can offer South Korea at this point.

HARRISON: Even though it is desirable for Japan to break the ice with Pyongyang, this need not rule out a U.S. relationship with North Korea soon afterward. The Japanese initiative could appropriately be followed in a year or so by a parallel U.S. move. The two approaches are not mutually exclusive. In any case, I agree with Whiting that Tokyo should move as soon as possible along the lines suggested by Kamiya.

WEINSTEIN: A Japanese liaison office, established in Pyongyang primarily for the purpose of overseeing and facilitating trade, could serve other important purposes as well. Even a semiofficial presence in Pyongyang, like Tokyo's representation in Taipei, could help facilitate communication and stimulate a dialogue with North Korea. It could also be a useful source of intelligence. This move would signify Japanese recognition of the Pyongyang government, even though Tokyo would continue to maintain full diplomatic relations only with Seoul. The importance of developing such communication with North Korea should not be underestimated. Our understanding of North Korea is extraordinarily limited. According to U.S. government sources, the level of government effort devoted to North Korea in Washington is miniscule. There is very little contact of any kind between the United States and North Korea. Although Japan has economic dealings with North Korea and has sent some high-ranking parliamentarians there to visit, the relationship is sporadic. Of course, the closed society maintained by Pyongyang hardly facilitates understanding. But whatever its causes, this striking lack of knowledge about North Korea should be a matter of serious concern.

The isolation of North Korea also drastically reduces whatever limited potential there may be to influence Pyongyang's behavior. It may well be, as Saeki notes, that for Japan, North Korea is "merely a market far smaller and more limited than that of South Korea" and that, in any case, North Korea would avoid the kind of "economically interdependent relationship with Japan" which might enable the latter to constrain Pyongyang from initiating hostilities against the South. Nevertheless, although economic or diplomatic relations cannot be used to compel North Korea to pursue a more conciliatory policy toward the South, such ties may give Pyongyang a greater stake in maintaining peace. While such relations alone are unlikely to prove decisive, if going to war would mean jeopardizing a host of beneficial economic ties and hard-won diplomatic relationships, Pyongyang would be more likely to calculate the costs of war as being too high.

The beginning step proposed by Kamiya may not, in itself, affect the situation in a dramatic way. But it would at least help begin the process of breaking down North Korea's isolation and creating a network of interests and relationships that would make it harder for Pyongyang to contemplate the resolution of the Korean problem by force.

OKIMOTO: There is, of course, a good deal of debate concerning the potential impact of economic relationships on North Korea's behavior. There is no question that North Korea's problems are severe. The widening gap between the two Koreas can be interpreted in two ways.

Some argue, pessimistically, that North Korea, falling ever farther behind in its peaceful competition with the South, will be increasingly motivated to take desperate actions against the South. This would be to ensure that the gap does not grow so large as to cast doubt on the legitimacy of the Pyongyang government. The North might consider stepped-up offensive deployments and the staging of more provocative "incidents," if not outright attacks, against the South. These heightened tensions might diminish the eagerness of foreigners to invest in the South.

The other, more optimistic, interpretation holds that North Korea's difficulties can lead to positive consequences by imposing a ceiling on its military expenditures, strengthening its stake in arms-control measures, and forcing it to seek expanded ties with non-Communist countries in order to keep the South's lead from growing even wider. Over time, economic troubles might even lead the North Koreans to abandon the illusion that the South will collapse from its own contradictions. In other words, rather than encouraging military adventurism, North Korea's economic weakness might lead to more moderate policies and, perhaps, to an acceptance of the need for peaceful coexistence with the South.

The pessimistic scenario suggests that Japan and the United

States should make efforts to bolster North Korea's economy so that Pyongyang does not become desperate and indulge in reckless actions. The optimistic scenario, on the other hand, suggests that little should be done to help the North Koreans. Rather, they should be allowed to fall further and further behind. Only after they have seen the utter futility of their position and have accepted the need for peaceful coexistence should they be given any assistance.

Most Japanese officials with whom I have discussed this subject lean toward the view that it is safer to lend at least modest assistance to the North Koreans before they become desperate. These officials tend to believe that an economically stable North Korea would be more inclined to accept the status quo than one that is economically weak and pressed to consider a return to economic autarky or heightened dependence on Communist allies. Economic relations with the non-Communist world would not only help foster growth, these ties might also create a degree of interdependence that would give North Korea a greater stake in peaceful coexistence and in regional stability. Some Japanese are even persuaded that South Korea would not necessarily be unhappy to see the North Koreans stabilize and develop their economy.

If this is the case, what can the Japanese do to help lift the North Korean economy out of its difficulties? Potentially, there is much that Japan can do, though this may fall short of Pyongyang's desires. Unfortunately, for the moment, the prospects for a rapid expansion of economic relations are not very bright. Although Japan is North Korea's chief trading partner among the non-Communist states, the magnitude of that trade is quite modest. In 1977 Japan exported $125.1 million worth of goods to North Korea, mostly machinery, equipment, and other chemical and heavy industrial products. Japan imported $66.6 million worth of commodities from North Korea, primarily raw materials and some manufactured products, especially nonferrous metals. Given Japan's limited need for North Korea's exports and the latter's severely restricted capacity to pay for Japanese imports, the prospects for rapidly expanded trade between the two countries seem slim.

Moreover, Japanese businessmen, burned by their recent experiences with the North Koreans, are deeply skeptical of Pyongyang's ability to plan and implement sound economic policies. Unpaid North Korean debts to Japan have made many Japanese reluctant to contemplate expanded economic contacts. Japanese business interests are not likely to expand economic relations with North Korea until the debt problem has finally been resolved and confidence in Pyongyang's ability to accumulate the foreign exchange needed to meet existing commitments has been restored. Japanese economic assistance on a government-to-government basis is a possibility, but Tokyo would probably feel constrained from acting without Seoul's approval. Even if there were no objections from the South Koreans, it is unclear what impact Japanese aid would have on the North Korean economy. North Korea's dire economic situation may reflect fundamental deficiencies that cannot be significantly alleviated by Japanese economic aid. But if there is any non-Communist country that can play a large and positive role in North Korea's economic future, it is Japan.

KOSAKA: It is probably correct to say that not too much can be expected from an expansion of Japanese economic intercourse with North Korea. In 1972 there was a chance that the bilateral economic relationship would develop rapidly, but, for the time being, the current economic situation has virtually destroyed that possibility. Still, the proposed policy of setting up a trade liaison office in Pyongyang, while keeping full diplomatic relations with Seoul, remains a desirable one. The rationale for it, however, may be more political than economic. If closer economic relations are sought between Japan and North Korea, this should be a prelude to closer general relations, not merely for the stated economic purposes. I would propose creating a fait accompli. Japan should go ahead and establish a trade liaison office in Pyongyang. This will show that Japan recognizes the existence of two governments, but that Tokyo makes a distinction in according a higher level of recognition to South Korea. Perhaps such a move may set a precedent.

The establishment of a Japanese, and even a U.S., liaison office in North Korea is worth considering because it may contribute to the stabilization of the political situation on the peninsula, even though the legal situation may remain ambiguous. But it is important to understand that there is nothing grandiose about this move. We should not expect it to bring the two Koreas together. Any plan to bring South and North Korea closer by Japanese or U.S. action is a kind of political fiction. The proposal to establish a Japanese liaison office should be considered strictly on its own merits. Though the benefits likely to result from such an office are not very great, it would at least improve communication, which is not a negligible accomplishment. Furthermore, the disadvantages of such an office are virtually nonexistent. But since a U.S. move in that direction would have a much greater impact, there is a need for caution on Washington's part.

MOMOI: This proposal would be easier to support if it called only for unofficial contacts. One could imagine maintaining a trade liaison office on an unofficial basis and after, say, two or three years, appointing a former diplomat as head of the office, thus making it semiofficial. Even an unofficial or semiofficial trade office would help stimulate a dialogue, facilitate better communication between the Japanese and North Koreans, and improve understanding about the situation in the D.P.R.K. If the South Koreans are clever enough to remain quiet, this arrangement would amount to subtle recognition of the reality of two Koreas. And since Japan would not undertake such a relationship with Pyongyang without extensive and continuous consultation with Seoul, one result would be an improvement in South Korea's intelligence about the North.

ROWEN: A problem with this proposal is the danger of an asymmetry should North Korea be widely recognized and South Korea not. And it cannot be assumed that closer economic relations will necessarily bring closer political relations. But as long as we keep close relations with Seoul, there is not much danger of such an asymmetry. Steps to reduce North Korea's isolation would be in the interests of all parties, including those of South Korea.

The tone of much of this discussion suggests an overriding concern that the continuing tension between the two Koreas presents risks to Japan and the United States and that we should try to reduce these risks by working to promote an eventual settlement. Implicit is the assumption that we should be relatively indifferent about the nature of the outcome on the peninsula. This view gives too little weight to the stake that both the United States and Japan have in South Korea, a country that has been making remarkable economic and significant political progress. The United States and Japan often express distress at the authoritarian character of the South Korean regime without considering the extent to which the foundations for a democratic society are being created and without adequately recognizing the highly repressive character of the Pyongyang regime.

It is, of course, desirable to prevent conflict in Korea, but I strongly doubt that this objective will be advanced by moves likely to create further doubts about the firmness of U.S. support for the R.O.K. Heightened uncertainty about future U.S. support could well result in Seoul's becoming more authoritarian and devoting additional resources to armaments. South Korea's incentives to seek nuclear weapons might also increase. In short, the effect of moves suggested to "defuse" tensions could turn out to be perverse, if they increase Seoul's feelings of insecurity.

This is not an argument against greater contact with the North. Some good might come of such contact. But given the nature of the U.S. ties to South Korea, it is far preferable that Japan take the lead in opening up communications with Pyongyang. I believe that any parallel moves by the United States should be made only with Seoul's concurrence.

KOSAKA: It is certainly not against the interests of South Korea to have Japan establish a trade liaison office in Pyongyang, while still maintaining full relations with Seoul. But I think it would be preferable to give such an office official status from the outset. An unofficial liaison office can be dangerous. The development of a relationship with North Korea should not be left to those who are pro-Pyongyang, which would be the result if things were done unofficially. It is better to have the government assume responsibility.

KAMIYA: In developing a Japanese dialogue with North Korea, the particular channels of communication used are indeed significant. In the case of the normalization of relations between Japan and the People's Republic of China, channels opened by pro-China groups and sinologists were instrumental in laying the basis for a change in formal relations between the two countries. But those groups were able to play such a role only because of two factors: (1) the changes that occurred during the early 1970s in the way China was treated internationally, and (2) the character of the Sino-Japanese historical legacy. The situation is different where Korea is concerned. Given the history of Japanese-Korean relations and the existence in Japan of a highly polarized Korean community, it would be difficult for Tokyo to consolidate a national consensus by leaving things entirely to the pro-North Korea group and to specialists on Korea. It is necessary to proceed on a broader basis, with active participation of the more moderate elements in both the pro-Seoul and pro-Pyongyang groups. The effort must, therefore, proceed under the auspices of the Japanese government.

Furthermore, as I indicated at the outset, it is essential that the United States undertake parallel discussions with the Soviet Union and/or China. The importance of effective coordination between Japan and the United States should be evident. It would be advantageous, from the standpoint of better understanding between the United States and Japan, particularly at a time of heightened tension over trade issues, to maintain a high degree of coordination between discussions at two levels. The first set of discussions would include narrowly defined public consultations between the United States and South Korea on the reduction of the U.S. military presence. The second would mean broader, possibly secret, consultations between the United States and Japan on policies for the stabilization of the Korean peninsula.

I recognize that the policy I have proposed may be very unpopular. The South Koreans are likely to reproach Japan for adopting what they see as a dangerous policy. And the United States is unlikely to recognize the advantages of this policy, because it may appear to offer benefits to North Korea prior to any move on Pyongyang's part to moderate its policies. Even North Korea may well be critical on the grounds that Japan continues to accord top priority to its relations with South Korea and remains committed to the maintenance of two Korean governments. These criticisms from abroad may stimulate a good deal of dissatisfaction with this policy inside Japan.

Despite all of this potential criticism, Japan should promote the sort of approach to North Korea that I have outlined, for in the long run this will serve the Japanese national interest in regional stability. Of course, Japan should make every effort to mitigate foreign criticism by consulting in advance with the United States and South Korea. Tokyo should avoid making the same mistake that the United States made with its troop-withdrawal policy. And we must recognize that it may take several years for North Korea to soften its foreign policy. Because of the danger that any dramatic change may lead to instability within North Korea, it is likely that Pyongyang will move cautiously. Nevertheless, if it becomes possible to convince Pyongyang to moderate its attitude toward Seoul and to accept some form of dual status with the South—perhaps even formal recognition of Seoul's legitimacy— that would provide a real basis for the withdrawal of the U.S. Army from Korea.

WHITING: Furthermore, we should not exaggerate the problems likely to be created by South Korea's reaction to the Japanese initiative proposed by Kamiya. Momoi may be correct in noting that a violent reaction by the South Koreans cannot be ruled out; they might even seize some Japanese ships. Nor is there any question that, as Saeki has noted, Seoul will worry that Japan might be deceived by Pyongyang, which may simply be seeking to alienate Japan from South Korea and to isolate the R.O.K. internationally. But we can agree that a Japanese trade liaison office in Pyongyang would be a step toward cross-recognition, even if the ultimate attainment of that goal still seems beyond reach. Kamiya, citing an earlier proposal from some South Koreans that Japan develop its trading relationship with North Korea, asserts that it may well be possible to persuade Seoul to go along with this move; and he may be right.

In any case, what might be the most negative South Korean reaction to the establishment of a Japanese liaison office in Pyong-yang? If they seize a few ships and hold a few anti-Japanese demonstrations, what will happen afterward? The basic relation-ship will survive. In considering potential South Korean reactions to any Japanese move, we must recall the Koreans' basic ambiva-lence toward Japan. On the one hand, Japan will remain the main source of capital and markets; on the other hand, it will be re-sented for its dominant role. Tokyo has long been a convenient whipping boy for Seoul, but the hand that feeds is seldom seriously bitten. Thus, improved Japanese relations with North Korea, or with other Communist powers, would receive mixed reactions from the South Koreans. To the extent that Japan works to pro-mote recognition of Seoul by Peking and Moscow, its efforts will be regarded positively. But to the extent that Japan is suspected of enhancing Pyongyang's status, it will be viewed with concern. Basically, however, Tokyo has the upper hand. Provided that it is prepared to ride out periodic anti-Japanese storms, whether justi-fied or not, its position in Seoul will not erode. In short, the

South Koreans have no place else to go.

HARRISON: It is worth adding that although many South Koreans will indeed view any Japanese initiative with Pyongyang as an insult to the South, this will not be a universal reaction. Former Premier Kim Chong-pil, who succeeded Park as head of the Democratic Republican party, has told me on several occasions that he sees Japanese contacts with the North as a useful means of relaxing tensions on the peninsula. I suspect that this feeling may be more widespread than it seems on the surface.

WEINSTEIN: In this connection, a well-placed South Korean official indicated in mid-1978 that he could see benefits for Seoul— in particular, better information on North Korea—if Japan were to open a liaison office in Pyongyang. But he made it clear that Seoul, if consulted in advance, would feel bound to veto the move, because it would give the North a certain advantage in the "legitimacy game." He added that despite his government's criticism of the United States for its failure to consult in advance on the troop-withdrawal decision, it is unrealistic to expect genuine consultation in matters of this kind. If such consultation merely consisted of efforts by Tokyo to persuade the Koreans that the move was being made for the sake of South Korea's interests, this would only give rise to resentment on the part of Seoul. "We don't want to be told by another government what our interests are," the official asserted. He declined to predict how his government would react if presented with a fait accompli.

Several South Korean academics went further, indicating that they would personally favor a Japanese liaison office in Pyongyang comparable to the one Tokyo maintains in Taipei. It is only through such contact, one academic observed, that North Korea will change. If such an office were clearly viewed as a prelude to full diplomatic relations, however, the South Koreans would react more negatively. The academics predicted that the Seoul government would oppose setting up a liaison office and might even protest it strongly. But in their private analyses, government officials would probably acknowledge the utility of such an office and would have mixed reactions to it.

As for U.S. reactions, Kamiya is correct in his estimation that Washington would regard with skepticism any Japanese approach to Pyongyang. State Department officials are aware of Japan's interest in playing a diplomatic role, since Tokyo can make no

military contribution to security. A Japanese scholar visiting in
Washington in late 1977 estimated that a majority of the Diet, including perhaps one-third of the LDP, would favor such a move.[26]
Yohei Kono, leader of the New Liberal Club, who was visiting
Washington at the same time, proposed that Japan take the lead
in this area. The Japanese Foreign Ministry is known to favor the
establishment of a trade liaison office in Pyongyang. But a well-
placed U.S. official indicated Washington's strong concern about
such a possibility. Indeed, he seemed to regard with horror any
Japanese initiative vis-à-vis North Korea. "The worst thing that
could happen," he volunteered, "would be for the Japanese to
get ahead of us with respect to North Korea. They want to avoid
another 1971, and what worries us is that they won't do enough
to protect the interests of South Korea."

The fact is that Tokyo seems quite reluctant to move without
the concurrence of Washington. The U.S. lack of trust in Tokyo's
ability to "protect the interests of South Korea" irks the Japanese,
who fear that the United States may simply wish to save this
"breakthrough" for itself, as was the case with the China initiative
in 1971. The United States should, in due course, move to develop
a relationship with Pyongyang. But for now, Washington should
encourage Japan to play a pioneering role with Pyongyang, perhaps to help trigger political changes that might bring a more
meaningful stability to Korea. If Washington remains skeptical,
one might ask whether the absence of U.S. concurrence should
serve as a veto of any Japanese initiative. If the Japanese are convinced, as Kamiya indicates, that this step would clearly serve
Japan's long-term interest in the stability of the region, then is it
unthinkable for Tokyo to proceed in the hope that Washington
will later come to see the wisdom of this move?

WHITING: In any case, it is time to question the costs and gains
of U.S. insistence on either dual recognition or nothing at all.
Pyongyang's relative isolation from non-Communist influences
raises the risk of miscalculation and increases its dependence on
its Communist allies. Past unexplainable or bizarre behavior,
ranging from DMZ incidents and the building of tunnels to the
expulsion of Australian diplomats, cautions against discounting
the costs of continued isolation. Although the difficulties encountered by Australia should remind us that the benefits of establishing contact with North Korea may be limited, whatever is

gained will be better than no contact at all. Especially after Kim passes from the scene, the more foreign presence in Pyongyang, the better, especially if this presence is reliable in reporting to, and consulting with, the United States. Moreover, as Momoi points out, the time element is important. We should do whatever is possible to encourage a softening of North Korea's policy while Kim is still alive, because his successor, lacking Kim's unquestioned authority, will find it harder to effect any major change of direction. Little other than the reaction of Seoul stands in the way of altering the U.S. policy of insisting on dual recognition. Given Seoul's vitally important economic relationship with Japan and its continued reliance on the U.S. security commitment, it should be possible to deal with South Korea's concerns.

WEINSTEIN: In this discussion, we have outlined several possible scenarios that might lead to a modus vivendi between the two Koreas. Clearly, there are some important differences among the members of the working group. These relate especially to the feasibility of various scenarios for confederation and cross-recognition; there is also substantial disagreement on whether Seoul should be given a veto over any potential U.S. approach to Pyongyang. But we generally agree on at least two points: (1) any modus vivendi will emerge as the product of long-term developments that cannot easily be predicted now; and (2) whatever approach is taken, the details will have to be worked out primarily (some would say exclusively) by the Koreans themselves.

As for near-term moves aimed at easing tensions on the peninsula, there is a consensus concerning the desirability of Japan's taking the initiative by seeking to establish a liaison office in Pyongyang, primarily to oversee trade, and, where possible, to expand economic cooperation with North Korea. With one strong dissent, we also agree that, as a second step, the United States should consider negotiating a peace agreement with North Korea and making a commitment in principle to the eventual withdrawal of U.S. forces, with the pace of withdrawals determined by Washington's assessment of the military balance on the peninsula. In exchange, North Korea would be required to provide a formal, written pledge of nonaggression against the South, and would implicitly accept the right of U.S. forces to remain in Korea until the military balance permits their withdrawal. The dissenting position holds that no U.S. initiative vis-à-vis Pyongyang should be undertaken without Seoul's approval. But we all agree that Seoul should at least be consulted in advance of any U.S. or Japanese moves.

These proposals are not likely to bring about dramatic changes in the Korean situation. Only the Koreans themselves can do that. The most important forum is the dialogue between the two Koreas. Even if Washington and Pyongyang should conclude a nonaggression pact, we hope that Seoul would continue to seek such an agreement directly with Pyongyang. The proposals we have made for Japanese and U.S. initiatives are offered not as a solution to the problem of Korean security, but as modest steps that may help facilitate the easing of tensions and promote the search for a stable foundation of peace on the Korean peninsula.

Notes

1. This is the North Korean translation of the original Korean version. The South Korean version stated that unification was to be achieved "through independent efforts, without being subject to external imposition or interference." By using the term *imposition* instead of *force*, the South was able to argue that it did not intend to rule out the retention of U.S. forces and the U.N. Command in Korea.

2. See the text of Lee's briefing circulated by the Korean Press Service, Seoul, July 4, 1972, parts 4, 8, 13. For a recent South Korean view of the North-South talks, see *South-North Dialogue in Korea,* International Cultural Society of Korea, no. 012 (Seoul, May 1977).

3. There is some inconclusive evidence suggesting possible divisions within the Park camp, especially between civilian and military leaders. Tokuma Utsonomiya quotes Kim Il-sung as saying that he "placed this matter [the mutual reduction of forces] before the North-South Coordinating Committee, but Lee Hu-rak said he could not convince the South Korean military to agree" ("Relaxation of Tensions and Korean Unification" [Paper presented at the Conference of U.S. and Japanese Parliamentarians on Korean Problems, Washington, D.C., September 19–20, 1977], p. 23). Kwan Ha-yim, former chairman of the Columbia University Seminar on Korea, has cited interviews in Seoul in 1974 suggesting divisions over the force-reduction issue (at a session of the seminar on October 21, 1977).

4. "Special Foreign Policy for Peace and Unification," Korean Information Service, Seoul, June 23, 1973, especially pp. 32–33.

5. Korean Central News Agency, Pyongyang, English-language broadcast, April 2, 1977.

6. Park Bong-sik, quoted in the *Korea Herald,* November 9, 1977, p. 5.

7. *South-North Dialogue in Korea,* p. 49.

8. Choe U Gyun, "The U.S. and Korea," *New York Times,* April 22, 1977.

9. The references to Pyongyang's "cold bloodedness" and "madness" are from a personal communication to Weinstein, dated April 23, 1979, from Paik Too-chin, speaker of the South Korean National Assembly. For an analysis of "Ping Pong Diplomacy, Korean Style," see the *Asian Wall Street Journal,* May 11, 1979. See also *Far Eastern Economic Review,* May 18, 1979, pp. 22–23, and *New York Times,* May 11, 1979.

10. See the *Asian Wall Street Journal,* March 31, 1979; *Far Eastern Economic Review,* April 20, 1979, p. 33; and *Far Eastern Economic Review,* May 18, 1979, p. 44.

11. United Kingdom, Foreign and Commonwealth Office, "Korea: Dialogue Attempts Fail," *Background Brief* (London: June 1979), p. 1.

12. *Mainichi Daily News,* July 3, 1979.

13. Ibid.

14. *New York Times,* January 2, 1980, January 13, 1980, January 19, 1980, January 25, 1980; and *Far Eastern Economic Review,* January 25, 1980, p. 31.

15. *New York Times,* January 19, 1980, and January 24, 1980; *Far Eastern Economic Review,* January 25, 1980, p. 31. The interview with Pak Jae-ro, vice-chairman of a North Korean citizens organization in Tokyo, was conducted by William Chapman of the *Washington Post* and reprinted in *San Jose Mercury,* February 15, 1980.

16. "R.O.K.-U.S. Joint Communiqué," *Korea Herald,* July 27, 1977, p. 2. See especially paragraph 10 of the communiqué.

17. These statements were made at the Conference of U.S. and Japanese Parliamentarians on Korean Problems, Washington, D.C., September 19–20, 1977, sponsored by the Institute for Policy Studies and the Afro-Asian Group of the Japanese Diet.

18. See Robert Shaplen, "Diplomacy and Solving the Korean Problem," *International Herald Tribune,* February 15, 1977, p. 6; Robert Shaplen, "Letter from South Korea," *New Yorker,* November 13, 1978, pp. 173–222; Gareth Porter, "U.S. Policy and a Korean Peace Settlement" (Paper presented at the Conference of U.S. and Japanese Parliamentarians on Korean Problems, Washington, D.C., September 19–20, 1977), especially pp. 32–35, 52–53; and Gareth Porter, "Time to Talk with North Korea," *Foreign Policy,* no. 34 (spring 1979), pp. 52–73.

19. Representative Les Aspin, "The Korean Troop-Withdrawal Plan: A Re-assessment," mimeographed, June 1979, p. 8.

20. Shinn estimated that some 10 million people in the North could be involved in visits by southerners of northern origin to the North. "The Inter-Korean Dialogue in Perspective" (Paper presented to the Columbia

University Seminar on Korea, New York, October 21, 1977), pp. 23–24.

21. Sang-woo Rhee, "The Future of North-South Korean Relations" (Paper presented at the Symposium on Northeast Asian Security, Washington, D.C., June 20–22, 1977), p. 17.

22. Utsonomiya, "Relaxation of Tensions," pp. 22, 26. See also "Record of Talks between Premier Kim Il-sung and Rep. Tokuma Utsonomiya," mimeographed, privately circulated, p. 5. These talks were held on August 9 and August 21–23, 1974, and July 15, 1975.

23. Selig S. Harrison, "Kim Seeks Summit, Korean Troop Cuts," *Washington Post,* June 26, 1972.

24. *New York Times,* April 11, 1978.

25. As noted above, Kim Il-sung indicated his willingness to sign a non-aggression pact with the South in 1972, notwithstanding the U.S. presence. But in 1974, he shifted back to his earlier position.

26. This was Eichi Imagawa of the Institute for Developing Economies, Tokyo.

8
Conclusions of the Working Group

As the preceding chapters have made clear, there are sharp differences among the members of the working group on some of the key issues considered in the study. But important areas of consensus have also emerged. This concluding chapter, written by the editors with the concurrence of the entire group, summarizes the main points of agreement and takes note of some of the most important differences.

We recognize that the U.S. and Japanese members of the group approach the subject of Korean security from significantly different national contexts. U.S. images of Korea tend to be more heavily laden with moral judgments. Having fought a war to preserve a "free" South Korea, the United States is inclined to focus more sharply than Japan on Seoul's human rights policies, Korean lobbying practices, and the strategic importance of the peninsula. The United States generally sees North Korea as a rigid Stalinist dictatorship—a renegade aggressor regime that should be quarantined. The Japanese, burdened with a colonial past and a highly polarized Korean minority, are intensely aware of the volatility of their relations with Koreans. Nevertheless, they are less extreme than the United States in their judgments about Korea. The Japanese tend to accept with greater equanimity the existence of authoritarian regimes in both the North and the South. They see a real danger in isolating North Korea, and they are more open to relationships with Pyongyang. The impressive progress that the South Koreans have made in developing their economy is coming to dominate Japanese—and, increasingly, U.S.—images of Korea.

The members of the working group share two fundamental assumptions, which underlie this study. First, although some members would draw attention to certain economic and political vulnerabilities that cloud Seoul's future, we all agree that the dynamic growth of the South Korean economy is likely to exert an extremely important influence on the overall balance between the two Koreas. Second, while there are differences of opinion as to how fast and how far Tokyo and Washington should move to develop relationships with Pyongyang, we share the belief that Pyongyang's continued isolation is highly undesirable.

Given the growing gap in size between the two Korean economies and the increasing readiness of Seoul to devote a higher percentage of expenditures to defense, it will be very hard for Pyongyang to keep pace. Despite revised intelligence estimates showing greater North Korean military strength, the current military balance between the two Koreas is viewed by the group as roughly even and likely to remain so until the mid-1980s, when the asymmetries are expected to begin favoring the South. The rising self-confidence of the South is already evident. Although there are varying degrees of concern about the North's present advantage in firepower and numbers of aircraft, most of us agree that the United States could have continued to withdraw its ground-combat forces, as previously planned by President Carter, without upsetting the existing balance, assuming that the proposed compensatory aid were provided. This does not mean, of course, that all members of the group favor such withdrawals. On the contrary, some members of the group feel strongly that troop withdrawals are undesirable, even though they would not upset the military balance.

While views about the merits of the Carter administration's troop-withdrawal plan differ sharply, all of the group's members are critical to some degree of the manner in which the original withdrawal decision was made and announced. There is a consensus that U.S. consultations with Japan in connection with the withdrawal decision were far from adequate. This failure is more than a mere "procedural" matter, because Japanese leaders see the inadequacy of consultations as evidence that Tokyo is considered insufficiently important to warrant careful treatment. The haste with which the withdrawal plan was announced, without even carrying out full-scale consultations inside the U.S. government, suggests to some members a certain rash and arbitrary quality in U.S. decision making. Nor was the withdrawal plan clearly related by the administration to any broader conceptual framework for U.S. diplomatic and strategic policies in Asia. While all members recognize that the disposition of U.S. armed forces is ultimately Washington's decision, these decisions should not be undertaken in what appears to be an arbitrary and unilateral manner.

We realize that it is often difficult to carry out effective consultations. In the case of the troop-withdrawal decision, the Japanese government, responding to domestic political pressures, sent conflicting signals concerning its desire to be consulted. From a political standpoint, the Japanese may even have derived some advantages from not having been consulted. But on balance we believe that the special obligation that the United States has assumed for Japan's security imposes a requirement that Washington be extraordinarily sensitive to Japanese concerns about safeguarding their interests.

To facilitate a more meaningful consultative process in the future, each side needs to have a clearer understanding of what the other means by *consultation* and what results are expected from the process. The U.S. assumption that consultation requires nothing more than keeping the Japanese informed can easily lead to misunderstanding. While merely informing an ally may be sufficient with respect to certain issues, care should be taken to ensure that Japanese views are solicited on matters of such direct importance to them as the peace and security of the Korean peninsula. Consultations held after the decision, while useful, do not compensate for the failure to solicit an ally's opinion in advance.

We also feel that the consultation process should be viewed more broadly. In order to gain a better appreciation for the subtleties of policymaking in both countries, each ally needs to develop a more extensive range of contacts with the other's legislators, interest groups, media, and so on. Given Japan's heavy dependence on the U.S. security guarantee, more effort should be made to provide access for Japanese journalists, perhaps through special meetings with members of the executive and legislative branches. This could increase Japanese understanding of the United States and reduce the likelihood of future "shocks" to the relationship.

Looking further ahead, it may be useful to develop trilateral (U.S.–Japanese–South Korean) consultations to the extent that the political climate in each of the three countries permits it. Some members believe that this would be particularly valuable in the search for a peaceful solution to the Korean question. At present, political sensitivities may be too delicate to undertake trilateral consultations on questions of military security, although as some of the Japanese members have suggested, joint discussions concerning intelligence data and the "definition of a crisis" might be possible. Even consultations that do not deal directly with military security questions could help maintain confidence in the viability of the Korean and Japanese security alliances with the United States. Certain issues may be less sensitive if dealt with in a multilateral framework. And trilateral consultations may also help give the Koreans and the Japanese a stronger regional perspective. The three countries might begin with talks about economic issues, such as trade, resource development, fishery problems, and energy, in which each has a high stake and over which conflicts could arise.

We have found that most discussions of Korean security are marked by a great deal of oversimplification. This may be seen in accounts of Korean, Japanese, Chinese, and Soviet views of the Carter withdrawal plan. This also applies to discussions concerning the possible acquisition of nuclear weapons by the two Koreas, the potential for arms control on the peninsula, and the search for a modus vivendi between Seoul and Pyongyang. Any real understanding of the Korean security problem requires sensitivity to the nuances, subtleties, and complexities of the situation. Indeed, it may well be that the chief contribution of this study is to demonstrate that much of the so-called conventional wisdom about Korean security rests on oversimplifications, exaggerated fears, and mistaken assumptions.

The positions of various nations on the withdrawal of U.S. forces are not so easily assessed. Although it is clear that the South Koreans were unhappy with the Carter administration's withdrawal policy, they made the best of the situation. Many accounts focus only on South Korea's opposition to the withdrawal; they fail to note the effective steps that Seoul took to strengthen itself. Nor do they recognize that Seoul's successful adaptation to the troop-withdrawal policy prior to suspension of that policy led to a perceptible increase in South Korea's self-confidence. Notwithstanding their reservations about the withdrawal policy, the South

Koreans, overall, took it calmly. And, barring major unanticipated developments, most of us find little reason for concern about future South Korean reactions should troop withdrawals be implemented. One member of the group, however, voiced apprehension about the loss of U.S. influence in an unstable situation.

North Korean reactions were mixed. Some statements showed a softer line toward the United States and welcomed the Carter withdrawal plan as "a very good thing," while others denounced the plan as insufficient, even deceitful. So long as the withdrawal of U.S. ground forces remained Washington's policy, the North Koreans seemed likely to avoid taking any precipitous action that might lead the United States to abandon the withdrawal policy. While Moscow and Peking appear unlikely to support any move to alter the status quo on the peninsula through military action, they still back North Korea's demand for the withdrawal of U.S. military forces. The Chinese have sometimes been portrayed as privately supporting a continued U.S. troop presence in Korea. But it is extremely difficult to discern Peking's real views. There have been some indications of a willingness by Peking to view a U.S. withdrawal with somewhat less urgency than Pyongyang. But there is no evidence that Peking is currently prepared, even privately, to indicate its acceptance of a continued U.S. troop presence in Korea.

Japan's views concerning the withdrawal of U.S. forces from Korea have been particularly susceptible to oversimplification and misinterpretation. Like Seoul, the Japanese government clearly had reservations about the Carter withdrawal policy. But, like the Koreans, the Japanese adapted well to the decision. Although there are clear indications of Tokyo's preference for a continued U.S. troop presence in South Korea, Japan's position concerning a longer-term U.S. military presence in Korea is not so easily defined. As one of the Japanese members of the group noted, the oft-quoted statement that "the security of Korea is essential to Japan's security" is less true in the strategic, than in the political, sense. Some Japanese members consider a continued U.S. military presence in Korea important because it "multilateralizes" the military balance on the peninsula and symbolizes the U.S. commitment to the region. Other Japanese members of the group believe that a complete withdrawal of U.S. forces could be carried gradually without damaging the credibility of the U.S. comm to Japan, provided that certain conditions are met. There is unanimous agreement that although Japan might take a number of steps to contribute to the security of Korea, it is not realistic to expect the Japanese to assume any new military-related duties and obligations in exchange for a U.S. pledge to maintain its defense commitment to South Korea or to keep its forces there. Japan will not ask the United States to stay in Korea. The Japanese do, however, clearly state their view that regional security is served by a continued U.S. commitment to Seoul. In any case, there is no evidence of any disposition on the part of the United States either to abandon its commitment to South Korea or to press Japan for a direct contribution to the military defense of South Korea.

Some members of the working group have made a case for the withdrawal of U.S. forces; others have argued against it. But virtually all agree that, apart from the always present, but remote, possibility of a North Korean attack, the principal concerns attached to any withdrawal are twofold: (1) as South Korea grows more independent and begins to take greater responsibility for its own defense, Seoul may feel it desirable to seek, as the ultimate trump card in deterring Pyongyang, a nuclear-weapons capability; and (2) the North Koreans, facing an adversary armed with increasingly sophisticated weaponry, may bring pressure on their Soviet and Chinese allies for accelerated military assistance, thus intensifying the arms race between the two Koreas.

With respect to the nuclear question, we find it an oversimplification to predict flatly, as some have, that the withdrawal of U.S. forces and tactical nuclear weapons from Korea would lead South Korea to go nuclear and that this, in turn, would lead Japan to follow suit. Tactical nuclear weapons are probably not needed for the defense of South Korea, though the Koreans seem inclined to attach some importance to them. To the extent that nuclear deterrence is required in Korea, most of us believe that it should be possible to provide at least some measure of it from weapons stationed offshore. There is some feeling, however, that offshore nuclear weapons do not meet the test, and that U.S. nuclear weapons should be kept in Korea as evidence of the U.S. commitment. There is no consensus as to whether South Korea is likely to seek nuclear weapons, but it is clear that the option has not been ruled out. It would be erroneous, however, to ignore South Korea's disincentives to go nuclear. Occasional South Korean intimations that they are considering the nuclear option may be bluffs aimed at persuading the United States to maintain its presence in Korea.

If the South Koreans do decide to move toward a nuclear capability, there are a number of possible scenarios. The fastest route is the seizure of U.S. weapons, a possibility that should not be ignored. According to one Japanese estimate, a South Korean effort to build their own weapons might take them no more than a year once they have acquired the necessary fissionable material. Experts cited in U.S. government reports estimate that it would take the South Koreans "a few years." In order to develop and deploy facilities for the production of fissionable material, the South Koreans would probably need three to five years.

We all recognize that the reactions of various countries to a South Korean nuclear capability would depend on the specific circumstances surrounding the event. Unless the circumstances are particularly threatening, the likelihood is that this event alone would not lead Japan to go nuclear. While information on any North Korean nuclear program is very limited, it is unlikely that the North would be in a position to match the South's nuclear capability, because neither Moscow nor Peking is likely to respond to requests for nuclear assistance unless Seoul adopts an aggressive posture. Although it is conceivable that Korea's nuclearization might have some stabilizing effects, the working-group members agree that the risks associated with nuclear weapons in Korea are such that the United States and Japan should exercise all the leverage at their disposal to dissuade Seoul from seeking such weapons. A Korean move toward nuclear weapons could lead to the abrogation of the U.S. commitment to Seoul. It is not certain how effective economic levers would be or, for that matter, how willing Washington and Tokyo would be to exercise them, if doing so would ruin the South Korean economy. The best deterrent to a nuclear South Korea is a greater feeling of security on Seoul's part. In the short run, this must include a continuing U.S. treaty commitment backed by some military presence. Over the longer run, all members of the group share the hope that improved relations between the two Koreas will create an environment in which neither Seoul nor Pyongyang will feel a need for nuclear weapons.

What can be done to reduce the danger of an intensified arms race between the two Koreas? The working group considered several arms-control possibilities. The establishment of a nuclear-weapons-free zone (NWFZ) on the peninsula was judged to be infeasible under present conditions. The major obstacle to this lies in the asymmetrical impact of such a measure on the two Korean states. The creation of an NWFZ would require the elimination of the U.S. tactical nuclear weapons presently stationed in South Korea. The North, which has no known nuclear weapons on its soil, would not have to give up anything. Furthermore, Seoul is more likely than Pyongyang to possess the capability and the motivation to develop its own nuclear weapons. An NWFZ, therefore, would require genuine sacrifices of the South but would cost the North very little. The members of the group see little prospect for establishing such a zone until there has been substantial improvement in the general climate of Seoul-Pyongyang relations. Even then, there would be problems in defining the zone, providing verification, and assuring the readiness of outside powers to accept the restraints that an NWFZ would impose on them. Nevertheless, the members of the working group agree that the NWFZ idea is one that should be explored, as possibilities permit.

The second arms-control approach considered by the working group relates to the role of those nations that supply military aid to Seoul and Pyongyang. The members of the group generally agree that the major powers have shown restraint in providing highly sophisticated military equipment to their respective Korean allies and that this de facto arms control should be continued. Where possible, such restraints should be made explicit through U.S. discussions with Moscow and Peking. This will, however, be difficult. One member of the group questions the basic assumption that an intensified conventional arms race is necessarily undesirable. The Korean situation is not, he argues, one in which a first-strike capability is the central issue. Besides, it is very unlikely that Pyongyang will be able to attain such a capability. Moreover, a reluctance to transfer sophisticated nonnuclear weapons to allied nations may be inconsistent with the goal of reducing incentives for acquiring nuclear weapons. At the other end of the spectrum, another member of the group believes that future arms sales to the South should be conditioned on Seoul's willingness to participate in negotiations on mutual force reductions with the North. In any case, it is clear that any explicit and comprehensive agreement to limit the transfer of arms to the Korean peninsula would require the consent of Seoul and Pyongyang. The question of arms-transfer restraints is likely to become less relevant as the two Koreas gain increased capabilities to produce their own weaponry and as Seoul develops more diverse sources from which to import sophisticated equipment. Thus, if the arms race between the two Koreas is to be kept within bounds, it will ultimately depend on the willingness of Seoul and Pyongyang to impose restraints on themselves.

There is general agreement among the members of the working group that Seoul and Pyongyang are unlikely to agree on mutual force reductions until basic changes have occurred in their attitudes toward one another. Some view Seoul as the principal obstacle to force reductions, while others view Pyongyang's proposals as little more than self-serving propaganda. The economic realities suggest that the North would derive particular benefit from force reductions. But whether these benefits are sufficient to lead Pyongyang to negotiate a broader settlement with Seoul is another question. In any case, the members of the working group agree that the issue of force reductions may be less important for the sake of arms control itself than as a means of inducing North Korea to undertake serious discussions aimed at working out a modus vivendi with the South.

Despite the variety of views on withdrawal of U.S. forces from South Korea, members of the working group agree on the need for more substantial efforts aimed explicitly at easing tensions between the two Koreas. We have discussed several scenarios that might lead to a modus vivendi between North and South. There are sharp differences among the members of the group concerning the feasibility of schemes for confederation and cross-recognition, and on the issue of Seoul's right to veto potential U.S. overtures to Pyongyang. But we generally agree on at least two points: (1) any modus vivendi will emerge as the product of long-term developments that cannot easily be predicted now; and (2) whatever approach is taken, the details will have to be worked out primarily (some would say exclusively) by the Koreans themselves.

As for near-term moves to ease tensions on the peninsula, there is a consensus concerning the desirability of Japan's taking the initiative by seeking to establish a liaison office in Pyongyang, primarily to oversee trade and, where possible, to expand economic cooperation with North Korea. With one strong dissent, we also agree that, as a second step, the United States should consider negotiating a peace agreement with North Korea and making a commitment in principle to the eventual withdrawal of U.S. forces, with the pace of withdrawals determined by Washington's assessment of the military balance on the peninsula; in exchange, North Korea would be required to provide a formal, written pledge of nonaggression against the South and would implicitly accept the right of U.S. forces to remain in Korea until the military balance permits their withdrawal. The dissenting position holds that no U.S. initiative vis-à-vis Pyongyang should be undertaken without Seoul's approval. But we all agree that Seoul should at least be consulted in advance of any U.S. or Japanese moves, in order to avoid any possible misunderstanding of their intent.

The members of the working group believe that the recommended measures, if implemented, could make a modest contribution to the maintenance of peace on the peninsula and, indirectly, to the development of an atmosphere of détente between Seoul and Pyongyang. We have no illusions, however, that any actions taken by Japan or the United States can resolve the difficult issues that divide the two Korean states. A central theme of this study is the need to avoid the kind of oversimplified thinking that has characterized much of the discussion of the Korean security problem. We hope that our analysis will stimulate new thinking, without suggesting that any easy solutions lie ahead. Though a sudden breakthrough cannot be ruled out, there is not much basis for anticipating any dramatic improvement in relations between the two Koreas in the near future. Significant progress toward arms control and a modus vivendi between the two Koreas is likely to come only as the basic attitudes of Seoul and Pyongyang change, and this will take time.

There is, however, no need for pessimism about Korea's future. Although a modus vivendi between the two Koreas seems distant, the likelihood of conflict is diminishing. The debate about the U.S. Korea policy has evoked a certain amount of alarmist rhetoric, exaggerating the dangers of war. One must, of course, always be prepared for the unexpected, and the assassination of Park, followed by December 1979's unprecedented breakdown of army unity, has raised new uncertainties; nor can it be denied that South Korea's economic performance has lost some of its previous luster. But the international environment in the 1980s is likely to counsel moderation to both sides. The developing U.S. and Japanese ties with China may become a significant force for stability in Korea, assuming that care is taken to avoid provoking the Soviet Union. Most important, the central fact about the Korean situation remains the growing economic and military strength of South Korea. Sooner or later, the increasing strength of the South will affect the strategic calculus of the North, making it harder for Pyongyang to ignore the futility of continued hostility toward the South. And Seoul's growing self-confidence could well, in time, increase the readiness of the South Koreans to make the "symbolic concessions" that would facilitate Pyongyang's acceptance of peaceful coexistence on the peninsula.

Index